Empress Alexandra

This book is dedicated to David Hayden, beloved husband
and father, bon vivant and passionate lover of history.

(1941–2020)

'Dieu nous a donné le vivre;
c'est à nous de nous donner le bien vivre' – Voltaire.

Empress Alexandra

The Special Relationship Between Russia's Last Tsarina and Queen Victoria

Melanie Clegg

PEN & SWORD HISTORY

First published in Great Britain in 2020 by
Pen & Sword History
An imprint of
Pen & Sword Books Ltd
Yorkshire – Philadelphia

ISBN 978 1 52672 387 1

A CIP catalogue record for this book is
available from the British Library.

Typeset by Mac Style
Printed and bound in the UK by TJ International Ltd,
Padstow, Cornwall.

Pen & Sword Books Limited incorporates the imprints of Atlas,
Archaeology, Aviation, Discovery, Family History, Fiction, History,
Maritime, Military, Military Classics, Politics, Select, Transport,
True Crime, Air World, Frontline Publishing, Leo Cooper, Remember
When, Seaforth Publishing, The Praetorian Press, Wharncliffe
Local History, Wharncliffe Transport, Wharncliffe True Crime
and White Owl.

For a complete list of Pen & Sword titles please contact

PEN & SWORD BOOKS LIMITED
47 Church Street, Barnsley, South Yorkshire, S70 2AS, England
E-mail: enquiries@pen-and-sword.co.uk
Website: www.pen-and-sword.co.uk

Or

PEN AND SWORD BOOKS
1950 Lawrence Rd, Havertown, PA 19083, USA
E-mail: Uspen-and-sword@casematepublishers.com
Website: www.penandswordbooks.com

Contents

Chapter One

'A dear, good, amiable child.'

1842–1855

The summer of 1842 was the hottest one that anyone could remember, with even the young Queen Victoria complaining about the 'overpowering heat'[1] in her journal as she contrived to spend as little time as possible in the sweltering capital. The queen's journal entries are full of references to spending the balmy evenings strolling in beautiful gardens with her beloved husband Albert, enjoying card games after dinner and excursions to the theatre, sitting for artists (such as for a particularly unsuccessful full-length portrait by Sir Martin Shee, which she described as 'monstrous',[2] 'distressing' and 'totally void of talent'[3]) and larking about in the royal nursery with their children, eighteen-month-old Victoria (a precocious and adorable little girl known in the family as 'Pussy') and her younger brother Albert Edward (a sickly child who was known simply as 'Baby'). However, outside their privileged bubble of dinner parties, concerts and family holidays, civil unrest was sweeping across the nation in the form of strikes and riots, which would ultimately involve over half a million workers in coal mines, factories and mills downing tools and protesting wage cuts and poor conditions. Victoria was kept fully briefed about the situation by her Prime Minister Sir Robert Peel and wrote about the 'dreadful' accounts of rioting in her journal. Meanwhile, closer to home she was anxious about the health of her former Prime Minister Lord Melbourne, who suffered a stroke towards the end of the year, and the premature death of the thirty-one-year-old Ferdinand Philippe, Duc d'Orléans, eldest son and heir of King Louis Philippe of France, who was accidentally killed in a carriage accident in July 1842. The Duc's wife Helene of Mecklenburg-Schwerin was a cousin of both Victoria and Albert and they therefore took a great interest in the tragedy as it unfolded across the Channel in France.

Victoria was twenty-three years old and had been married to her first cousin Albert of Saxe-Coburg Gotha since February 1840. They had only met a handful of times before their wedding and remained blissfully in love, although the disparity in their fortunes and Victoria's determination not to surrender any of her authority to her husband, inevitably resulted in conflict. The early years of the couple's marriage were marred by a series of epic rows as Albert expressed his frustration and Victoria failed to understand his unhappiness and bristled at what she perceived to be his implied criticism of her ability to rule alone. By the summer of 1842, however, the couple's relationship was far more harmonious as both developed a greater understanding of the other's character and Victoria, keen to see Albert shine in public life, gave her husband more responsibilities. The arrival of their children also did much to reconcile the couple, not least because Victoria's pregnancies gave Albert an opportunity to step in and shoulder some of her work while she was either indisposed or recovering from childbirth. In contrast to her modern reputation as an uninterested mother who resented and bullied her children and found them utterly repellent when they were babies, Victoria was enchanted by her eldest child Vicky and her journals are full of updates about her daughter's health and progress and how pretty she looked when she was brought downstairs in one of her favourite velvet frocks, which were often gifts from Victoria's mother, the Duchess of Kent. When Bertie came along a year after his sister, he too was greeted with joyous relief by his adoring parents and there is no hint of his mother's later antipathy towards him in her descriptions of his infant beauty, her constant worrying about his poor health or her proud recording of various childhood milestones such as his first steps or the eruption of his first teeth. In fact, it is clear that Victoria, aside from the pressures that her position placed upon her, was much like any other new young mother and was thoroughly enchanted by her eldest children.

In the early autumn of 1842, Victoria and Albert embarked on an adventure that they had been looking forward to for quite some time – their first visit to Scotland. In the early stages of their rather unusual courtship, they had bonded over a shared passion for the romantic historical novels of Sir Walter Scott, which were mostly set in the Borders region of Scotland. Victoria longed to see Scotland with her own eyes, while the homesick Albert was no less keen, having heard that the landscape in the Highlands was reminiscent of that of his native Germany. The couple travelled north on the royal yacht, disembarking at Leith on 1 September before driving into Edinburgh, where they were to stay at Dalkeith Palace, residence of the Duke of Buccleuch. They were enchanted by their first glimpse of the Scottish capital, which Victoria described as 'quite beautiful' and 'totally unlike anything else that I have seen' before adding that 'Albert, who has seen so much, says it is unlike anything he ever saw'[4] and had pronounced the view 'fairylike'. The couple were charmed by Edinburgh and their passion for Scotland only increased as they ventured further north, with the queen being particularly enthralled by visits to castles and sites associated with her tragic ancestress Mary Queen of Scots, who was clearly one of her heroines. Victoria was fascinated by anything related to her Stuart ancestors and was inclined to sympathise with them to the detriment of her own Hanoverian forebears, even to the extent of raising some eyebrows by declaring herself to be a Jacobite. The royal couple only spent a fortnight in Scotland but it was long enough for the northernmost part of their kingdom to completely win their hearts. Victoria wrote in her journal that 'as the fine shores of Scotland receded more and more, we felt quite sad that this very pleasant and interesting tour was over, but we shall never forget it'[5] and indeed, the couple had already resolved to return as soon as possible, although another decade would pass before Albert purchased their own piece of the Highlands when he bought Balmoral Castle in Aberdeenshire as a holiday home for their growing family.

Victoria had probably already guessed that she was pregnant again in the middle of August just before they set off on their Scottish adventure, but made no explicit mention of the fact that she was expecting another child in her journal (although it is also a possibility that the intimate details of her pregnancy were removed when her youngest daughter Princess Beatrice heavily edited her mother's journal after her death in January 1901) until 11 March 1843, when she checked over the linen and clothes that had been used for her last two babies, pronouncing it 'in the best state' and noting that there was 'hardly anything more to be ordered'[6] before rather gloomily adding that she supposed 'that the event will take place somewhere near the 20th of April'. In the meantime, the only hints of her condition are the occasional references to after dinner naps and the fact that her regular rides were replaced by rather more sedate outings in a carriage with Prince Albert taking the reins. Victoria's third pregnancy certainly seems to have been as uneventful as her previous two, although she was plagued by a persistent cold for several months, which greatly annoyed the usually robust queen, who rather prided herself on her rude good health. On the 23 March, a month before she expected her baby to be born, Victoria very regretfully ended a family holiday to her uncle Leopold's mansion Claremont in Surrey (where, incidentally, her first cousin Princess Charlotte had died in childbirth in 1817) and begrudgingly returned to Buckingham Palace for her lying in, predicting that she would not be allowed to leave the capital for quite some time.

Although this was Victoria's third pregnancy and she was probably already feeling rather bored and insouciant about the whole process, she and Albert still felt some excitement about preparing the nursery for their new arrival. At the end of March, the couple purchased an ornately carved seventeenth-century gilt wood cradle that had allegedly been first used by the infant Augustus II of Saxony in 1670. Albert, the proud German, was doubtless particularly pleased to have acquired a piece connected with such an important figure from German history, albeit one from neighbouring Saxony. The cradle took pride of place in the royal nursery but Victoria's hopes that it would be in use by the middle of April were quickly dashed for the baby showed no sign of making an appearance even though their private apartments in Buckingham Palace were in some disarray thanks to the preparations for the new arrival. 'We feel quite impatient at my being still about,' she wrote in her journal on 13 April, 'for we had expected the event almost before this.'[7] At the same time, Victoria was very worried about the failing health of her favourite uncle Augustus, Duke of Sussex, the sixth son and ninth child of George III and Charlotte of Mecklenburg-Strelitz. In the absence of her own father, who had died when Victoria was a toddler, the Duke of Sussex, who was kind-hearted and known for his liberal views and interest in Freemasonry, had taken a benevolent interest in his young niece, who lived in apartments close to his own in Kensington Palace. He gave Victoria away at her wedding to Albert in February 1840 and a few months later, to show her gratitude for his kindness, she granted his morganatic second wife Lady Cecilia Underwood the title of Duchess of Inverness in her own right. Relations between Victoria and her uncle had slightly cooled by 1843 thanks to his dislike of her beloved Albert but she was still deeply upset when the news arrived on 21 April that the elderly Duke had breathed his last. In typically eccentric style, he left instructions that his remains should be buried privately and without any pomp in Kensal Green Cemetery near Kensington Palace and the arrangements for his funeral preoccupied Victoria for the next few days until she finally went into labour during the evening of Monday, 24 April.

After stoically suffering the pangs of early labour through dinner and then a quiet evening with Prince Albert, Victoria finally gave in just after midnight and called for her obstetrician Sir Charles Locock, who had presided over her last two labours along with her personal physician Sir James Clark. The baby, 'a fine, healthy girl'[8] according to her relieved mother, was born at five minutes past four in the morning in the presence of Prince Albert who, Victoria later wrote when the ordeal was at an end, 'watched so tenderly over me the whole time'.[9] Whereas the Princess Royal's birth had been witnessed by several dignitaries, including the Prime Minister, Lord Melbourne, and Archbishop of Canterbury and that of the Prince of Wales had been observed by the Home Secretary, only the Earl of Liverpool, Lord Steward of the Household was present for this latest birth and it was to him that the new baby was presented so that he could inspect her and verify that she was indeed the queen's own child and not an imposter that had been smuggled into the royal bedchamber. Unlike many other royal mothers, Victoria was unusually unconcerned about the need to have witnesses when her children were born, with Locock rather wryly noting that in his opinion 'she would not care one single straw if the whole world was present'.[10] It's likely that Albert, who was markedly more inhibited than his wife, was rather less keen on the presence of several male witnesses during his wife's labours.

Mother and baby were able to rest for a few hours before their first official visitor, Victoria's mother, the Duchess of Kent, arrived early in the morning to meet her new granddaughter. Relations between Victoria and her mother had not always been cordial but Prince Albert, who was the duchess' nephew, had done much to mend his wife's fractured relationship with her mother. Like a lot of people who had been unsatisfactory parents, the duchess turned out to be an excellent grandmother who adored her daughter's growing brood of children and took enormous pleasure in spoiling them with gifts and special treats. The rest of the day passed quietly as Victoria recovered from her ordeal while Albert took charge of spreading the news about the safe arrival of their new baby to relatives and other heads of state all around the world. When Victoria finally managed to update her journal again on 14 May she gave thanks to God for 'again so mercifully protecting me this time'[11] before, ever mindful of family anniversaries, noting that her second daughter had arrived on the birthday of her favourite aunt Princess Mary, Duchess of Gloucester, who was said to have been the most beautiful of George III's numerous daughters. The daily visits from her mother did little to console Victoria for the seclusion that she was forced to endure as she recovered. The young Queen loved to be busy and active and being confined to her bedchamber for days on end was not at all her idea of fun, although the long hours in bed were considerably enlivened by visits from her two eldest children, who were brought to her at bedtime. She was therefore absolutely delighted when her doctors deemed her well enough on the 1 May to have her bed wheeled into the sitting room by Albert and her midwife Mrs Lilly. She was visited by Lady Sarah Spencer, Lady Lyttelton, who had just been appointed as Lady Superintendent of the Royal Children, and her unofficial advisor Baron Stockmar and the group discussed the new baby's name, which Victoria decided should be Alice Maud Mary. The middle names were in honour of Victoria's cousin Princess Sophia Matilda of Gloucester, a niece of George III, who was to act as one of Alice's godmothers (Maud being an old German variant of Matilda) and Princess Mary, Duchess of Gloucester, whose birthday she shared.

Victoria and Albert were thoroughly delighted with their new daughter, whom the queen pronounced on 12 May to be 'an extremely pretty little thing and decidedly larger than the other two at that age: she already takes notice and smiles'.[12] The queen's seclusion lasted for several weeks, enlivened only by short visits by close friends and family, short perambulations in the garden in a bath chair pushed by Prince Albert and quiet evenings lying on her sofa listening to her husband reading aloud, before she was considered well enough to leave the confines of her apartments and then resume her usual daily life after being ceremoniously churched on 19 May. The queen wore white for the occasion and used her wedding veil, which she reserved for special occasions, as a shawl. Alice was christened a few weeks later on 2 June in the chapel of Buckingham Palace, wearing the same lace trimmed gown and cap that her brother and sister had worn. Once again the queen wore white, this time a gown of watered silk teamed with her Turkish diamond tiara, a spray of flowers and the sapphire and diamond brooch that her husband had given her on their wedding day, while Albert wore his Field Marshal's uniform. It was a beautiful ceremony but did not pass without incident – the elderly Archbishop of Canterbury forgot the baby's names and had to have them whispered to him by the Bishop of London and the pages of the prayer book stuck together and could not be opened, which brought matters to a standstill. More seriously, Victoria's uncle, the King of Hanover, who had been invited to act as godfather to the new princess, didn't turn up to the ceremony so that the Duke of Cambridge had to act as his proxy, and then took everyone by surprise by arriving at the palace in the early evening when all the guests had already departed, claiming to have been delayed during his journey. His invitation had been Albert's idea, as a means of extending the laurel branch to the fearsome Hanover, and Victoria couldn't help but think that his tardiness was entirely due to malice rather than incompetence. Thankfully, there were no issues with the other godparents who were Victoria's half-sister Princess Feodora, who was represented by their mother, the Duchess of Kent; Albert's brother Prince Ernest, who was represented by the Grand Duke of Mecklenburg-Strelitz, who was engaged to Victoria's cousin Princess Augusta of Cambridge, and Princess Sophia Matilda of Gloucester. Very much moved as always by the christening, Victoria wrote in her journal that night that she hoped that 'our dear little Alice might grow up in virtue and goodness, and be preserved from all dangers'.[13]

Victoria was entranced by her new daughter and proudly peppered her journals with references to Alice's beauty, healthy size and intelligence, while the reports of her governess Lady Lyttelton were no less glowing. Lady Sarah Lyttelton was a niece of the celebrated Lady Georgiana, Duchess of Devonshire and was a widow with five children when the royal couple, who had grown to like and trust her a great deal, asked her to become governess to their three children, who would call her 'Laddle'. Good natured, kind hearted, indefatigable and wise, Lady Lyttelton was an excellent choice for the position and took the greatest care of her charges who, in return, adored her. Until 6 August 1844, when they were joined by another brother, Alfred, Alice reigned supreme as baby of the nursery, winning hearts with her chubby cheeks and hands, which earned her the nickname of 'Fatima', and her exuberant nature. Both Victoria and Albert were extremely fond of commissioning portraits of their children, recording their changing appearance as they grew up with, naturally, the most popular works being those by Winterhalter, whose charming depictions of the growing royal family, all bouncing curls, huge shining eyes and rosy cheeks have come to epitomise this golden era. However, the earliest portrait of Alice was not painted by Winterhalter but was instead the work of Sir Edwin Landseer, one of the best loved artists of the era and a favourite of both Victoria and Albert. Shortly after Alice's birth, Albert secretly commissioned Landseer to paint a portrait of the baby princess as a surprise birthday present for the queen, who was to turn twenty-four on 24 May. Although Landseer, like many other artists, had a tendency to occasionally dawdle and procrastinate over his works, he pulled out all the stops to deliver Victoria's birthday gift in just a few weeks, producing a truly delightful painting of the chubby infant, who was nine days old when the sitting occurred, fast asleep in the ornate golden cradle that had been bought just before her birth, with Dandie Dinmont, a Skye terrier that had been Albert's birthday present to his wife exactly a year earlier, sitting faithfully and protectively at her side. Victoria was predictably thrilled by the gift, describing it in her journal as 'exquisite', 'a small gem' and 'a chef d'ouvure (sic), and so charming and lovely, as to composition and painting'.[14] Lady Lyttelton, who had tactfully ensured that the month-old Alice had a small posy of primroses ready in her hand to present to her mother when she visited the nursery on her birthday, also sang the painting's praises, writing that Alice was watched over by 'Dandie, the black terrier, with an expression of fondness and watchfulness such as only Landseer can give'.[15]

From the very first, Alice was considered to be delightfully pretty, especially by her father, who considered her to be perhaps the most lovely of his five daughters thanks to the delicate bone structure that she would pass on to her own daughters. Victoria, on the other hand, was in raptures over Alice's chubbiness, describing her as 'good, fat Alice'[16] on her first birthday, when she attended the celebrations in a pretty new pink dress, probably a present from her grandmother, flanked by her siblings, who were both dressed in white. For members of such a large family, birthdays were a very special treat as they afforded the children a rare opportunity to be the star of the show and centre of attention and Alice certainly seems to have made the most of her time in the spotlight. Albert had introduced a tradition of having elaborately decorated birthday tables where presents were displayed surrounded by flowers and other treats for the birthday boy or girl. Toys and books were obviously very popular gifts for the royal children but even from a young age, the princesses in particular could expect to receive jewellery, small art works for their nursery and clothes. However, as far as Alice was concerned, perhaps her most spectacular present was the tame pet lamb, bedecked in pink ribbons, that she received for her fifth birthday in April 1848, although she no doubt was also enchanted by the orchestra who played a serenade beneath her bedroom window at Windsor Castle on her eighth birthday[17] or a trip to see Madame Tussaud's waxworks on her tenth birthday[18] – both special treats organised by her father. The birthdays of her children were also an opportunity for the queen to take stock of their development as they grew older. On Alice's ninth birthday in 1852, she noted that her second daughter was 'a dear child, industrious, sweet tempered, affectionate and unselfish… At sixteen months and two years old it was impossible to see a prettier, dearer little thing'[19], while on her thirteenth she wrote that 'Alice is a dear, good, amiable child, who deserves to be very happy.'[20]

Although Albert's childhood had been overshadowed by his parents' divorce, the departure of his mother and the debaucheries of his father, his overwhelming feelings about it were happily nostalgic while Victoria, on the other hand, felt that she had endured rather than enjoyed her childhood and was keen to put it firmly behind her. Their experiences, happy and sad, naturally influenced how they wanted their own children to be raised and for the most part they were in perfect agreement that they wanted their offspring to be well educated, enjoy a great deal of time outside and, most importantly, have some fun – although not too much. Their visit to Scotland at the start of Victoria's pregnancy with Alice had inspired them to look for a permanent country residence where their children could benefit from plenty of fresh air and exercise. They first discussed the plan of acquiring property on the Isle of Wight in October 1843, six months after Alice's birth, inspired by Victoria's happy memories of spending childhood holidays in Norris Castle on the island. She had been given the opportunity to purchase Norris Castle shortly after becoming queen, but turned it down as the prospect of having a family of her own to share holidays with had seemed a very distant prospect at that time. Now, however, she regretted the decision as the couple began to look for a suitable residence for themselves and their children. It was her Prime Minister, Sir Robert Peel who first suggested that they acquire Osborne House, at that time an elegant Georgian mansion belonging to Lady Isabella Blachford, which commanded a magnificent view across the Solent. Albert inspected the house in March 1844 and being 'much pleased'[21] with both the building and its location, encouraged Victoria to acquire it for their family. The building was quickly discovered to be too small for their purposes and so, in 1845, Albert decided to design an entirely new residence in collaboration with the master builder Thomas Cubitt.

Unlike Victoria, who before 1845 had left the country of her birth only once, in order to visit King Louis Philippe in France in September 1843, Albert had travelled widely before their marriage and had been particularly struck by the art and architecture of Italy. When he came to design his family's summer residence, he had in his mind the elegant country villas of Tuscany and the magnificent Renaissance palazzos of Florence, both of which would inspire his designs for Osborne House. Although it appears rather grand to modern eyes, Osborne was Victoria's Trianon where she could escape from the cares of her position and enjoy a carefree, normal existence with her beloved husband and children. In contrast to the royal palaces, which were primarily designed to be backdrops to the display and pageant of royal life rather than comfortable family homes, Osborne was specifically planned by Albert in a way that placed his marriage and children at the very heart and forefront of the building with the children's nurseries placed next to the couple's apartments and the decor and furnishings deliberately chosen to be as unassuming and comfortable as possible. Meanwhile, the grounds that surrounded the house were a perfect playground for the royal children and equipped with a private beach, floating swimming pool and even a Swiss cottage which had been specially transported over from Switzerland to act as a play house where Alice and her siblings could learn to cook and do simple housework tasks. Although all of the children were undoubtedly destined to preside over their own grand households and would almost certainly never actually have to do their own cooking or cleaning, Albert still thought it imperative that they should all be able to look after themselves.

Although the couple loved their time at Osborne, which had the significant benefit of enjoying pleasant weather for much of the year and becoming positively balmy during the summer months, they never forgot their love of Scotland and in June 1852, a year after Osborne House was finally completed, Prince Albert purchased Balmoral Castle in Aberdeenshire, which the couple had been leasing and occasionally visiting since 1848. Like the original Osborne House, Balmoral Castle was too small to accommodate the royal family, which by this time included seven children, and their household and was therefore replaced by an entirely new castle; a Victorian fantasy of how a Scottish baronial mansion should look, conceived by Prince Albert who also drew inspiration from the castles of his native Germany. While the interior of Osborne House was decorated with typical Victorian chintzy middle class taste, Balmoral was a riot of clashing tartans, heavy wood furniture, stuffed stag heads and antlers fashioned into chandeliers and other decorative items. Most visitors found the castle both gloomy and also, thanks to its location and Victoria's predilection for open windows at all times, incredibly chilly, but the royal couple didn't care about what they thought, for at Balmoral, so far away from the capital and the majority of their subjects, they felt like they could truly be themselves. As with Osborne House, the royal children were encouraged to spend as much time as possible outdoors, enjoying the fresh air and spectacular views of the Scottish countryside until the weather drove them inside and they could entertain themselves painting, performing theatrical tableaux or learning Scottish dances. In keeping with the different pace of life at Balmoral, Victoria felt able to take a close personal interest in the people who lived on or near the estate and encouraged her children to do the same. From an early age, Alice and her sisters were encouraged to spend time with the local people, playing with their children, overseeing the daily distribution of alms and paying visits to bereaved or otherwise beleaguered tenants. Although all of the children took this duty very seriously, it had a particularly powerful effect on Alice who was extremely kind hearted and took a down to earth interest in the lives of everyone that she encountered.

Although there was plenty of time for fun and games, the royal children's education began when they were still babies and followed the strict forty-eight-page-long guidelines laid down by Baron Stockmar, who believed that education's purpose was to develop and strengthen the good aspects of the personality while simultaneously reducing any bad tendencies that the child might have via the means of a rigorous programme of learning. The royal children began lessons in French at just eighteen months and then added German, which was commonly spoken in the royal household, around their fourth birthday. By the time they were seven, their lessons, which began at half past eight in the morning and ended at six, also included Greek, Latin, Arithmetic, Geography, Philosophy and History. The precocious Princess Victoria, who was extraordinarily bright by any standards, flourished in this hot house atmosphere but her brother Bertie, who had been promoted to the nickname 'The Boy' after Alice usurped his title of 'Baby', floundered painfully. Alice, although not as brilliant as her elder sister, still managed to shine in the school room and was considered very clever by her governess Lady Lyttelton. Luckily for the royal children, they were not expected to stay at their desks all day but were allowed plenty of breaks to play outside, embroider or work on their dancing, art and music. All of Victoria's daughters were accomplished artists and musicians, with Alice being particularly gifted on the piano. The Victorians believed very strongly that the Devil makes work for idle hands and so kept themselves and their children relentlessly busy, which was doubtless extremely trying if one happened to be of a naturally indolent disposition. Fortunately, Alice took after her father Albert in that she loved to be busy and industrious and was never happier than when she had lots of different projects on the go at the same time.

Although she was very close to her elder sister Vicky, with whom she shared a bedroom, Alice's true partner in crime was her brother Bertie, whom she would absolutely adore for the rest of her life. As Prince of

Wales and heir to the throne, Bertie was lumbered from birth with the heavy expectations of his parents and subjected from infancy to a strict educational regime that was intended to mould him into a perfect future king. Bertie's tragedy was that he actually desperately wanted to please his parents, especially his mother, but was dominated and overshadowed by his talented eldest sister and would always be judged in comparison to her rather than as an individual. In Alice, his adoring little sister whom he called 'Alee', he found someone who loved him for himself and appreciated his own genuine merits such as his good nature and unfailing kindness towards his younger siblings and even his arch rival Vicky. When Bertie was banished to his room for some childhood wrongdoing, it was Alice who crept upstairs to chat to him through his locked door and pass him biscuits and even as adults they would always be the first to stand up for each other against their mother and siblings. Within their family, Alice was admired for her kind heart and apparently endless benevolence when it came to those less fortunate than herself, but on the flip side, her sensitivity and tendency to lengthy bouts of melancholy were both disapproved of by her mother. She would cry unconsolably when her parents or beloved Bertie went away and would be devastated by any criticisms – especially if they came from her father Albert, whom she revered and worshipped, even admitting that 'it makes me feel myself so small, so imperfect when I think that I am his child and so unworthy of being it.'[22] Albert could do no wrong as far as Alice was concerned and from an early age she modelled her behaviour and character on his, in particular espousing his strong interest in philanthropy and social welfare.

Perhaps Prince Albert's greatest achievement was the Great Exhibition in Hyde Park which was opened by Victoria in May 1851 and attracted over 6 million visitors (equivalent to a third of the entire British population at this time) before it closed in October of that year. Albert himself had devised the exhibition as a means of showing off Britain's role as an industrial leader and it featured thousands of exhibits from all around the globe with pride of place, naturally, going to those created at home. The royal family visited the exhibition at least three times, on one occasion accompanied by Prince Wilhelm of Prussia and his family, which included his nineteen-year-old son Friedrich and twelve-year-old daughter Luise. While Princess Luise bonded with Alice, forming a friendship that would endure into adulthood, Friedrich, who was known by his family as Fritz, was very taken by Vicky, not quite eleven at the time, who captured his attention with her bright intelligence and lively personality. Obviously, Vicky was still far too young to be getting engaged, but her parents and Fritz's mother, Princess Augusta, were completely in favour of a future match between the two and therefore encouraged the young pair to correspond when the visit had come to an end.

Four years later, in September 1855, and a month short of his twenty-fourth birthday, Fritz returned in order to visit the royal family at Balmoral and was more enamoured than ever with Vicky, now almost fifteen. Although it was obvious to everyone that he had come to see Vicky, it had not been his plan to actually propose to her during this visit. However, he was so struck by her loveliness that he could not help approaching Victoria and Albert to ask for permission to marry her and with their blessing he proposed while they were out riding together. The news was greeted with delight by Victoria and Albert but for Vicky's younger siblings, and in particular the sensitive and warm-hearted Alice, there was a sad sense that the happy childhood that they had all shared was coming to an end and that adulthood with all its trials and tribulations was all too close at hand.

Chapter Two

'More like a funeral than a wedding.'

1858–1862

The seventeen-year-old Vicky married her Fritz in the Chapel Royal at St James' Palace on 25 January 1858. Although the groom's parents had naturally tried to argue that their only son, who was second in line to the Prussian throne, should be married in Berlin, Victoria's insistence that her daughter's wedding should take place in her own country had nonetheless won the day. Vicky was the first of Victoria's children to get married and it was only fitting that she should be provided with a most splendid day. The fourteen-year-old Princess Alice provided invaluable support to her elder sister at this happy but stressful time and their mother's journal reveals that the two princesses were often together in the days before the wedding. Although Vicky was naturally thrilled and excited to be marrying a man that she loved very much, she was still very young and dreaded leaving her parents and siblings to start a new life in Germany. No doubt the two girls spent a great deal of time talking about what lay ahead, more immediately for Vicky but also, at some point in the future, for Alice too. While Vicky was resplendent on her wedding day in white moire trimmed with three flounces of Honiton lace, her three younger sisters looked enchanting in pink satin trimmed with Newport lace, which Alice teamed with a wreath of cornflowers and marguerites, while her sisters Helena and Louise had smaller sprays in their hair – the youngest princess, Beatrice was considered too young to be present at the ceremony but made a brief appearance, dressed in pink satin like her sisters, at the reception afterwards. Victoria wrote in her journal that evening that Alice 'cried dreadfully'[1] during the ceremony, obviously deeply distressed to be losing the sister that she had known all her life and to whom she had been extremely close. When Vicky left for Germany on 2 February, Victoria obviously felt great sympathy for her 'dear good Alice, whose grief was piteous when she took leave of her sister, from whom she had never been parted.'[2]

After Vicky's departure, Alice took over her role as eldest resident daughter, which involved acting as a companion to her mother, particularly when her father was otherwise engaged. Victoria's journals are full of references to walks in the garden, drives and private dinners with Alice, who bore her new duties with quiet resignation. Although she loved her mother, she also found her difficult, highly strung and demanding and although Victoria's journals were still littered with references to Alice's sweet nature and good temper, clashes between the two would only increase as the young princess approached adulthood. However, while Alice often felt frustrated by her mother, her adoration of her father never faltered and she would always consider him to be the very best of men and measured all others against him. Until her departure for Berlin, Albert had spent an hour every day alone with Vicky, chatting about art, history and current affairs and it made Alice inexpressibly happy when he transferred his attention to her and it was she who had the happy privilege of sitting down with her father every evening after dinner. Although this may have seemed like idle chit chat, it was all designed to mould her character, expand her general knowledge and, importantly for the daughter of two notable art collectors, develop her taste. As for her siblings, she would never stop missing Vicky but would draw even closer to her brother Bertie in her absence, much to the relief of their mother, who already found her eldest son and heir intensely annoying and hoped that Alice's good sense and obedient nature would prove to be a good influence on him, which indeed it was as she was the only person in the family that he seemed to have any respect for. However, Victoria was rather less pleased by the fact that Alice could always be depended upon to take Bertie's side against her and could be extremely sharp tongued while doing so. On the whole though, both Victoria and Albert appreciated the efforts that Alice made to keep Bertie in line and smooth his troubled relationship with his parents.

Just as her mother's churching ceremony signified her return to public life after giving birth, so too did Alice's confirmation on 21 April 1859, four days before her sixteenth birthday, mark the end of her childhood. Victoria and Albert had been thinking about Alice's future prospects ever since her birth and although they did not anticipate arranging a match as prestigious as that made by her sister, whose husband would one day rule Prussia, they still hoped, in time, to see her presiding over a suitably grand court, preferably in Germany. Albert and his advisor Stockmar had put their heads together and came up with what was known as the Coburg Plan, an imperialistic dream of unifying the thirty-eight different German states in order to create one great nation with Prussia at its head. It was Albert's belief that an alliance between Britain and this new united German empire would create a natural equilibrium in a Europe that still remembered the dark days of the Napoleonic wars and would, he hoped, ensure a strong and long lasting peace. The marriage of Vicky and Fritz had done much to further Albert's plans as he now expected to see his daughter sitting on the Prussian throne, her marriage a physical embodiment of the bond that existed between their nations, but he knew that further marriages and alliances between the royal houses of Britain and Germany would be necessary and so he turned his attention to Alice. At sixteen, she was slender (the days when her mother had nicknamed her 'Fatima' were very much in the past) and delightfully pretty with an elfin face, her mother's limpid blue eyes and fine chestnut brown hair, which she wore neatly drawn back over her ears in the style of the day. Although she had a reputation for being serious minded, she also delighted in pretty dresses, hair ornaments and fine jewels, even, with the assistance of her parents, buying herself a beautiful diamond necklace and earrings to mark the occasion of her confirmation. There was no doubt at all that Alice was one of the most eligible and desirable princesses in Europe but whether her parents would be able to find a princeling worthy of her hand was another matter entirely.

Victoria instructed her eldest daughter Vicky to keep an eye out for any potential candidates amongst the various German noble houses, stipulating that: 'Beauty I don't want though I should be glad of it when it's there; but nice, manly, sensible, healthy, gentlemanlike appearance is essential.'[3] Obviously, as far as Victoria and her daughters were concerned, there was no man on earth to equal Prince Albert but that did not deter them from looking for the next best thing. Keen to see her sister living nearby in Germany, Vicky fell to her task with gusto, sending several photos of prospective bridegrooms back to England so that Victoria could inspect them at her leisure. The first candidate to catch Vicky's eye was her husband's cousin, Prince Albrecht of Prussia, who was twenty-two and considered to be rather good looking. However, although he was on paper exactly the sort of young man that Victoria would have liked to see her daughter married to, she was put off by the scandal that had surrounded Albrecht's parents' divorce in 1849, which had occurred after his mother, Princess Marianne of the Netherlands, eloped with her coachman and then conceived his child. Victoria was horrified by all of this until she was reminded of the fact that Albrecht's fractured family background was almost exactly the same as that of her own beloved Albert, who was of course the most virtuous man alive as far as Victoria was concerned, at which point she decided to keep him on her list of potential husbands, which included virtually every eligible Protestant prince in Europe.

Although Victoria would naturally have preferred that Alice marry into one of the German noble houses, she also gave serious consideration to eighteen-year-old Prince Wilhelm of Orange, the eldest son and heir of King Wilhelm III of the Netherlands and his wife Princess Sophie of Württemberg, who was one of Victoria's favourite cousins. Wilhelm's parents had been estranged for several years, but Victoria had learnt her lesson and decided not to hold this against him, particularly as she was so fond of his mother and knew what a difficult time she had had with her philandering husband. However, when Victoria heard that young Wilhelm had behaved in a rather less than princely fashion during a recent trip to the exclusive spa town of Baden, she was rather less inclined to be forgiving and decided that he would not be a suitable husband for her innocent daughter, despite Vicky's protestations that his poor behaviour at Baden was down to youthful high spirits and having the misfortune to fall in with the wrong crowd. Victoria remained unimpressed and was horrified when Wilhelm announced that he intended to visit England in January 1860. Victoria had no wish to encourage any pretensions that Wilhelm might have had to Alice's hand, but at the same time knew that she could not risk offending his father by not inviting him to stay with the royal family at Windsor Castle. She was somewhat reassured when reports began to circulate that the young prince had publicly announced that he had no intention of getting married for the foreseeable future, but nonetheless decided to take the extra precaution of warning Alice about his unsuitability before he arrived so that she knew not to make any special efforts to engage with him. As it turned out, and as anyone who knew Victoria's weakness for handsome young men might have guessed, Wilhelm's visit passed without incident and he even managed to make a highly favourable impression upon the queen, who was impressed by his excellent manners and the unaffected way that he played with her younger children – while, perhaps pointedly, paying very little attention to Alice.

What Alice thought of her family's not especially subtle attempts to find a husband for her is not known, but Victoria's journals and letters refer on more than one occasion to the young princess' unwillingness to marry and leave home. Some of this trepidation was inspired by the horrendous ordeal that Vicky had undergone while giving birth to her eldest son Wilhelm in January 1859, which had left her traumatised and her baby with a withered left arm thanks to a mismanaged breech birth. Vicky's unmarried sisters were understandably shaken by reports of their sister's terrifying labour and Alice in particular felt compelled to announce that she was in no hurry to get married and have children in case the same thing happened to her. She was also motivated by a genuine desire to remain with her parents, informing her mother that she did not want to go away. However, the unhappy, frustrated lives of the unmarried daughters of George III and Queen Charlotte, some of whom Victoria had known very well and profoundly pitied while growing up in Kensington Palace, served as a serious warning to the next generation and there was little chance that Alice would be encouraged to remain unmarried for long. On Alice's seventeenth birthday in April 1860, Victoria wrote to her uncle Leopold, King of the Belgians that her second daughter was a 'good, dear, amiable child, and in very good looks just now' but that 'her future is still undecided, she is quite free, and *all* we wish is a good, kind husband – *no* brilliant position (which there is not to be got), but a quiet, comfortable position'.[4] Although he had won her over during his visit to Windsor earlier that year, Prince Wilhelm was clearly no longer in the running, especially as Victoria had turned her attention elsewhere – to the house of Hesse-Darmstadt, whose current Grand Duke had three strapping, good-looking nephews, the eldest of whom, twenty-three-year-old Prince Louis, was in line to succeed to the duchy after his father, Prince Charles.

Although the Grand Duchy of Hesse-Darmstadt was not the largest or grandest of the many German noble houses, it was one of the oldest and could trace its origins back to the creation of the Landgraviate of Hesse in 1567 before becoming a grand duchy in 1806. However, despite its small size, Hesse-Darmstadt had been considered sufficiently prestigious for Tsar Alexander II to marry into the family when he took Princess Marie of Hesse-Darmstadt, Prince Louis' aunt, as his bride in 1841. Having the Empress of Russia as an aunt was obviously a huge point in the favour of the three Hesse princes, especially with Queen Victoria who still had fond memories of the time that the young Alexander, who was then Tsesarevich, had visited London and swept her off her feet with his good looks, *joie de vivre* and talent for dancing. 'I really am quite in love with the Grand Duke,' she breathlessly confided to her journal during his visit. 'I never enjoyed myself more.'[5] Unfortunately, the eldest Hesse prince was unlikely to set anyone's heart aflutter but then again, Victoria had rather different requirements for a prospective son-in-law than she had for the subject of a youthful flirtation and if the Hessian princes were not renowned for dancing all night and charming young ladies then so much the better, as far as she was concerned. As usual, Vicky was instructed to procure photographs and gather as much information about the princes, particularly the eldest, Prince Louis, who would naturally be the most suitable match. However, although Vicky was able to furnish her mother with a most pleasing account of Louis' various virtues, she was also forced to inform her that he was said to be madly in love with the strikingly attractive Princess Maria Maximilianovna of Leuchtenberg, whose grandfather was Empress Joséphine's only son Eugène de Beauharnais. Disappointed by this unwelcome news, Victoria was inclined to strike Louis from her list until her husband and Stockmar advised her that Louis' family were not at all in favour of a match with the Leuchtenbergs, who were widely regarded as parvenu Bonapartist upstarts and thus inferior to the established old houses of Europe, and were far more keen to ally themselves with the British royal family. They were also of the opinion that the rumours of Louis' attachment to Princess Maria had been grossly exaggerated and until either he himself explicitly confirmed it or an engagement was announced, his heart should be considered free. Although Victoria was still hesitant, she agreed that Louis and his younger brother Henry should be encouraged to visit England so that she could inspect them for herself – only to once again be caught out when they announced their imminent arrival rather sooner than she had expected.

This time Alice was not pre-warned about growing too attached to the visiting princes and so when Louis and his brother arrived at Buckingham Palace on 1 June 1860, she was free to be impressed by what her mother described in her journal that evening as a pair of 'nice, pleasing, natural and unaffected young men'[6] – just the sort, in fact, that she would most like to see marrying her daughters. After a few days in London they moved to Windsor Castle for the rest of their visit where, on 5 June, Victoria blandly noted that Louis took Alice in to dinner and the next day wrote, after sitting beside him at dinner, that she liked him 'more and more'.[7] What Alice thought is not recorded but she was certainly fascinated by the quiet and serious young Hessian prince and was undoubtedly disappointed when he returned home to Germany, although the couple swapped photographs and promised to stay in touch. 'There can be no doubt that... Louis and Alice have formed a mutual attachment and although the visit has fortunately passed over without any declaration, I have no doubt that it will lead to further advances from the young gentleman's family,'[8] Prince Albert noted to his confidante Baron Stockmar after Louis' departure. 'We should not be averse to such an alliance as the family is good and estimable, and the young man is unexceptional in morals, manly and in both body and mind distinguished by a youthful vigour.'[9] Albert was happy to let matters unfold naturally but Victoria was far more impatient and after upbraiding her husband for not caring about Alice's fate, asked poor Vicky, who must have been at least a bit fed up about acting as her mother's go-between, to do some detective work to find out what Louis thought about Alice now that they had met. To Victoria's delight, Vicky was able to surpass her expectations by directly appealing to Louis' mother, Princess Elisabeth, who had been born a princess of Prussia and was a distant cousin of Vicky's husband Fritz. Elisabeth had made no secret of her ambition to marry at least one of her sons to a British princess and was only too happy to let it be known that her son had been captivated by Alice's quiet charm and was planning to write and ask her parents for permission to propose to her.

The royal family were enjoying a summer holiday at Osborne House when Louis' promised letter arrived, much to the delight of both Albert and Victoria, who were both impressed by his good manners and courteous way of expressing himself. They had almost certainly not forgotten that when Fritz had approached them to ask permission to propose to Vicky all those years earlier, he had ignored their request to wait until she was older and so they were pleased by Louis' restraint and discretion, which was so marked that even Alice had no idea that he planned to propose until Albert gently informed her of the fact. This happy conversation took place on 25 July, the day after a telegram had arrived from Fritz in Germany to inform them that Vicky had safely given birth to her second child, a daughter, who would be named Viktoria Charlotte. To celebrate, Alice and her siblings cooked dinner for their parents in the fully equipped kitchen of their Swiss Cottage in the grounds of Osborne House, after which Albert delivered the happy news that Louis was planning to come to England later that year and propose. In the meantime, on 22 September, Alice had the great treat of accompanying her parents on a visit to her father's childhood home in Coburg, although the trip was to be a bittersweet one as news arrived en route that Albert's beloved step mother Marie, who had married his father (who was also her uncle) in 1832, had died after a short illness, which naturally plunged the party into some gloom. However, although everyone wore mourning for the rest of the visit, their spirits were greatly lightened when they arrived at Coburg and found Vicky and her children, Wilhelm and the new baby Charlotte, waiting for them. It was the first time that Victoria and Albert had met their Prussian grandchildren and they were thrilled by the experience, with Victoria later writing in her journal that they 'felt so happy' to finally see them, before concluding that despite everything 'it seemed like a dream to be at last at dear Coburg'.[10]

While Victoria enjoyed exploring the place where her mother, a princess of Coburg, had spent her childhood and Albert rather morosely revisited the haunts of his own youth, Alice spent a great deal of time with her elder sister Vicky and her children and there can be no doubt that the sisters talked at length about Louis and Alice's forthcoming engagement. The safe arrival of Vicky's daughter had done much to calm the fears about pregnancy and childbirth that Wilhelm's disastrous birth

had caused and Alice now felt far more cheerful about the prospect of
having children of her own. Victoria, however, was keen that Vicky should
not be too candid about the realities of married life and childbearing and
would later caution her to 'say as little as you can on these subjects before
Alice (who has already heard much more than you ever did)… I am very
anxious that she should know as little about the inevitable miseries as
possible, so don't forget, dear.'[11] The two princesses were together on
1 October when news arrived that their father had been forced to leap
from a moving carriage when his horses were frightened by the sound of
an approaching train at a level crossing – the prince, much to everyone's
relief, was unhurt but he was undoubtedly shaken by the experience
while Victoria, always fearful for those whom she loved, was distraught at
the thought of how much worse it could have been and leaned heavily on
her daughters for support. Albert had completely recovered by the time
they left Coburg ten days later and Alice had her reward when they were
joined in Coblenz by Louis' parents, who were keen to discuss Louis'
visit to England the following month and the forthcoming engagement
with her mother and father. Victoria later noted in her journal that while
Louis' mother, Elisabeth was 'most friendly and kind',[12] his father, Prince
Charles was 'very civil and amiable but very shy'[13] – unfortunately for the
poor prince, shyness in men was not a trait that she particularly admired.

After weeks of anxious excitement on both sides of the Channel, Louis
returned to Windsor Castle on 24 November with his friend Leopold,
Prince of Hohenzollern in tow, perhaps for moral support. Their arrival
did not go as planned for they somehow managed to turn up two days
early, throwing Victoria, who hated to be taken by surprise, into a panic
although she swiftly took charge of the situation, only later noting in
her journal that 'it was an anxious moment and a nervous one for Alice
and me as we know what the object of the… visit is!'[14] After a few nerve-
racking days, Louis found himself alone with his prospective in-laws
when Leopold departed to Portugal, where he was expected to propose
to the Infanta Antonia – an event that Victoria and Albert took a great
interest in as her father, Ferdinand II was a prince of Saxe-Coburg Gotha
and their mutual first cousin. However, although everyone knew that a
proposal even closer to home was imminent, Louis failed to act, much to
Victoria's impatient consternation, although she noted in her journal that

'it is so nice to see the liking the young people have to one another, and it is so apparent, that everyone must see what is coming.'[15] After a few more uncertain days, Albert offered to arrange matters to bring forward what he called 'the great Alician event' but in the end his intervention proved unnecessary for on the 30 November, when pouring rain had forced the party to remain indoors, Louis finally plucked up the courage to ask Alice to marry him. 'Perceived Alice and Louis talking more earnestly than usual before the fireplace and when we passed to go into the other room, both came up to me in great agitation, Alice saying he had proposed to her and he begging me for my blessing, which I gladly gave him,'[16] Victoria recorded later that evening. 'Alice came to our room and told us of Louis expressing his hope to her that she liked him sufficiently to exchange her English for a German home – small as it was.'[17] Everyone was delighted by the news and when Empress Eugénie of France visited Windsor a few days later, Victoria was very proud to introduce Louis as 'my future son-in-law'[18] and then later note that he appeared at dinner in the Windsor Uniform of a dark blue frock coat with scarlet collar and cuffs and 'looked so nice, being evidently much pleased at being one of us.'[19]

Finding himself unable to leave his betrothed's side, Louis remained in England until just after Christmas, endearing himself to his future mother- and father-in-law, who were in raptures over what Albert described to Stockmar as 'his unaffectedly genial and cordial nature, his great modesty and a very childlike nature, united with strict morality and a genuine goodness and dignity.'[20] Victoria meanwhile was struck by how happy the young couple were and described them as existing in a state of 'perpetual sunshine'. The wedding date was set for 4 June and Victoria and Alice excitedly began to prepare for the big event, only for their plans to be put on hold when Victoria's mother, the Duchess of Kent, suddenly fell ill at the beginning of the year and then died on 16 March. Victoria's relationship with her mother had been rocky to say the least, but her marriage to Albert had done much to reconcile them and she was genuinely devastated to lose her – her grief becoming even more intense when she read through her mother's journals and letters afterwards and remorsefully realised just how much the duchess had actually loved and cared for her. Naturally, with the court now in mourning, Alice's wedding would have to be postponed although Victoria still formally announced the engagement at a meeting of the Privy Council on 30 April so that they could begin the process of arranging her dowry, which Parliament unanimously agreed should be £30,000 (approximately £1.8 million in 2019) along with an annuity of £6,000 (£355,000 in 2019) – a huge amount of money compared to the average income at the time and enough to enable Alice to live in some modest style but not tremendous luxury. 'She will not be able to do great things with it,'[21] Albert wryly noted, perhaps foreseeing trouble ahead when Alice had moved to Germany and found herself unable to live in quite the same style to which she had become accustomed, especially as much of the money had already been earmarked for the construction of a new palace for the young couple in Darmstadt. Alice, who had just turned eighteen and doubtless probably thought that it sounded like a great deal of money, was perfectly content though and eagerly looking forward to Louis' next visit later that month. He arrived at Osborne House on 19 May and promptly fell ill with measles on Victoria's birthday five days later, much to her displeasure and Alice's distress, although luckily it was to be a mild dose and he was up and about again by the end of the month and fully fit by the time Vicky and her family arrived on 24 June for an extended visit – their first since Vicky's marriage over three years earlier. Victoria was delighted to have her eldest daughter back again, but the happy family gathering gave rise to melancholy musings about the absence of her own mother for as she noted in her journal that first evening: 'to feel that my own precious Mama is no more with us to share our joy, greatly spoils the pleasure and makes me dreadfully sad.'[22]

That September, Louis joined the royal family at Balmoral for the first time, which gave him an opportunity to see Alice at her best for it was in Scotland that she truly felt happiest and most at home. Like many young girls at the time, she had been inflamed with a passionate hero worship of Florence Nightingale which had inspired her to take a close interest in medical matters. In different circumstances, she might have considered training as a nurse but as this would have been considered a deeply inappropriate vocation for a princess, she instead channelled her energies into philanthropy and taking a close interest in the welfare of the people around her. At Balmoral there was plenty for her to do and she spent a great deal of time visiting the crofter families on the estate, distributing alms, playing with the children and ministering to minor ailments. Louis was entranced by this new aspect to his betrothed's character and spent hours accompanying her on these visits – in between hunting excursions with her father and brothers, during which he impressed everyone with his shooting skills, even bringing down four stags on one memorable occasion. However, while everyone else was busily occupied on the estate, Victoria was still feeling incredibly despondent about her mother's death and her journal is littered with gloomy reflections about her own mortality and the ever present fear of losing another loved one, writing on 6 October that 'all allusions to death, eternity, present, & future life, affect me much, since I have been face to face with death & know what it is to have a dear one in another world!'[23] Victoria's melancholy mental state was trying for all of the family, but especially so for Alice, who was desperately looking forward to marrying and starting her new life but felt guilty about abandoning her mother at such a difficult time. Matters only got worse later in the autumn when rumours that her elder brother Bertie had been indulging in rather un-princely behaviour reached their father's ears, causing Albert to visit Bertie in Cambridge, where he was studying at Trinity College, in order to implore him to mend his ways. While there, Albert caught a chill that grew progressively worse after his return to Windsor Castle, despite being encouraged to spend as much time as possible resting in bed or taking warm baths, which eased his rheumatism. Alice did all that she could to help, both by ministering to her father and also doing her best to support her mother, but by 2 December they were both very frightened as Albert's condition continued to worsen and he began to look extremely ill. Two days later, Victoria wrote in her journal that he was 'in such a listless state and hardly can smile'[24] and could take no nourishment other than raspberry syrup in seltzer water – much to the apprehension of the royal doctors, who urged him to eat. She would have been even more alarmed had she known that Albert himself believed that he was close to death and had waited until she was absent from the room before discreetly asking Alice to write to Vicky and tell her that he was dying, only to be disappointed when she later admitted that she had not felt able to do so and had only told Vicky that he was 'very ill'. 'You have done wrong,' Albert gently chided her. 'You should have told her that I am dying, yes, I am dying.'[25]

Alice did everything that she could to assist, but felt helpless in the face of her father's rapidly deteriorating state and fatalistic acceptance of his own imminent demise. Although her mother clung to the hope that he was merely suffering from a seasonal fever and would eventually recover, Alice, who rarely left Albert's side, became increasingly sure that he was right about the seriousness of his illness and did not feel quite so optimistic as she watched him fade away before their very eyes, at times not even able to breathe comfortably and too weak to even get dressed. By the 10 December, Albert was unable to do anything but lie on his sofa and listen to Alice reading aloud from his favourite books by Sir Walter Scott or playing quietly on a piano that was specially brought into the next room. A member of the household would later write that 'Princess Alice's fortitude has amazed us all. She saw from the first that her father's and her mother's firmness depended on her firmness, and she set herself to that duty... He could not speak to the Queen of himself, for she could not bear to listen and shut her eyes to the danger. His daughter saw that she must act differently, and she never let her voice falter or shed a tear in his presence. She sat by him, listened to all he said, repeated hymns, and then when she could bear it no longer, would walk calmly to the door, and rush away to her room, returning with the same calm and pale face, without any appearance of the agitation that she had gone through.'[26] They concluded that: 'Of the devotion and strength of mind shown by Princess Alice all through these trying scenes, it is impossible to speak too highly.'[27] As Albert's life neared its end, the strain on his wife and family became almost unbearable as they all desperately struggled to prepare themselves for what was now becoming an inevitability. The only person who appeared oblivious was Bertie, who was still away in Cambridge and unaware of just how serious his father's illness actually was. Victoria had irrationally decided that the chill that had set the current crisis in motion was entirely the fault of their eldest son and the reckless behaviour that had compelled his father to visit him in the first place and so was unwilling to request his attendance at Windsor Castle. However, as Albert's conditioned worsened, Alice decided to take matters into her own hands and secretly despatched a telegram to her brother succinctly informing him that their father was not very well and that he should come at once.

Thanks to Alice's intervention, Bertie was kneeling at the foot of their father's bed when he passed away at 10.50 pm on 14 December. Alice, who had tirelessly ministered to her father's needs during his final illness was kneeling at Albert's side with her mother on the opposite side. Victoria was, predictably, distraught when her husband breathed his last and cried out 'Oh my dear darling' before giving out a terrible, piercing wail that seemed to echo in the corridors beyond. When Victoria was eventually gently prised away from Albert's body, she was led into the anteroom next door where she lay down on the sofa with her head on Alice's lap. Although the prince had been ailing for quite some time and had suffered intermittent bouts of poor health for many years previously, his death stunned the royal household with his wife and children in particular hardly knowing what to do with themselves in the wake of this enormous tragedy. While Victoria restlessly, almost wildly, roamed the royal apartments in search of some peace and her sisters and brothers sobbed helplessly, it was Alice, calm and composed as always, who held the family together, impressing everyone with her good sense, dignity and apparently endless patience when dealing with her mother's terrible grief. 'Could you but see that darling's face,' one of Victoria's ladies in waiting wrote about Alice during the crisis. 'Her great tearless eyes with their expression of resolutely subdued misery! No one knew what she was before, although I *marvelled* that they did not.'[28] In the absence of Vicky, who was suffering alone in Berlin, Alice assumed the role of eldest daughter, supporting her mother when she made the short journey down to Frogmore to select the location for a brand new mausoleum for herself and Albert and helping with the funeral arrangements. Along with her other siblings, Alice placed a lock of her hair in her father's coffin before it was sealed for its final journey – Victoria's contribution was a photograph of the beautiful Winterhalter portrait of herself, dewy eyed and with her lustrous hair falling heavily over one plump shoulder, that she had given to Albert as a birthday present in 1843, the year of Alice's birth. A few days after Albert's death, Alice and her sisters Helena and Louise accompanied Victoria to Osborne House, where she would remain for several months, sequestered away from the eyes of the world and free to give way to her grief in privacy in the house that she and Albert had built together in happier times. It must have been incredibly painful for them all to be there without him, but once again Alice was apparently able to put her own grief to one side in order to provide support to her mother. None of the royal ladies were present at Albert's funeral, which took place in St George's Chapel in the precincts of Windsor Castle on 23 December, the presence of women still being discouraged at funerals in case they interrupted the solemnity of the occasion with tears and fainting. Victoria was almost certainly distressed not to be present at Albert's interment but Alice no doubt considered it a blessing that her mother's terrible suffering could remain far from the curious public gaze. At the precise moment of Albert's interment, which was attended by a devastated Bertie and eleven-year-old Prince Arthur acting as chief mourners, Victoria picked up her pen and wrote to her eldest daughter Vicky, starting her letter with the despairing words: 'It is one o' clock and all, all is over!'[29]

According to Victoria's journals, Alice was in constant attendance on her mother at this time and forced to always be on hand to act as companion, confidante and nurse with barely any time spare to spend with her fiancé Louis, who had hastened to Osborne to lend support to his future wife and mother-in-law. Dressed in heavy black mourning clothes, she accompanied Victoria on her walks and carriage rides, sat with her at mealtimes and spent countless hours supporting her as she wept, raged and reminisced – all under the gaze of Prince Albert, whose portraits and busts were placed everywhere about the house, even over Victoria's bed. However, by the middle of February, when Vicky finally arrived from Germany to find her family in a state of disarray 'like sheep without a shepherd' as she put it, Alice had completely burnt out and her own health, which had never been robust, was beginning to fail under the relentless pressure of ministering to her grieving mother and, after Bertie had departed on an official visit to the Holy Land, acting as Victoria's unofficial secretary and go-between with her ministers, which was a huge burden for an inexperienced eighteen-year-old. 'How I grieve for her,' a family friend wrote at this time. 'Her young life crushed and blighted by a weight of care and responsibility of which few have any idea.'[30] Alarmed by her sister's wan looks and generally depressed air, Vicky suggested to their mother that Alice should be allowed to leave Osborne for a while in order to recuperate and gather her strength. At first, Victoria was unwilling to let Alice go but in the end she had to capitulate and on 19 February, Alice departed to spend ten days with her friends, the Belgian Consul Sylvain Van de Weyer and his American wife Elizabeth. While there, Alice must have given some thought to her own future – weighed down by her mother's dependence on her, she was doubtless beginning to wonder if she would ever be permitted to marry Louis after all. The wedding was still scheduled to take place that July but Victoria was so utterly consumed by her grief that she actively discouraged her children from smiling or appearing cheerful, not that there was much cause for even the most moderate mirth in the royal household at the beginning of 1862, and there was certainly absolutely no question of Alice's wedding being discussed in her mother's presence or indeed at all. It was a huge relief to everyone therefore when Victoria confirmed in February that the marriage would take place on 1 July as planned – not because she wished it, however, but because Alice's marriage had been one of Albert's own pet projects and as far as his widow was concerned, his word was still law.

If her father had still been alive then Alice's wedding would have taken place in either St George's Chapel in Windsor Castle or, more likely, the Chapel Royal in St James' Palace where her parents and elder sister Vicky had celebrated their weddings. However, Albert's death and Victoria's withdrawal from public life had made this quite impossible and instead it was decided that the wedding would take place at Osborne House with only a very few guests and as little fuss as possible. On 14 June, Victoria inspected Alice's bridal trousseau and was dismayed to find it 'so sad' with 'only black dresses made up',[31] which reflected the lack of enthusiasm that the entire family felt about the upcoming nuptials, which they all felt would be a most dismal and depressing day without their father's presence. Victoria was particularly unhappy, confiding to her eldest daughter Vicky that she wished that Alice were not leaving her side quite so soon and, as evidenced by her journals, clinging to her second daughter even more than usual. 'How I rejoiced at this marriage,' she wrote in her journal shortly before the wedding day, 'and now it will be a dreadful ordeal, all alone by myself!'[32] Victoria's sense of impending doom was increased by the untimely demise of Bertie's much-loved Governor, Major General Bruce, who had caught a fever while accompanying the young Prince of Wales on his trip to the Holy Land. Victoria had become morbidly preoccupied with Bruce's illness and was devastated by his death on 27 June, just a few days before Alice's wedding, the dreaded news arriving along with the first of the guests, virtually all of whom, with very few exceptions, were close family members. She managed to rally over the next few days thanks to being forced to socialise not just with the wedding guests but with Alice's future in-laws, who had arrived on the Isle of Wight with their son the day after Bruce's death. Nonetheless, the whole affair was permeated with a gloomy atmosphere and Victoria confided to her journal that 'all this hustle going on, with my heart utterly broken and my nerves so shattered, is very trying'.[33] On the eve of the wedding, Victoria took Alice and her siblings to Albert's room, where her wedding presents had been carefully arranged – from Albert there was an opal parure that he had selected before falling ill and from Victoria there was a diamond diadem 'designed by my precious Albert'[34] and a large pearl and diamond brooch. Bertie's contribution was a magnificent sapphire, diamond and pearl parure, while the younger siblings presented Alice, who was 'very much pleased and touched',[35] with three diamond, ruby and emerald rings and a turquoise brooch and earrings.

Alice's wedding day was dull and overcast, which suited Victoria's mood very well but was doubtless a disappointment to the bridal pair, who were keen to extract as much cheerfulness as possible from what promised to be a rather doleful occasion. Although it lacked the grandeur of the royal chapels, the bright and light-filled rooms of the Italianate Osborne House would ordinarily be eminently suitable for a summer wedding and indeed the guests would note how pretty everything looked bedecked with flowers from the gardens. While the queen naturally wore mourning along with what her youngest daughter Beatrice referred to as her 'sad cap', as a special concession she had allowed the ladies of the royal household to wear dresses in the acceptable demi-mourning hues of lilac or grey for the occasion. Alice herself looked lovely in a simple white 'half high dress with a deep flounce of Honiton lace, a veil of the same and a wreath of orange blossoms and myrtle'. Her only adornment, besides the flowers, was her mother's order and the opal cross and brooch that had formed part of her father's posthumous wedding present. She was originally supposed to have eight bridesmaids, like her sister Vicky in 1858, but the number had been halved to four when the wedding was relocated to Osborne House, with her sisters Helena, Louise and Beatrice performing the duty in 'sprigged net over white with pale mauve trimmings',[36] along with Louis' sister Princess Anna of Hesse. Although there were larger and grander rooms in Osborne House, such as the beautiful Council Room, Victoria had decided that the wedding should take place in the dining room, which was cleared of its furniture for the occasion. A temporary altar was erected beneath Winterhalter's justly celebrated 1846 painting of the royal family, which had been specifically created for Osborne House and depicted Victoria and Albert seated on rather theatrical thrones and surrounded by their five eldest children, including Alice herself, who leans over the infant Princess Helena while gazing adoringly across at her elder sister Vicky. Previously, the painting had been a cheerful and much-loved focal point of the room, acting as a backdrop to countless family dinners and celebrations over the years – now it would assume the role of an altar piece, with Albert's extended hand seeming to float in benediction over the bowed heads of the bride and groom.

The ceremony began at one in the afternoon, when Victoria, supported by her sons, entered the room, which was empty except for the Archbishop of York, and seated herself close to the altar, with the four boys standing in front of her in order to shield her from the view of the rest of the congregation, who entered soon afterwards, followed by the groom. In the absence of her father, Alice was led up the aisle by Albert's rakish elder brother Ernest, Duke of Saxe-Coburg Gotha – a sight that must have wrung Victoria's heart as they made their way to the altar. Although reports would later claim that the bereaved queen, shielded by her protective wall of sons, sobbed throughout the ceremony, she herself claimed in her journal that she 'restrained my tears and had a great struggle all through, but remained calm.'[37] When the ceremony was over, Alice and Louis paused to embrace her mother before making their way to the Horn Room to sign the register before going upstairs for a private luncheon with Victoria, while everyone ate downstairs. After this, Alice posed for the artist George Housman Thomas, who had been commissioned to paint a picture of the ceremony, which involved collecting faithful portraits of all the most significant attendees. When this was done, Alice changed into her going-away outfit of a white 'mousseline de soie' gown and orange blossom trimmed bonnet and headed off on honeymoon at St Clare Castle in Appley with her new husband. Left behind at Osborne House, Victoria felt bereft and not a little sorry for herself now that Alice, who had done so much to support her over the last seven terrible months, had gone. She spent the evening reading her journal entry about Vicky's wedding in 1858, noting that it was 'so different to this… such a joyous occasion'.[38] In a letter to Vicky, who had been forced to remain in Berlin as she was pregnant with her third child, she went even further and described Alice's big day as 'more like a funeral than a wedding'.[39]

Chapter Three

'It is a state of affairs too
dreadful to describe.'

1862–1872

It rained for every day of Alice's three-day honeymoon but she didn't seem to care at all for she was completely happy and contented for the first time in months. Even the fact that her mother, accompanied by a large party of family and courtiers, paid the newly-weds a surprise visit on the second day did little to dampen Alice's spirits, although Louis may well have felt rather less impressed to have his honeymoon so rudely interrupted by his overbearing mother-in-law. For Victoria's part, she was exceedingly pleased with Louis, especially as he had readily agreed that he and Alice would spend several months of every year with Victoria, which had done much to reconcile her to losing another daughter. After they returned to Osborne House, they spent another week with Victoria before departing for their new life together in Darmstadt. Alice was deeply distressed by the prospect of leaving her family behind and broke down and cried when she said goodnight to her mother on her last evening. The following morning, Victoria took this last opportunity to lecture Louis about the importance of taking proper care of Alice, pointing out that she was looking very thin and required some extra cosseting, especially if she became pregnant soon – none of them obviously realising that Alice had almost certainly conceived her first child, who would be born the following April, either during her honeymoon or shortly afterwards. There were sad scenes when they left Osborne House that afternoon, with Victoria noting in her journal that Alice was 'terribly overcome' while she herself 'tried to bear up as much as I could and clasped her in my arms, giving her my blessing.'[1] The plan was that the couple should return in October and Victoria, who could not even bear to watch their yacht leave, prepared herself to feel quite desolate until they were reunited again, although she would later express surprise at how little she actually missed Alice now that the separation had occurred: 'Much as she has been to me… and dear and precious as a comfort and an assistance, I hardly miss her at all, or felt her going – so utterly alone am I.'[2]

Alice no doubt felt a curious mixture of misery and excitement as she boarded the royal yacht for the first leg of her journey, but would have been comforted by the company of her new husband who was very much looking forward to having her to himself at last. They arrived in Brussels that evening, then went on to Cologne, where they boarded the train that would take them to Darmstadt, the capital of the Grand Duchy of Hesse. It was pouring with rain but huge crowds still gathered, clustered beneath umbrellas and cheering loudly, to greet Prince Louis' new bride. For Alice, whose life at Osborne had been quiet and even rather sequestered, this noisy, joyous welcome to her new home must have been overwhelming as she and Louis rode in their carriage through the streets decorated with English flags, accompanied by the shouts of the crowd and music played by the city's bands and orchestras. 'I am really deeply touched by the kindness and enthusiasm shown by the people, which is said to be quite unusual,'[3] Alice later wrote to her mother, clearly relieved to have had such a good start to her new life. Her first home in Darmstadt was the so called Prinz Karl Palace in the town centre, which was the residence of Louis' parents and rather smaller than the older and much grander ducal palace, which was inhabited by Louis' uncle Grand Duke Ludwig III, an immensely tall (he was 6 feet 10 inches) noted eccentric whose wife Mathilda of Bavaria had died that May – a loss that had occasioned a minor panic that Alice's wedding might have to be postponed again in order to accommodate the Hesse family's period of mourning. The Grand Duke had announced during the marriage negotiations that Louis and Alice would not be welcome to reside under his roof, but now, although he was still unwilling to let them move in, he was clearly keen to warmly welcome Alice to the city, endearing himself to her by comparing his grief for his wife with the great sorrow of her widowed mother and taking a great deal of interest in her numerous siblings, whom she was already missing terribly. Louis' parents were also extremely welcoming, having grown to love Alice and appreciate her qualities over the past few years and she would become especially close to her mother-in-law Princess

Elisabeth, who was as cheerfully good hearted as her son. Alice would also become great friends with her husband's younger brothers Henry, who reminded her of her own brothers, and William, who was quiet and studious. Her best friend in Darmstadt though was her gentle and good-natured sister-in-law Anna, who was exactly a month younger than herself. Alice would be devastated when Anna, who married the Grand Duke of Mecklenburg-Schwerin in 1864, died of puerperal fever in April 1865 after giving birth to her only child – a stark reminder of the dangers of childbirth and one of the reasons why Alice became increasingly engrossed with studying nursing and midwifery during the late 1860s. 'It makes one feel the uncertainty of life, and the necessity of labour, self denial, charity and all those virtues which we ought to strive after,'[4] she wrote at the time, obviously very moved by her sister-in-law's death.

It was fortunate for Alice that she got on so well with her husband's family as although their home was obviously much larger than that inhabited by the average citizen of Darmstadt, it was still rather a squeeze to fit in an extra married couple and their retinue of servants. Alice wrote to her mother that although her rooms were 'prettily arranged' and had been thoughtfully decorated for her in an 'English style', they were rather smaller and more cramped than any suite of rooms that she had hitherto inhabited and she was finding it rather trying. However, this uncomfortable arrangement was only intended as a temporary solution as work was already underway on the so called Neues Palais, which had been significantly funded by Queen Victoria who intended it to act as a suitably magnificent permanent residence for her daughter and family. However, its conception had incurred some controversy when it was decided that the palace should be built on the site of Darmstadt's former botanical gardens, which naturally incurred the wrath of some of the town's more nostalgic residents, who deplored the fact that their heritage was being destroyed in order to create a house for a foreign princess and that their former public park would now be railed off to create a private royal garden. There were even some fears that the opposition to the new palace might harm Alice's popularity in Hesse, but this quickly proved not to be the case as demonstrated by the warm welcome that she received when she first arrived. However, the architect Konrad Klaus, who had been engaged by Victoria, had only just drawn up his plans and it didn't seem likely that the work would be finished for several years – indeed, Alice and her family would not be able to take up residence until March 1866, after effectively bankrupting themselves thanks to the spiralling costs of building and decorating their new home. Alice's discomfort only increased when she discovered, probably within a few weeks of her arrival in Darmstadt, that she was already pregnant, which doubtless rendered the prospect of adding another person to the already cramped household absolutely intolerable. She had also never forgotten Vicky's terrible account of her sufferings when her eldest son was born and so resolved that the baby should be born in England with her mother, familiar faces and the royal doctors that she had known all her life safely close at hand. Alice, always thoughtful and considerate of the feelings of others, was concerned about hurting the feelings of her husband's family by suggesting that she thought that the medical care in Darmstadt might not be up to scratch, but in the end they managed to tactfully arrange matters so that they were able to leave in the autumn.

On 20 September, Alice was reunited with her mother and some of her siblings at Rheinhardtsbrunn Castle, where they were holidaying. While there, Alice informed her mother of her pregnancy and asked for help returning to England for the baby's birth the following spring. As her father had predicted, her allowance really didn't go very far, especially when the costs of building a new palace were factored in, and she was already finding herself in rather straitened circumstances. It was a great relief therefore when Victoria placed the royal yacht at her disposal and agreed that they should return in the middle of November – just in time to mark the doleful occasion of the first anniversary of Albert's death at Windsor Castle, which was followed by his final interment in the new mausoleum that Victoria had commissioned for them both at Frogmore. As she had no doubt anticipated, from the moment of her arrival, Alice immediately returned to her former position of chief prop, comforter and companion of her difficult mother, replacing her sister Helena, who was affectionate and dutiful but also timid and prone to bursting into tears. Once again, Victoria's journals are filled with a constant round of carriage rides, walks, meals and chats with Alice, while Louis makes rather less appearances, as he was apparently content to spend his time either alone or with Alice's brothers, with whom he had formed close friendships.

After a difficult Christmas and New Year, during which Victoria dwelled on the lack of her beloved Albert and how different life was without him, the difficult but bittersweet, for Alice at least, year of 1862 finally drew to a close and the royal family braced themselves for whatever 1863 had in store for them. The first major royal event of the year was the wedding of Alice's brother Bertie to Princess Alexandra of Denmark on 10 March, which took place in the splendid surroundings of St George's Chapel in Windsor Castle and was a much happier affair than the last royal wedding, although Victoria still didn't feel quite ready to face anyone and hid away from view during the ceremony in a small closet overlooking the altar. 'Here I sit, lonely and desolate, who so need love and tenderness, while our two daughters both have their loving husbands and Bertie has taken his lovely pure sweet bride to Osborne,'[5] she wrote in her journal that night. For Alice, Bertie's wedding had been a delightful occasion – she adored her brother and was truly delighted to see him married at last and to a bride who seemed to wholeheartedly love him and appreciated his many good qualities.

Alice's labour began during the evening of 4 April and continued, attended by the nurse and obstetrician, Dr Charles Locock, who had been present at her own birth, until quarter past five the following morning, when she gave birth to a daughter. Her labour had been exhausting and extremely painful, but eased considerably after she was given chloroform, which her mother noted had left her 'half stupefied'.[6] Victoria had passed a sleepless night until she was called to her daughter's rooms in the early hours and was at Alice's side, stroking her shoulder, as the baby was born. Later, when she had recovered from her ordeal, Alice confided to her mother that she had thought a great deal of her father during her labour and had even at times felt his presence in the room. The presence of a new baby in the royal household did much to raise everyone's spirits and even Victoria seems to have felt more cheerful that April as she spent several hours every day with her daughter and new granddaughter, who was to be named Victoria, although she would also on occasion note that her 'feelings are very mixed for my misery still weighs so heavily on me that I can feel no real joy, though I am truly grateful'.[7] Alice was churched on 26 April, the day after her twentieth birthday, and the new baby was christened Victoria Alberta Elisabeth

Mathilde Marie the following day in the green drawing room of Windsor Castle. Victoria acted as godmother to the baby, whom she held in her arms during the ceremony and presented not just with the fine white silk and lace christening robe, but also a diamond cross attached to a small string of pearls. Now fully recovered from childbirth and conscious that they had been away from Darmstadt for around five months, Alice ignored her mother's hints that they should remain in England for longer and returned home to Hesse not long after her daughter's christening. Although she sincerely sympathised with her mother's plight, she was beginning to feel uncomfortably torn between her loyalty to Victoria and the duty that she owed to her husband and child, with the result that she was beginning to lose patience with her mother and yearn for a time when she would rely less heavily on her children for affection and support. Certainly, she was now keen to curtail Victoria's expectation that they would spend at least half the year with her and resolved that from now on they would spend far less time in Britain. When she became pregnant again in the spring of 1864, she ignored hints that she should once again return to England for the birth and instead remained in Darmstadt, where she gave birth without incident to her second daughter Elisabeth on 1 November, this time ably supported by her mother-in-law. Although Victoria, far away at Windsor Castle, professed herself to be 'sorry that it is again a girl',[8] Alice and Louis were rather pleased to have two little daughters to dress up and fuss over.

Alice's elder sister Vicky had given birth to her third son, Prince Sigismund in September 1864 and the two sisters delighted in having babies that were so close in age. However, Victoria, who was already beginning to feel a little left out of all these cosy chats between them, was incensed when she found out that not only had Vicky decided to breastfeed her baby herself, rather than employing a wet nurse as was customary for royal ladies, but she had also persuaded Alice to follow suit. Not only that, but when the two sisters were together in Berlin in early 1865, they had swapped babies and fed each other's children. Victoria was disgusted. 'I maintain… that a child can never be as well nursed by a lady of rank and nervous and refined temperament,' she wrote to Alice, 'for… the more like an animal the wet nurse is, the better for the child.' Warming to her theme, she went on that 'it hurts me deeply that my own two daughters should set at defiance the advice of a mother of nine children, forty six years old… You said that you did it only for your health… and because you had no social duties. Well, Vicky… has none of these excuses and indeed has very important public and social duties to perform, which she cannot with the nursing.'[9] To Victoria's fury, both of her daughters, emboldened by each other and the great distance that lay between them and their fuming mother, remained defiant and continued to feed their own children, much to her annoyance. Victoria had already noted with some resignation that as she grew older Vicky, once her pride and joy, was becoming increasingly mutinous but she was even more surprised and displeased by Alice's defiance – which would become more marked as the years passed and she gained confidence. By the time that Alice's third daughter, Princess Irene, was born on 11 July 1866, she had fully established herself as a beloved citizen of Darmstadt, where she had won hearts with her genuine and hands-on interest in the welfare of its townsfolk, and, from March of that year, as chatelaine of her own household now that the Neues Palais was finished. Irene, whose name was taken from the Greek word for 'peace' and intended as a reference to the much longed for end of the Austro-Prussian War, was the first of Alice's children to be born in the new palace, which almost certainly made it feel more like a home for them all. However, the pregnancy had not been without its issues, most significantly the war that flared up between Austria and Prussia, the latest in a long series of power struggles between the two great powers as they tussled over the ultimate fate of the German states. Whereas a great many members of the German Federation favoured unifying under the rule of the Austrian Emperors, others were keen to keep Germany independent of its imperial neighbour by instead gathering under the rule of the Kings of Prussia. Unfortunately for Alice, her husband was one of those who favoured the Austrians, which placed her in the uncomfortable position of being on the opposing side to her sister Vicky, who was wife to the heir to the Prussian throne. Not only that, but there was the additional stress caused by the fact that Louis' younger brother Henry would also be on the opposing side as he was a lieutenant colonel in the Prussian army.

Although she was in an advanced state of pregnancy and desperately worried not just about her sister and brother-in-law but also, more painfully still, her own husband Louis, who had gone off, very unwillingly, to war as Commander of the 2nd Hessian Infantry Brigade, Alice once again rose with aplomb to the challenges before her. The calm good sense and purposefulness that had made her so indispensable during the crisis that followed her father's death would once again stand her in good stead as she supported her husband and his family, cared for her daughters and prepared for the inevitable flow of wounded from the battle fronts. Inspired by her resourceful heroine Florence Nightingale, she set to work in the local hospitals, where she made it plain that absolutely no task was too mundane, too gruesome or too dirty for her to take it on – from rolling bandages to comforting the sick and dying, Alice was everywhere and everything and, in return, her husband's people loved her more than ever. However, as the beleaguered, starving and often horrifically wounded Hessian troops began to filter back from the battlefields for treatment, they brought back with them war's horrible and inevitable by-blow – disease. When cholera began to spread like wildfire through Hesse at the start of July, Alice panicked and sent her daughters off to her mother in England, where they arrived just in time to attend the wedding of their aunt Princess Helena to Prince Christian of Schleswig-Holstein at Windsor Castle on 5 July. Victoria adored her two delightful little granddaughters, whose care she regarded as a sacred trust, and wrote in her journal on their first night that 'Victoria is just as lovely as she was and Ella too splendid, running about everywhere.'[10] Back in Darmstadt, while her daughters were enjoying their stay at Windsor Castle, Alice was overwhelmed and horrified by the devastation that the war had wreaked, writing that 'the confusion here is awful, the want of money is alarming; right and left one must help. As the Prussians pillaged here, I have many people's things hidden in the house. Even whilst in bed I had to see gentlemen in my room, as there were things to be done and asked which had to come straight to me. Then our poor wounded – the wives and mothers begging I should inquire for their husbands and children. It is a state of affairs too dreadful to describe.'[11]

Although the end of the war on 22 July 1866 was a huge relief, it brought with it further stress and unhappiness as the Prussian victors demanded heavy reparations from the losing side. According to the terms of the Treaty of Prague, the Habsburgs were now forbidden to involve themselves in German affairs, which would from now on fall entirely under the jurisdiction of the Prussian monarchy. More significantly for Alice and her family was the fact that according to the terms of the treaty, Hanover, Holstein-Schleswig, Hesse-Kassel, Nassau and Frankfurt were annexed as part of Prussia along with parts of Bavaria and Hesse-Darmstadt. It could have been much worse for the Hessians, but thanks to the close familial relationship that Alice enjoyed with her sister and the Prussian royal family, they got off quite lightly and were able to retain some independence. They were, however, crippled by the severe financial reparations imposed upon them by the Prussians, who demanded three million florins up front along with, insultingly, the huge sum of 25,000 florins a day for the maintenance of the occupying Prussian army for as long as they stayed; which turned out to be for over a month and a half. 'We are almost ruined,'[12] Alice wrote in despair to her mother. She was already living in uncomfortably straitened circumstances thanks to the fact that, as her father had predicted, her income never seemed to go very far, especially now that they were in the process of furnishing their new palace, which had gone so far over budget that Louis had been forced to take out a huge loan in order to pay the builder, who was himself facing bankruptcy. Although Alice did her best to economise by selling superfluous horses, reducing the size of her household and even making her daughters' clothes herself, it was simply not enough and she was forced to ask her mother for assistance more than once, much to Victoria's mounting annoyance. If Alice had been more biddable and, to Victoria's mind at least, less contrary and argumentative, then perhaps Victoria would have been more inclined to offer help, but as the years passed and her relationship with Alice gradually became more fractious and difficult she became increasingly unwilling and complained to Vicky that 'Alice and Louis get money from me for their birthdays and Xmas to help them in furnishing their house – and always more and more is asked for.'[13] Although Victoria herself had always had plenty of money and had never had to economise, she prided herself on living relatively thriftily and found Alice's insistence that she was doing everything that she could to reduce their expenses extremely annoying. Instead of being sympathetic when Alice claimed not to be able to afford a holiday location that she had suggested, she was irritated.

The matter of Princess Helena's marriage to Prince Christian, which ought to have been a happy family event, only served to widen the rift between Victoria and Alice after the latter reprimanded her mother for selfishly encouraging her younger sister to marry a man who was far too old for her (Christian was fifteen years older than Helena and looked it) simply because he was a younger son and therefore more than happy to make his home in England, thus ensuring that Helena would forever be at Victoria's beck and call. There was also the fact that Christian's father, the Duke of Schleswig-Holstein had taken on King Christian IX of Denmark, father of Alexandra, Princess of Wales, in a complicated dispute over the territory of Schleswig-Holstein, which was claimed by both but would eventually pass into Prussian hands in the aftermath of the Austro-Prussian War. The addition of Prince Christian, whose father had retained the ducal title, to the royal family led to a serious rift when Alexandra and her husband Bertie vehemently made their displeasure about the marriage known and even threatened to boycott the wedding, much to Victoria's fury. Alice, always loyal to Bertie, especially against their mother, immediately placed herself on his side, which made matters even worse and provoked Victoria into denouncing her second daughter as 'so sharp and bitter… no one wishes to have her in their house'.[14] As daughter-in-law of the King of Prussia, who had taken control of the contested territories, some had expected Vicky to also be on Bertie and Alexandra's side but to their surprise, she announced that she had always liked Prince Christian's family and was therefore firmly in favour of Helena's match. Alice's attitude also softened when she spoke to Helena about her engagement and learned that far from feeling inveigled into the match against her will, she was actually very happy with her fiancé and was looking forward to their life together. However, although the wedding itself passed off happily with both Bertie and Alexandra in attendance, thanks to Alice's intervention, the matter was not entirely at an end and flared up again later that year when Alice discovered that her mother was planning to give Helena a significant sum of money as well as a home and slightly higher annuity and made the mistake of letting her trouble-making younger sister Louise know how annoyed she was – with the result that it quickly came to Victoria's ears. Instead of trying to placate Alice, Victoria announced that the Hesse family were not invited to any of the usual family gatherings for the foreseeable future, which naturally hurt Alice's feelings very much. The impasse between the stubborn queen and her even more obstinate daughter might well have continued for quite some time had not Victoria accidentally swapped letters intended for Vicky and Alice, with the result that Alice received a letter detailing all of her faults and complaining at length about her undutiful, mutinous and selfish behaviour. To her credit, Alice did not immediately fire off a recriminatory letter to her mother but instead wrote to Vicky and begged her to intercede on her behalf, claiming not to have known just how upset their mother was with her. Victoria was naturally mortified and horrified when her error was pointed out and this made her rather more conciliatory than she might otherwise have been when Vicky relayed Alice's apology to her. 'Tell dear Alice that now she properly and lovingly owns she is much grieved at what she did and said (I will truly believe out of hastiness and imprudence) that I will forgive and forget and receive her with open arms,' she wrote to Vicky. 'And am indeed looking forward to seeing her for, I hope, a good two months in the middle of June with dear Louis and the darling children.'[15]

However, although Alice and Victoria's relationship appeared to be back on track again, the queen continued to privately obsess about her second daughter's failings and wearied Vicky by constantly returning to the unwelcome topics of Alice's jealousy of her sisters, endless complaining, bad temper, bossiness and arrogance. She informed Vicky that Alice ruined visits to Osborne and Windsor Castle by complaining about everything and that 'if Alice wishes to come, she should accommodate herself to my habits'.[16] In some ways, Alice had assumed Albert's mantle when it came to checking Victoria's tendency to melodrama and emotional self-indulgence but whereas Victoria had always deferred to her husband's opinion and had feared his disapproval, she found Alice's advice and interference increasingly superfluous and irritating. Fearing his wife's excessive response to his death, Albert had asked Alice to do what she could to prevent her mother from descending into a state of morbid, torpid melancholy after his passing and this she had attempted to do by increasingly putting pressure on Victoria to resume her neglected public duties, just as her father would have done. By 1867, six years after Albert's death, Victoria had resumed most of her official duties but was still reclusive and declaring herself quite unable to venture out in public, to the annoyance and alarm of her children who feared the detrimental effect that this would have upon the royal family's popularity. It was Alice who had suggested a few years earlier that her mother might feel happier and more comfortable if she brought her favourite Scottish retainer, the blunt and honest ghillie John Brown down from Balmoral in order to have him at hand all year round at her English residences – however, she could not possibly have anticipated the powerful hold and influence that Brown would quickly exert over the bereaved and lonely queen, who desperately needed male affection and companionship, nor the fact that he would more often than not take her side against her own children, especially when it came to the matter of her self-imposed seclusion. Horrified by the rumours that were swirling about the exact nature of Victoria's relationship with Brown, disturbed by her ever increasing dependency upon him and dismayed by the familiarity that he showed towards her, Victoria's children moved into action and tried to oust him, only to find that it was far too late and that Brown was so deeply entrenched in the royal household and, more crucially, Victoria's affections that he could not be removed. Although Alice, naturally, bore the brunt of her mother's annoyance when she discovered what her children were about, she was in fact one of the least troubled by Brown's presence at Victoria's side. She didn't much like Brown, who was coarse in both appearance and manners, but she appreciated the fact that he made her mother relatively happy (obviously she could never be entirely happy without Albert but she was laughing again and beginning to take an optimistic and engaged interest in life once more) and had even, in his own bluff way, coaxed her out of hiding.

On 25 November 1868, Alice finally gave birth to the much longed for son and heir, who was named Ernest for Alice's uncle, the Duke of Saxe-Coburg Gotha, who had given her away at her wedding, but would always be known as 'Ernie'. Although Alice's three little daughters were much-loved, there could be no doubt that the arrival of a son was a huge relief to everyone, including his grandmother Victoria, who noted his arrival in her journal with some satisfaction. The following July, Alice and Louis celebrated their sixth wedding anniversary surrounded by their children and would no doubt have reflected with pleasure on the changes that the years had wrought in their family. However, not everything was going well for the couple – their money problems never seemed to improve and although Louis was just as much in love as ever with his wife, Alice was beginning to feel increasingly frustrated by his lack of intellectual curiosity and the fact that while she had always been a bookworm and enjoyed a copious correspondence with her family, he did everything in his power to avoid ever picking up a book or writing a letter. Ever since childhood she had considered her father to be the very epitome of every conceivable manly virtue and poor Louis, who lacked gravitas and was even in some ways positively childish if not shallow, in no way matched up to what she remembered of her father. The fact that Albert's death made him even more irreproachable and perfect as far as his wife and children were concerned only served to make the contest even more unfairly loaded against Louis. 'I longed for a real companion, for, apart from that, life had nothing to offer me in Darmstadt,' she wrote to him sadly after receiving a particularly disappointingly 'childish' letter from him. 'I could have been quite happy and contented living in a cottage, if I had been able to share my intellectual interests and intellectual aspirations with a husband whose strong, protective love would have guided me around the rocks strewn in my way by my own nature... So naturally I am bitterly disappointed with myself when I look back and see that in spite of good intentions, and real effort, my hopes have nonetheless been completely shipwrecked.'[17] She was also disappointed by her life in Darmstadt, which she found boring, mundane and stale, compared to the vivid and privileged existence that she had enjoyed as daughter of the world's greatest queen and that her sister Vicky still enjoyed in Berlin – although ironically, she appears to have been unaware that her elder sister was deeply envious of her as she believed Alice to be the beauty of the family and was convinced that her father-in-law, the King of Prussia, who liked to be surrounded by pretty young women, and his daughter Princess Louise, who was great friends with Alice, but had always rather kept Vicky at arm's length, by far preferred her sister to herself.

Ever since childhood, Alice had loved getting dressed up in pretty dresses and fine jewels in order to enjoy the parties and, later, balls that formed a regular part of royal life – sadly though, there were few excuses for dressing up in Darmstadt and even if there had been an endless parade of balls and galas, she barely had the means to dress in the manner to which she had once been accustomed. Luckily for Alice, she had her many philanthropic interests to give her life meaning and distract her from her unhappiness but it wasn't quite enough to assuage her frustration and envy of her sisters, whom she felt were living much better, more glamorous lives. At the end of 1869, Alice's feelings of dissatisfaction were interrupted by yet another crisis as relations between France and Prussia rapidly began to break down, the rising tensions between the two inflamed by the Minister President of Prussia, Bismarck, who was willing to do anything to bring about his glorious vision of a fully unified and powerful Germany and believed that his goal would be quickly and efficiently achieved by bringing the Germanic people together against their common enemy, France. Yet another dynastic row between the nations swiftly brought matters to a head in the summer of 1870 and by the end of July, Prussia and France were at war and mobilising their troops. This time, to Alice's relief, Louis would be on the same side as her sister Vicky and brother-in-law Fritz, but they were privately saddened to be at war with their family friends, Napoléon III and his delightful wife Eugénie. Yet again, Alice swung into action, organising nurses, hospitals and medical supplies and exhausting herself in the process, exacerbated by the fact that she was once again pregnant and would give birth to another son, Friedrich (known within the family as 'Frittie') on 7 October 1870.

Back in England, Victoria was absolutely horrified by the reports that she was getting from the Continent but insisted upon remaining as neutral as possible, even if at heart she could not help but sympathise with the Prussians. 'The only way is to leave matters as quiet as possible, and to let people quiet down,' she wrote. 'For me to attempt to do anything, beyond preaching neutrality and prudence would be useless.'[18] For her daughters, trapped in Germany, desperately scared for the wellbeing of their husbands who had joined the troops on the front and working hard around the clock to care for the wounded and needy, Victoria's determination not to get involved and send troops to join the German armies was a source of deep bitterness and frustration. 'The feeling is very general here that England would have it in her power to prevent this awful war, had she in concert with Russia, Austria and Italy, declared that she would take arms against the aggressor, and that her neutrality afforded France advantages and us disadvantages,' Vicky complained. 'France can buy English horses as her ships can reach England, whereas ours cannot on account of the French fleet.'[19] To make matters worse, Britain's neutrality and the widespread knowledge that they were profiting from the sale of horses and armaments to the French, convinced many Germans that the British were against them and, naturally, it was only a short matter of time before this resulted in Alice and Vicky being regarded with deep hostility and suspicion as potential enemy agents. It was even whispered that they were passing military secrets on to their mother, who was in turn sending them to the French. Alice was deeply hurt by these allegations but silently continued her work in the hospitals and anywhere else that she was needed, pausing only when she was so exhausted that she was forced to accept Vicky's invitation to recuperate in Berlin. By the time the war ended with a resounding Prussian victory and the promotion of Vicky's father-in-law from King to Emperor of Prussia in January 1871, Alice had not set eyes on her husband for seven months and had a new baby in the nursery that he had yet to meet. It was an emotional homecoming for them both and Alice was so grateful and delighted to be reunited with Louis again that she was even able to temporarily put her unhappiness about their situation aside in favour of enjoying the simple pleasures of family life. In the middle of September 1871, they travelled with their five children to Scotland in order to visit Victoria at Balmoral Castle, where they were warmly welcomed and little Ella, who was already extraordinarily pretty, the 'splendid boy'[20] Ernie and baby Frittie, who was described as 'a great love, so merry, dear and pretty',[21] were quite evidently treated as great favourites by their formidable Grandmama. Victoria was felled by a bout of what she referred to as 'rheumatic gout' during the visit and was impressed by the great care and gentleness with which Alice, always ready to act the nurse, looked after her. 'Dear Alice was in and out constantly, and very affectionate and kind helping my maids move me.'[22]

Alice and her family remained in England until January 1872, by which time Alice would have realised that she was expecting her sixth child. At the beginning of December, she and her family travelled down to Sandringham in Norfolk in order to spend some time with her brother

Bertie, sister-in-law Alexandra and their five children. However, soon after their arrival, Bertie fell ill with what Alice immediately suspected to be an attack of typhoid fever and despite the best efforts of the royal doctors, his symptoms continued to worsen over the next few weeks. The ten assorted Hesse and Wales children were all summarily packed off to the care of their grandmother at Windsor Castle and Alice rolled up her sleeves in order to nurse her brother back to health in between placating the terrified Alexandra and sending updates about Bertie's progress to Victoria, who immediately began to compare his sufferings to those endured by her beloved Albert during his final days. On 29 November, Victoria was sufficiently alarmed to make the trip to Sandringham, her first visit to her son's country house, which despite her anxiety she was still able to note in her journal was 'a handsome, quite newly built Elizabethan building'.[23] There she was met by Alice and Alexandra, who took her upstairs to see Bertie, who was clearly extremely unwell. She left a few days later, reassured that Bertie was not in any imminent danger, but was asked to return on 8 December when his condition began to deteriorate again, much to the alarm of his doctors and family. Bertie's illness reached a crisis point on the 13th, the eve of the tenth anniversary of his father's death – a coincidence that his mother felt most keenly as she sat by his bedside and tried her best to soothe him as he struggled for breath, clutched at his bedclothes and wildly demanded to know who she was, so deep was his delirium. When she went to bed that night, Alice feared that she would spend the next day beside another deathbed, but to her relief she was greeted the following morning by the news that Bertie had slept soundly that night and was much better. Victoria's antipathy for her eldest son was completely forgotten when she later visited his bedside and he kissed her hand, smiled and warmly thanked her for coming to him. More gratifying still was the widespread relief and celebration that greeted the news of Bertie's recovery. Rumours of his rakish, debauched lifestyle and neglect of his beautiful wife had impaired his popularity with his mother's more strait-laced subjects but, in the aftermath of his illness, all was apparently forgiven and forgotten as the people turned out in their thousands to attend thanksgiving services in churches all over the country. Even Victoria managed to overcome her terror of appearing in public in order to attend a celebratory thanksgiving service at St Paul's Cathedral on 27 February 1872.

Alice and her family were not present at her brother's celebration as they had already returned home to the Neues Palais in Darmstadt, where at 3.40 am on 6 June 1872 she gave birth to her fourth daughter, who was to be named Alice after herself but was instead christened Alix for, as Alice put it 'they murder my name here'[24] – although within the family she would generally be known as 'Alicky' to differentiate her from her uncle Bertie's wife Alexandra, who was also known as Alix. In honour of her four aunts, none of whom would get to meet her for quite some time, the new baby was given the middle names Viktoria Helene Luise Beatrix when she was baptised on 1 July – which also happened to be the tenth anniversary of her parent's wedding day at Osborne House. Her glittering array of godparents, none of whom were present, was Bertie and his wife Alexandra; Fritz's beautiful cousin Princess Anna of Prussia, Landgravine of Hesse-Kassel; Alice's youngest sister Princess Beatrice; Victoria's aunt, the Duchess of Cambridge, who had been born a Princess of Hesse-Kassel, and the Tsesarevich Alexander of Russia along with his vivacious wife, Maria Feodorovna, who was the younger sister of Alexandra, Princess of Wales. The new baby was an absolute delight – large and plump like all of Alice's children, with bright auburn hair, huge eyes and a cheerful, happy disposition, which quickly earned her the nickname of 'Sunny' within the family. 'She is a sweet, merry little person,' Alice wrote fondly of her new daughter. 'Always laughing and a dimple in one cheek, just like Ernie.'[25]

Chapter Four

'And does not one grow to love one's grief?'

1872–1878

Alix's first home was the bright and sunny nursery in the Neues Palais in Darmstadt, which was newly decorated with sturdy wooden furniture from Maple & Co., a popular English furniture company based on the Tottenham Court Road in London, which mostly catered to a middle class and landed gentry clientele. Alice looked back on her childhood in England as a halcyon, uncomplicated and happy time and was keen that her own children should experience the same thing – to which end she recreated her own childhood as much as she could, surrounding them with English furniture, plain English nursery food like the hated rice pudding, mutton chops and baked apples and, of course, a parade of English nannies – none of which stayed for very long until they secured the services of the loyal and redoubtable Mary Ann Orchard. 'I try to copy as much as is in my power all those things for my children that they may have an idea when I speak to them of what a happy home ours was,' Alice wrote to her mother, later adding that 'the decoration and domestic arrangements are so English that it is hard to believe that one is in Germany'.[1] Her children's daily routine adhered to a strict timetable that incorporated plenty of time to play and exercise – either indoors when the weather was bad or outside in the beautiful gardens that had once been the town's botanical park. Like their cousins in England, Alice's children had plenty of pets to look after and were encouraged to learn to ride from an early age, which Alix, in particular, excelled at. There were lessons too, with the earliest ones being delivered by Alice herself, partially because she couldn't afford to pay someone else to do it but mainly because she enjoyed being the one to teach her children how to read and write and do their first simple sums. Later on, when they were older, Alice imposed a stricter educational curriculum, still partially taught in school rooms at the top of the palace by herself alongside professional tutors, which incorporated English, German, history, geography, mathematics and French as well as the usual music, singing and dancing lessons. Well read, erudite and highly intelligent herself, she was determined that her own children should also grow up with a love of books and knowledge for its own sake – and in this at least, she was to be remarkably successful as all of her children would later be regarded as extraordinarily well educated and even accomplished, especially in comparison to their cousins, the children of Bertie and Alexandra, who were allowed to run wild and received a very unsatisfactory education, to the despair of their doting grandmother, Victoria.

'On the same floor as the nurseries were [Princess Alice's] rooms, and there the little princesses brought their toys and played while their mother wrote or read,' Alix's confidante Baroness Buxhoeveden later wrote about the Hesse children's happy childhood. 'Sometimes all the old boxes containing their mother's early wardrobe were brought out for dressing up. The children strutted down the long corridors in crinolines and played at being great ladies, or characters from fairy tales, dressed in bright stuffs and Indian shawls, which their grandmother, Queen Victoria, could not have imagined being put to such a use.'[2] Such gentle, well-organised fun was typical fare for Alice's offspring, who would never be allowed the riotous liberties that their Wales cousins enjoyed in England, but were instead expected to always behave well and to use their time as productively as possible. All of the children were made to tidy their own rooms and make their beds and forbidden from asking the servants for help with anything, from cutting up meat to doing up buttons or shoe laces, that they were capable of doing themselves. Furthermore, they were all given basic lessons in handicrafts such as woodworking, dressmaking, gardening, vegetable growing and cooking, just as their mother and her siblings had been in the miniature Swiss Cottage at Osborne House and which had, in Alice's case at least, been of some use in adult life. However, it was undoubtedly thanks to the Hesse family's ongoing financial issues, that these lessons were supplemented with some extra instruction in managing money and balancing the books – something that Alice and her siblings had almost certainly never been taught and which she herself had been forced to learn the hard way. 'I strive to bring them up totally free from pride of position, which is nothing save what their personal worth can make it,' Alice wrote proudly to her mother, before stressing 'how important it is for princes and princesses to know that they are nothing better or above others, save through their own merit; and that they have only the double duty of living for others and of being an example – good and modest. This I hope my children will grow up to do.'[3] It was a very typical, modest, rather strait-laced Victorian childhood, neatly transported from England to a small provincial town in Germany and, as Alice had hoped, her children thrived upon it. Like many children, Christmas was the high point of their year and naturally Alice did her best to replicate the wonderful family Christmases that she had enjoyed when her father was still alive with huge Christmas trees 'laden with candles, apples, gilt nuts, pink quince sausages and all kinds of treasures'[4] surrounded by small tables, one for each member of the family, all laden with presents and treats. After Alice had distributed presents to all of the palace servants, the Hesse family would retire for a sumptuous Christmas dinner, complete with mince pies and plum pudding sent all the way from England.

Although Alice was undoubtedly an exemplary mother and even unusually hands-on in her approach to the important task of child rearing, her children were beginning to see less and less of her at this time as she devoted increasing amounts of time to her various philanthropic endeavours. Over the years, Alice's interest in nursing had increased, encouraged by a much cherished correspondence with her heroine, Florence Nightingale, who arranged for some of Alice's protégé nurses in Darmstadt to train in England, where they would be exposed to more advanced techniques and theories about treatment. Alice was fascinated by hospitals and had extensively toured several in England, gathering ideas and information about the best way to modernise and improve the ones that fell under her patronage in Hesse, including her very own Alice Hospital in Darmstadt, which she had founded in 1869 and where much of her precious funds went. Naturally, she hoped to instil the same philanthropic, generous principles in her children and so they were taken on regular visits to hospital wards and clinics, where they met the patients and performed small tasks for them, while their mother busied herself changing dressings, emptying bedpans and taking temperatures. Although it was difficult to criticise Alice's involvement in nursing, even if her mother deplored the ease with which her gently reared daughter performed even the most unpleasant and potentially unhygienic of tasks, her interest in women's rights and suffrage went quite beyond the pale as far as Victoria, who regarded it all as a 'mad, wicked folly',[5] was concerned. 'Were women to "unsex" themselves by claiming equality with men, they would become the most hateful, heathen and disgusting of beings and would surely perish without male protection,'[6] the most powerful woman in the world wrote with revulsion in 1870. She and Alice had been at loggerheads for quite some time at this point and it was probably no surprise at all to Victoria when her second daughter began to express views about the equality of the sexes and placed herself firmly in the opposite camp to her mother – even going so far as to mischievously send an incensed Victoria a leaflet about women's rights. As for her own daughters, Alice informed her mother that she did not want her girls to believe that marriage was 'their sole object for the future'[7] and wanted them 'to feel they can fill up their lives so well otherwise' as 'marriage for the sake of marriage is surely the greatest mistake a woman can make'. It was one of her greatest wishes that her own daughters should grow up free from the tiresome constraints that society had placed on herself and her sisters and that although there was much to be said for the happiness of a good marriage and successful motherhood, they should also be able to find fulfilment in their own interests and industry as well. If they should be free to do so in a world where women enjoyed equal suffrage with men then so much the better.

In the spring of 1873, Alice fulfilled a lifelong ambition by travelling to Italy, where she planned to spend two months thoroughly indulging the passion for Italian art that she had shared with her father. Albert had undertaken an extensive 'grand tour' of Italy in his youth and would remain a devotee of Renaissance art for the rest of his life, with Raphael being a particular favourite. Up to now, Alice had been forced to suppress her urge to visit Italy in favour of sedate family holidays in England or on the Normandy coast but, after having six children, she clearly felt like she had earned some time to herself and so intensified her study of the Italian language and Renaissance art before making a travel plan that would take her to Munich, where she met King Ludwig II of Bavaria, and then through the picturesque Alpine Brenner Pass to Italy, where she travelled on to Florence before catching the night train to Rome. It had been Alice's plan to travel incognito and as cheaply as possible but when her identity was discovered just a few days after arriving in the Italian capital, she found herself being entertained by King Victor Emmanuel II and the rest of the Italian royal family, who were only too pleased to show her around their city and enable her to access palaces and galleries that were normally out of bounds to foreign visitors and even have a private audience with Pope Pius IX in the Vatican. Alice was completely entranced by Rome and wrote to her mother that 'every day I admire the scenery more and more; every little bit of architecture, broken or whole, with a glimpse of the Campagna... it is a picture in itself which one would like to frame and hang up in one's room. It is too, too beautiful.'[8] Naturally, her thoughts often returned to her father, who had also fallen passionately in love with Rome. 'I thought so often and so much of dear Papa, when I saw the originals of all the pictures he so much admired and took such an interest in,' she wrote to her mother. 'I can see in many things where dear Papa got his ideas from for Osborne and for his decorations.'[9] Alice returned to Florence in time to spend her thirtieth birthday there on 25 April, which was an especially magical experience, although she does not seem to have been quite as enamoured with Florence as she was with Rome. After visiting the main sites in Florence, including the Duomo, Uffizi, Pitti Palace and Santa Croce, Alice moved on to Pompeii and Sorrento, where she fell in love with the view of the Bay of Naples, which she described as being 'like a beautiful dream'[10], before returning once again to Rome.

On 2 May, Alice returned to Darmstadt, where she was absolutely thrilled to be reunited with her children, whom she had missed terribly during her Italian adventure and who were equally delighted to have her back again. However, just as the newly-reunited family looked forward to another happy summer together, tragedy struck when little Frittie, who was just two and a half years old and suspected to be suffering from haemophilia like his uncle Leopold, died in a tragic accident on 29 May. Alice had spent that morning watching her two young sons playing in her room and had turned her back for just a few moments in order to call for their nurse to come and take them away when Frittie somehow fell from her bedroom window on to the balcony below – a fall that probably would not have killed another child, but could prove catastrophic for a haemophiliac. As there was no outward sign of head trauma or broken bones, the doctors were initially fairly confident that the boy would recover from his tumble but then were forced to change their minds when the side of his head began to swell in an ominous manner that suggested a hidden brain haemorrhage. Alice remained at his side all day in between firing off frantic telegrams to her mother in Balmoral and husband Louis, who was not at home that day. She was holding her youngest son in her arms when he finally slipped peacefully away, without ever regaining consciousness. In Scotland, Queen Victoria was deeply distressed by the terrible bulletins that were arriving from Darmstadt, noting that before she could even reply to the first telegram announcing the accident, another one arrived from Louis' mother to say that Frittie was dead. The little prince had been a particularly winsome and appealing child and the whole family was shocked and deeply distressed by his loss. Everyone was impressed by the quiet calm and dignity that Alice displayed over the next few days as she came to terms with her loss and prepared for her son's funeral, which took place in the family mausoleum, the Rosenhöhe, in Darmstadt and was a most moving event – Frittie's brother Ernie insisted upon picking flowers in the palace gardens to place on the small coffin. 'They are all in the great admiration of dear Alice, who is so natural in her grief, so calm and resigned, dwelling on the happiness and safety of her dear little one,'[11] her mother wrote in her journal a few days after Frittie's death. 'She heard the dreadful fall and will never be able to forget it.'[12] Although Alice appeared outwardly serene, she struggled to cope with her overwhelming grief and the terrible guilt that she felt about the accident that had robbed her of her youngest son. 'You understand how long and deep my grief must be,' she wrote to her mother. 'And does not one grow to love one's grief, as having become part of the being one loved – as if through this one could still pay a tribute of love to them, to make up for the terrible loss, and missing of not being able to do anything for the beloved any more?'[13]

In the aftermath of Frittie's death, Alice, always prone to melancholy, became increasingly depressed and withdrawn as she mourned her son and the 'part of my heart' that lay in his grave with him. People, places and pursuits that she had once enjoyed now no longer filled her with delight and, just as her mother had done after the death of her beloved Albert, she dwelled constantly and morosely on Frittie's absence from the family gatherings that she now found so exhausting and pointless. Although she was physically strong and resilient, as evidenced by the gruelling manual work that she happily carried out on her hospital wards, Alice had always been prone to what her mother vaguely referred to as 'nerves' and had a tendency to suffer bouts of neuralgia when under stress – now, she completely fell apart and no one quite knew what to do to help her. Victoria was seriously alarmed by Alice's emotional state, especially as she knew better than anyone just how profoundly shocking such a sudden bereavement could be, and put all of her issues with her daughter aside as she swung into sympathetic action. She wasted no time before inviting Alice to spend some time with her in England, where she could be cared for by Victoria's own doctors, and in November she welcomed her, accompanied by Louis, Irene, Ernie and the baby Alix, to Windsor Castle. 'Poor dear Alice was much upset on first arriving, but recovered herself again,' a worried Victoria wrote that evening. 'She looks very thin and her face so drawn and ill.'[14] It was the first time that Victoria had met Alice's youngest daughter, who was just beginning to walk, and she was thoroughly enchanted by her. 'Alice's little Alix is a sweet child with lovely dark blue eyes and a constant smile on her fat face,' she wrote in her journal the day after their arrival. 'She indeed deserves her nickname of "Sunshine" and "Sunny".'[15] The family remained with Victoria until 19 December and although Alice still looked 'weak and sad',[16] her mother nonetheless believed that the visit had done her much good. Alice was about four months pregnant when she left England and both she and Louis desperately hoped that the new baby would be another boy – however, they were to be disappointed when another daughter, who was christened Marie for her new aunt-in-law Marie Alexandrovna, who had married Alice's brother Prince Alfred that January, arrived on 24 May 1874, which was also the fifty-fifth birthday of her grandmother Queen Victoria and just a few days before the first anniversary of Frittie's accident. As it often does, the arrival of a new baby to love and care for did much to improve Alice's mood and although she still continued to mourn Frittie, at least some of the terrible despair and emptiness that she had experienced after his death dissipated.

On 13 April 1875, Alice, along with Louis, Ernie and the two youngest girls Alix and Marie (who was known within the family as May), arrived at Osborne House for a prolonged visit to Victoria, with the three eldest girls arriving later in the month. 'Alice is looking thin and drawn,'[17] her concerned mother wrote in her journal that night before adding that in contrast Louis looked very well and that 'Ernie is big, broad and tall; Alix, too lovely and the little baby, not quite eleven months old, a sweet, fair little thing with most engaging dimples.'[18] It was the first time that Alix, who would turn three that June, had ever visited Osborne, the location of her mother's happiest childhood memories, and there is every indication that the holiday was a great success as the Hesse children, whose behaviour was still markedly better than that of their boisterous Wales cousins, impressed everyone, especially their exacting grandmother. On 22 April, Victoria wrote in her journal that after lunch she had 'tried to make a sketch of that adorable splendid little Alix. She was very fidgety and said "I don't like to be maked."'[19] She has the most beautiful colouring and large deep blue eyes.' She persevered though and on 2 May, despite Alix once again being 'very fidgety',[20] managed to start a delightful watercolour of her mutinous granddaughter dressed in a white flounced dress bedecked with pink ribbons, which she continued a week later despite the fact that 'dear beautiful amusing little Alix… sat very badly'.[21] The rest of the visit passed happily for the three Hesse children, who were allowed to join the adults for breakfast and at the end of luncheon, which was taken beneath a tent in the gardens on fine days, and spent the rest of their time playing in the Swiss Cottage that had been erected in the grounds by their grandfather Albert, planting trees or paddling in the Solent – unless it was raining, in which case they were forced to amuse themselves indoors in the nurseries that had once echoed with the shouts and laughter of their mother and her siblings. On 23 April the party returned together to Windsor Castle where, two days later, the family gathered to celebrate Alice's thirty-second birthday, the first that she had spent at Windsor for seven years. 'Gave dear Alice her presents in the Oak Room,' Victoria wrote later. 'All the six children were there, making me think of former happy days when we celebrated our birthdays, surrounded by our children.'[22] However, as far as Alice's children were concerned, the high point of the visit was almost certainly the children's dance that took place in the splendid surroundings of the Red Drawing Room in Windsor Castle on 11 May, attended by all six of Alice's children along with the five children of their uncle Bertie, their aunt Helena's four Schleswig-Holstein children and as a bonus treat, three of their Prussian cousins, Charlotte, Viktoria and Waldemar, the children of their aunt Vicky, who had arrived earlier that day. Also in attendance were the three eldest children of Victoria's cousin, Princess Mary of Cambridge, Duchess of Teck – the eldest of whom, eight-year-old Princess Victoria Mary (also known as May) was destined to one day marry her cousin Prince George of Wales. 'We sat on the sofas, whilst the children galloped up and down,' Victoria later recalled for her journal. 'At first some of the children were very shy, but it did not last long and they all seemed very merry and happy.'[23] At five, the adults escaped to the adjacent Green Drawing Room for tea until the children had theirs at six in the opulent State Dining Room, 'at a very long table, which was an amusing sight'.[24]

Alice, Louis and the four youngest children left Windsor Castle on 14 May, while the two eldest girls, Victoria and Ella accompanied their grandmother on a visit to Balmoral Castle. Victoria and Alice were not to be reunited until 5 April 1876, when Victoria paid a visit to Darmstadt – her first since Alice had taken up residence there after her wedding in 1862. It was the thirteenth birthday of Alice's eldest daughter Princess Victoria and her grandmother was very pleased to see her birthday table, laden with presents, set up in the drawing room. Victoria had never before seen the Neues Palais, which she had helped pay for, and she enjoyed inspecting it from top to bottom, taking in the 'handsome' hall and staircase, and the 'prettily furnished' drawing room before visiting 'Alice's large and pretty sitting room with a bow window, charmingly arranged with all her pretty things and family souvenirs,' as Victoria described it later. 'This opens into her nice bedroom, where she showed me the terrible window out of which dear little Frittie fell. It has been closed up and against it stands a table, on which relics of the dear child are placed'.[25] Victoria was concerned by how unwell Alice looked, but there was clearly little time to address this properly on such a brief visit as they were only able to have a quick conversation before Victoria was whisked off to the nursery to visit her 'dear lovely little Alicky and little May'.[26] Luncheon was served in the palace dining room, which was decorated with grand full-length portraits of Victoria's Hanoverian predecessors George III, Queen Charlotte, George IV and William IV – perhaps intended as a deliberate reminder to the not always very respectful Hessians of Alice's close connection to the British royal family. It was a short but sweet reunion and one that both would think about often in the coming months, but while Alice felt buoyed up by seeing her mother, albeit for just a few hours, Victoria came away feeling extremely anxious about her daughter's health and mental wellbeing. They were not to see each other again until 19 September, when Alice arrived at Balmoral for a recuperative holiday, this time without her husband or any of her children in tow. Her travels around Italy had given her a taste for travelling alone and she was clearly in need of some time off from the endless demands of her busy life in Darmstadt. For her part, Victoria was very pleased to have Alice all to herself for a few weeks, although she privately noted that she was 'grieved to see Alice looking so terribly thin and drawn'[27] and certainly hoped that the bracing Scottish air would do her some good.

On 20 March 1877, Alice was deeply shocked and distressed when her father-in-law Charles died after a short illness, making her husband Louis heir to his uncle. They no doubt expected to be in this position for a few more years to come, the old Grand Duke apparently being in reasonably good health for his age, but were astounded when he too passed away three months later, on 13 June. Louis and Alice were now Grand Duke and Duchess of Hesse and by Rhine and the change in title reflected a definite change in their previously less than optimal fortunes as they now had possession of the main palace and all the revenue that came with the title. They were still not as fabulously wealthy as Louis' Romanov relatives but at least they now had more than enough to live in some style and still be able to contribute to Alice's many philanthropic causes, such as her hospital and the training of new skilled nurses for the province. It was a huge relief to Alice, who had spent over a decade struggling to make ends meet but it was too late to compensate for the damage that had been done to her mental health over the years. Although she still cared deeply about the wellbeing of the Hessian people, her depressive state of mind and frustrations with her husband had clouded her view of the duchy to the extent that she now viewed it with some hostility. Furthermore, she had not forgotten or forgiven how quickly the people there had suspected her of collusion with the enemy during the war of 1870 and even now, seven years on, she felt unpopular and unwelcome in Darmstadt. When she took the children to Houlgate in Normandy for their annual summer holiday, Louis, clearly stung by her dislike of his ancestral home, wrote to ask that she allow 'the bitterness of the salt water (to) drive away the bitterness that you still feel against Darmstadt. Please, my darling, don't speak so harshly of it when I come to join you – it would quite spoil my happiness at seeing you again.'[28] Annoyed, Alice responded that she would 'certainly say nothing to you about Darmstadt when you come… I have no intention of saying anything unpleasant, least of all to you. You shake off anything unpleasant like a poodle shaking off the water when it comes to the sea – natures like yours are the happiest in themselves, but they are not made to help, comfort and advise others.'[29] To Alice's great pleasure, her return from Normandy was greeted with cheering and enormous enthusiasm by the people of Darmstadt, which was not quite enough to assuage her unhappiness but certainly gave her confidence a much needed boost as she set about her new role as Grand Duchess. Although Alice certainly relished the opportunity to utilise her new more generous resources in order to assist more people, she found her new position gruelling and thankless and as a result became increasingly prone to the neuralgia and attacks of 'nerves' that usually befell her when she was under pressure. 'I have been doing too much lately… and my nerves are beginning to feel the strain, for sleep and appetite are no longer good,' she wrote to her mother. 'Too much is demanded of one; and I have to do with so many things. It is more than my strength can stand in the long run.'[30]

In spring 1878, Louis decided that Alice would benefit from a change of scene and accompanied her on a visit to her sister Vicky at Berlin, where she was reunited with her great friend, Vicky's sister-in-law Princess Louise, Grand Duchess of Baden. After this, they travelled on to Eastbourne in Sussex, where they stayed for a week on the Grand Parade and enjoyed the sunshine before going up to Windsor Castle on 12 July, where they were to stay for the night before heading back to Eastbourne, where this time they would be staying at Compton Place, a

Georgian mansion belonging to the Duke of Devonshire, which would be a perfect base for the excursions that they planned to make along the south coast. 'Dear Alice looks thin, ill and drawn,'[31] Victoria noted after their arrival, before adding that in contrast, Louis, always a vision of rude health especially when placed beside his delicate wife, was 'most flourishing'.[32] They were reunited a few days later at Bertie's garden party at Marlborough House and after that on the 16th, when Alice took her children to visit her youngest brother Prince Leopold, who was unwell, at Windsor Castle. Victoria was enchanted by the six Hesse children, who had grown a great deal since the last time she saw them in April 1876. 'Victoria and Ella are taller than their mother and quite young ladies,'[33] she wrote later. 'Alicky is a glorious child, handsomer than ever, a great darling, with brilliant colouring, splendid eyes and a sweet smile. Ernie is just the same, dear good boy. Little May is also very pretty and a great darling.'[34] Victoria was especially interested to see fourteen-year-old Ella, who was reputed, within her own family at least, to be one of the most beautiful princesses in Europe, with a face so lovely that her cousin Princess Marie of Edinburgh later described it as 'exquisite beyond words, it almost brought tears to your eyes'.[35] To Ella's extreme discomfort, she had recently been proposed to by her cousin Wilhelm, the eldest son of her aunt Vicky, who had taken to frequently visiting Darmstadt when he could escape from his studies at the University of Bonn, much to the horror of his good natured, well-mannered Hesse cousins, who couldn't stand him. Like everyone else, Wilhelm was smitten by Ella's enchanting loveliness, but in his case it had grown into a full blown and passionate love. However, although their grandmother Queen Victoria, who saw no problem with marrying a first cousin as, after all, she herself had done so, was all in favour of the match as she hoped that Ella's sweet nature would curb Wilhelm's propensity for bullying everyone around him, her daughter Vicky was rather less keen – perhaps because she was unwilling to risk the possibility of one of her nieces being carriers of the haemophilia gene, which might prove catastrophic for the newly united imperial Prussia if Ella passed the illness on to any sons that she might potentially have with Wilhelm. It's possible that these concerns were also passed on to Wilhelm himself for even though his passion for Ella could not be disputed, he very suddenly transferred his attentions to a second cousin, Princess Augusta Victoria of Schleswig-Holstein, who was a granddaughter of Queen Victoria's half-sister Feodora.

On 16 August, Alice and her family joined her mother at Osborne House for a short stay. Yet again, Victoria was dismayed by how 'dreadfully ill, so pale and thin'[36] her daughter looked, despite having been away from Darmstadt for several months. She was delighted to have her younger Hesse grandchildren in the nurseries though, writing in her journal what a 'pleasure' it was as 'I love to hear the little feet and merry voices above.'[37] The three eldest princesses stayed with their uncle Bertie, beautiful Aunt Alexandra and Wales cousins on a royal yacht, also confusingly called the Osborne, which was moored off the coast nearby – which must have been the most delightful adventure for them. The two eldest Wales boys, Eddy and Georgie, were now teenagers and much better behaved than they had been as children, when they were the despair of their formidable grandmother and, having been thwarted in her plan to match Ella with Wilhelm, Victoria naturally began to wonder if she might not be better off with one of them instead. The younger children, including Victoria's favourite Alix, enjoyed glorious summer days playing in the extensive grounds and even swimming in the floating pool that their mother had also enjoyed as a child. Also staying on the Isle of Wight, in a small house that they had rented at West Cowes, were the Princess of Wales' parents, the king and queen of Denmark and they were also frequently to be found at Osborne House during their visit. When Alice and her children left on the 20th, Victoria was very sad to see them go, writing rather forlornly in her journal that her grandchildren would 'have grown and changed by the time I see them again'.[38] The Hesse family returned to Eastbourne until the end of September, having completely fallen in love with the town and local area. The children had a wonderful time learning how to play tennis or spending hours playing on the beach, under the careful supervision of their governesses and nurses, while Alice either rested, worked her way through her reading pile or involved herself in local philanthropic efforts – she could never resist a good cause and even though she was supposed to be on holiday, she helped raise funds for local schools, hospitals and churches and, just as she did at home in Darmstadt, often took her children, even the two youngest girls Alix and Marie, along with her when she made her visits. However, they were almost certainly left at home when she paid a visit to one of her pet causes, Albion House, which was a home for reformed prostitutes that she had agreed to act as Patroness for, with the view of establishing similar homes in Hesse when the family returned in September.

The end began with a sore throat. On 7 November, Princess Victoria, Alice's fifteen-year-old eldest daughter, started to feel increasingly hoarse and uncomfortable as she read aloud to her younger sisters from Lewis Carroll's *Alice in Wonderland* and despite everyone's hopes that she would sleep it off and feel better in the morning, she developed a fever overnight and was much worse the next day. To Alice's dismay, the doctors diagnosed a case of diphtheria, one of the most feared diseases of the period, which caused membranes in the throat to swell until they covered the tonsils, making it difficult for the sufferer to swallow or breathe until, in some tragic cases, they suffocated and died. Although Princess Victoria was immediately quarantined, her father and younger siblings Alix, Irene and May also fell ill with the same disease within the next few days, driving Alice to despair as she insisted upon doing the lion's share of the nursing herself, albeit assisted by eight nurses. Other than herself, only Ernie and Ella appeared unaffected by diphtheria and the decision was made to send them off to their grandmother's house until everyone else had recovered – only for Ernie to also fall ill within days of arriving, which necessitated him being sent straight back again to be nursed by his devoted and exhausted mother. Over in England, Victoria was kept appraised of events by a stream of regular daily telegrams from her daughter, who kept her updated with the progress of the unfortunate invalids. On 11 November, Alice was able to report that her daughter Princess Victoria was out of danger and sitting up, reading and writing again and two days later her telegram informed her mother that 'Alicky tolerable; darling May very ill, fever so high, Irene has got it too. I am miserable, such fear for the sweet little one.'[39] On the 15th, Alice informed her mother that while Alix and Louis were nearly out of danger and on the mend and Ernie and Irene were both still very ill, her youngest daughter, 'precious little' May 'suffers so much, am in such terrible fear'.[40] By the next morning she was dead after sitting up suddenly in bed and 'giving a choking cough'. 'This is too dreadful,' Victoria wrote, obviously in shock. 'How my darling child adored that little angel.'[41] May had been conceived in the terrible aftermath of Frittie's accident and had done much to assuage her mother's grief over losing her son – now she too was gone. It was too cruel, too terrible. 'The pain is beyond words but God's will be done,' Alice wrote to her mother later that day in between ministering to her other sick children. 'Our precious Ernie still a source of such terrible fear, the others, though not safe, better.'[42] Everyone was much relieved when his fever broke shortly after this and he too seemed to be on the mend, only for their hopes to be dashed a few days later when he once again relapsed and seemed even more ill than ever – to the point that even he was scared that he was about to die, much to Alice's distress.

Victoria was devastated by the loss of her pretty little granddaughter, who was just four years old. 'How I see her before me at Osborne, running up and down the hill, while Alice and I were taking tea, so full of life and spirits, so funny and pretty, with her blue eyes, fair hair and bright colours.'[43] When May was buried alongside Frittie in the Rosenhöhe mausoleum on the afternoon of 18 November, Alice was the only family member present at the funeral, the others being ill or kept away because of the fear of infection. 'Our sweet May waits for us up there and is not going through the agony we are, thank God,' Alice wrote to her mother after the funeral. 'Her bright, happy sunshiny existence has been a very short bright spot in our lives but oh how short! I don't touch on the anguish that fills my heart for God in his mercy helps me and it must be borne... How I pray that my precious Ernie may be spared to me. I went to the mausoleum this morning. How crushed I felt. In tears, anguish, I prayed to be spared from having to part with Ernie too. I can but say, in all my grief, there is a mercy and a peace of God, which even now He has let me feel.' [44]Although Louis and the other children were well on their way to recovery, Ernie's condition continued to cause alarm for a number of days and Alice, who had kept all the children apart during the contagion so that none of them were aware that their youngest sister had died, was very much afraid that it would cause a relapse if she told him that May, of whom he was extremely fond, was no longer with them. Keeping the secret from Ernie, who constantly asked how his little sister was doing, added to the terrible strain that Alice felt. On 25 November, Ernie's tenth birthday, he was finally declared out of danger but still Alice did not dare tell him that May had succumbed to her illness. 'It made me almost sick to smile at the dear boy,' she wrote to Victoria. 'But he must be spared yet awhile what to him will be such sorrow.'[45] She finally told him the truth on 1 December, telling her mother later on that 'the sorrow was such a blow, it quite upset him, though I told him as gradually as possible. The tears kept running down his little face and I comforted him as best I could, saying that we should be together again and that she had none of the suffering we now had. He wished to know about her death and gave a sigh of relief that it had been without suffering and came so quick.'[46]

A week later, all of the invalids were very much on the mend and Alice felt able to resume some vestiges of her usual life again. After spending so many days cooped up in the palace, caring for her sick husband and children, she was desperate for some fresh air and despite the freezing cold weather, enjoyed taking walks in the gardens and even a carriage ride. On the 7th, she ventured out to the train station in order to briefly meet up with her brother Alfred's Russian wife Marie, Duchess of Edinburgh, the spoiled only daughter of Tsar Alexander II and his wife, Princess Marie of Hesse, who was Louis' aunt. Marie was just passing through Darmstadt on her way to England so it was just a quick meeting but no doubt still a boost for Alice, who must have been feeling very lonely and forlorn as she nursed her family back to health. Everyone who saw her at this time noticed how ill, pale and thin she looked and so when she sent word to her mother the very next morning that she had woken up with the dreaded sore throat and beginnings of a fever, Victoria was thoroughly alarmed, writing in her journal that Alice 'will never have the strength to get through it. But I must hope the best, though I know how weak she is.'[47] The fact that Alice had almost certainly caught the infection while comforting Ernie after breaking the news of May's death made her illness all the more poignant and the whole family rallied around in support, all of them well aware that Alice, who had neglected her own health while caring so assiduously for everyone else, would have to battle hard in order to survive. Victoria was particularly distressed and immediately implored Dr Jenner, her most trusted physician to hurry to Darmstadt in order to care for her daughter. At the same time, she was incredibly anxious about her daughter-in-law Marie and her children, who were now in London and doing everything that they could to prevent the dreaded infection taking hold. Over the next week, a constant stream of bulletins once again arrived from Darmstadt, keeping Victoria and the rest of Alice's family updated about her progress. At first, it seemed as though she had only a mild case of the disease but it quickly became clear, as her fever worsened and she found it increasingly difficult to swallow and breathe, that she was in fact extremely ill – which was no surprise to anyone who knew her and had observed her increasingly weak and feeble state over the years. Jenner arrived in Darmstadt on 12 December and reported to Victoria that he found Alice feverish and uncomfortable, but did not consider her case entirely hopeless. For her part, Victoria was very struck by the fact that Alice was lying ill on the anniversary of her father's final illness in 1861 and Bertie's brush with death seven years earlier and took to the Blue Room in Windsor Castle, where Albert had died, in order to pray for her daughter's recovery. 'How it brings that awful time… back to my poor mind and heart,'[48] she wrote that evening.

The next day was spent in an agony of suspense as Victoria, so far away in Windsor, desperately waited for news about her daughter. 'At a little after 11, came a telegram from Louis, which gave me a frightful shock: "Jenner has seen Alice, is consulting with Doctors. He does not despair, but I see no hope; my prayers are exhausted."[49] Distraught with worry, Victoria and her youngest daughter Beatrice went to the royal mausoleum at Frogmore, where Albert was buried and which had become a place of regular pilgrimage for the entire family – even Alice's small children had been taken there more than once to lay flowers on their grandfather's tomb. While there, Victoria received a most alarming telegram from Dr Jenner, informing her that the disease had spread to Alice's windpipe and that she was finding it incredibly difficult to breathe, which meant that she was beginning to slowly suffocate. Dr Jenner was able to give them some hope later on that day when he telegraphed to say that Alice's breathing had improved and that she'd been able to get some sleep and even take some soup, eggs and liquids, but the overall prognosis was still not a hopeful one and Victoria once again retreated to the soothing calm of the Blue Room in order to pray for Alice's deliverance. Victoria barely slept that night as she was so worried about Alice and felt vaguely reassured to find that there was no news, good or bad, awaiting her when she got up the next morning. However, just as she sat down to breakfast, her faithful ghillie John Brown entered with two telegrams from Darmstadt.

'I looked first at one from Louis, which I did not at first take in, saying: "Poor Mama, poor me, my happiness gone, dear, dear Alice. God's will be done." (I can hardly write it!) The other was from... Jenner saying: "Grand Duchess became suddenly worse soon after midnight, since then could no longer take any food", Directly after, came another with the dreadful tidings, that darling Alice sank gradually and passed away at (half past seven) this morning! It is too awful! I had so hoped against hope. I hurried to poor dear Beatrice, already much distressed, at the worse news and then went back to my room, where poor Leopold met me, to whom I broke the news and who sobbed bitterly, whilst I embraced and pressed him to me. "I am so sorry for you dear Mama, she loved you so tenderly and devotedly," which I know she did, dear sweet child. We all said "Poor Louis, poor children" for to them it must be too fearful.' [50]After this, Victoria hastened to the sitting room of her eldest son Bertie, who had been Alice's closest ally amongst her siblings and found him in his dressing gown 'looking dreadfully pale and haggard, trying to repress his violent emotion, quite choked with it. His despair was great and he could hardly speak. As I kissed him, he said "The good are always taken, the bad remain". Went in for a moment to dear Alix... who was much affected and distressed and said "I wish I had died instead of her."'[51]

The rest of the day passed in a state of deepest misery as the entire royal household sincerely mourned Alice's passing. Surrounded by her children, Victoria spent some of the day at the mausoleum at Frogmore, where they placed wreaths on Albert's tomb then knelt beside it, 'thinking of her, who far off was lying lifeless, but whose pure spirit was reunited to the father that she loved so dearly'.[52] On the way back to the castle, Victoria and Bertie decided to commission the sculptor Boehm to create a beautiful memorial to Alice for the mausoleum and agreed that it should depict Alice recumbent, as though sleeping, clasping her daughter May to her breast, which Bertie thought would be 'very appropriate and beautiful'. He and Leopold had already decided to leave straight away for the funeral in Darmstadt, although the royal doctor Sir William Gull, who was called for in the absence of the preferred Dr Jenner, imposed several conditions on the princes to ensure that they would not catch any lingering infection, stipulating that they should not stay in Darmstadt itself and could only briefly shake hands with Louis.

At the end of a long, exhausting and emotional day, Victoria struggled to find the words to convey just how profoundly distressed she was by this, the first of her children to die. 'That this dear, talented, distinguished, tender hearted, noble minded, sweet child, who behaved so admirably during her dear father's illness and afterwards in supporting me and helping me in every possible way should be called back to her father, on this very anniversary seems almost incredible and most mysterious! To me, there seems something touching in the union which this brings, their names being forever united on this day of their birth into another better world.'[53]

Chapter Five

'The best and dearest of Grandmamas.'

1878–1884

In Darmstadt, while the frantic telegrams passed between Windsor Castle and the Neues Palais, Alice increasingly struggled to breathe. As the illness progressed and her throat became more swollen and sore, she lost the ability to speak and so communicated with her husband with pencil written notes, until finally she became so weak that even that was too much effort. When Dr Jenner arrived, Louis initially prevented him from seeing her, in case his unexpected presence alerted her to the seriousness of her condition and frightened her, but in the end relented – probably because he feared a scolding from his intimidating mother-in-law. At first, Jenner reported back to Victoria, Alice did not seem all that unwell and was able to take his hand and ask him to examine her sore throat but she soon afterwards lapsed into unconsciousness and that was when the true battle to keep her alive began. On the last evening, Louis had thought that she looked a little better and so had kissed her hands and risked going to bed to get some sleep, which meant that it was his mother, Elisabeth, who had always been so kind to Alice, who held her hand as she drew her last torturous breath in the early hours of the morning. Outside the palace, the snow-covered streets of Darmstadt were crowded with townsfolk, all silently keeping vigil as they waited for news – Alice had often feared that they did not love her and would have been immensely touched had she known just how saddened they were by her loss.

'You have all had the most terrible blow which can befall children,'[1] Victoria wrote to her granddaughters a few hours after the terrible tidings of Alice's death had arrived at Windsor Castle. 'You have lost your precious, dear, devoted Mother who loved you and devoted her life to you and your dear Papa! That horrible illness which carried off sweet little May and from which you and the others recovered has taken her away from you and poor old Grandmama, who with your other kind Grandmama will try and be a Mother to you! Oh, dear children, dearest beloved Mama is gone to join dear Grandpapa and your other dear Grandpapa and Fritte and sweet little May where there is no more sorrow or tears or separation.'[2] Victoria had maintained a correspondence with her granddaughters since they were old enough to read and write simple letters, usually sending them affectionate little missives along with their birthday and Christmas presents – from now on though, she would make the effort to write far more frequently.

Due to the fear of infection, Alice's funeral took place within a few days and her eldest and youngest brothers Bertie and Leopold were there to see her buried in the Rosenhöhe mausoleum close to her children Frittie and May. It was freezing cold and the snow lay thick upon the ground, which meant that Louis, who had only just recovered from his own battle with diphtheria and had barely eaten or slept since Alice had first fallen ill, could not attend as he was still too frail to venture out into such harsh weather. He was absolutely devastated though and hardly knew how to comfort his distressed and confused children, who were also unable to attend their mother's funeral and seemed to barely be able to comprehend the tragedy that had just befallen them. At the exact same time as Alice was being laid to rest, precious photographs of her parents tucked into her coffin beside her, her mother and family gathered together in the private chapel of Windsor Castle for their own ceremony, which was so moving that it left almost everyone in tears. 'How impossible it seems that it should be my own darling child who is gone!' Victoria wrote in her journal. 'How I recall every trait of her childhood, such a lovely sweet little child and baby she was, so good, pretty and dear. When her sister married, she became my constant companion and was so full of talent. She had developed so wonderfully and had shown such sense and energy, such initiative power. She was such a charming companion, we could talk on all subjects so openly together, she was so friendly to those in the house, always simple, never proud or haughty. I had hoped to see a great deal of her next year and now all is over forever in this world.'[3] However, in the midst of all this misery, Victoria was still able to note that their shared grief had brought her closer than ever to her eldest son, Bertie: 'We have but one feeling of love, affection and regret,' she wrote in her journal after he had returned, full of sorrow and thoroughly broken-hearted, from Alice's funeral. 'It has brought all so close together.'[4]

In Darmstadt, Alice's children were traumatised by the sudden loss of their mother and it was a sad and miserable Christmas for them all. 'We miss darling Mama dreadfully, especially this week, which used to be one of the gayest in the year,'[5] her daughter Victoria wrote to her grandmother after Christmas, enclosing a present that Alice had commissioned for her before her death – a 'very pretty gold brooch with the name 'May' in black enamel and small diamonds and the dear little child's photograph at the back' which 'upset' the queen very much. Her thoughts were constantly with Alice's motherless children, so far away in Darmstadt, and she longed to have them with her. 'You must treasure her in your hearts as a Saint – one who is rare in this World,' Victoria wrote to her granddaughters on 27 December. 'It is a great privilege to be her child, but it is also a great responsibility to become really worthy of her, to walk in her footsteps, to be unselfish, truthful, humble minded, simple, and to try and do all you can for others, as she did…This must have been a dreadful Christmas and *what* a New Year! That every blessing may be yours in this new and terribly altered year is the earnest prayer of your loving, devoted and sorrowing Grandmama.'[6] By the end of the year, Victoria, had resolved to bring Louis and his children to England so that she could be close to them and do whatever she could to provide assistance – she had very quickly realised that Alice's death would put an end to her annuity of £6,000, which had never seemed to go far enough while she was alive and would be much missed by her stricken widower and children. It was arranged that they would come to her in the middle of January and in the meantime there was a constant stream of letters between Queen Victoria and Darmstadt, with her grandchildren Victoria, Ella, who had returned home from her grandmother's house to a scene of desolation, and Ernie, who was completely devastated by his mother's death, being her most regular correspondents.

On 18 January, Alice's brothers Bertie and Leopold went by royal yacht to Flushing in the Netherlands, where they collected Louis and the children and brought them back to Osborne House, where Victoria was anxiously waiting for them. 'I felt my heart beat dreadfully and received poor dear Louis on the staircase, going down the steps to meet him,' she wrote in her journal on 21 January, after their arrival. 'He was dreadfully affected, as was I too. Took him to my room and he gradually became calmer. Then I went and called in the dear children, who were all crying, excepting dear little unconscious Alicky. It is terrible to see these blooming children, all in deep mourning, all looking so well and to miss darling Alice, who so doted on them and was so anxious about them... It is a great comfort to have (Louis) and the dear children with me, but very sad.'[7] Louis had brought with him several of Alice's belongings and also Angeli's 'wonderfully like and beautiful' family portrait of Alice and Louis with Ernie, Ella and Alix, which had been commissioned by Victoria two years earlier but was still not quite finished at the time of Alice's death. Later on, Victoria would write to Alice's eldest daughter to say that 'the dear family picture is a great delight and comfort to me and so wonderfully, splendidly painted and grouped – so very like. I think Ella's expression is just hers and Ernie's an expression that he often has.'[8] Several of Alice and Louis' household had come to England with them and Victoria spent the next few days speaking to them in private about her daughter's final days, gleaning every single detail about her death and torturing herself with how terrible Alice's suffering had been. She also busied herself talking to her grandchildren's faithful nanny, Miss Orchard, about their education and development, which she had decided to take an even greater interest in now that their mother had gone. Although there could be no doubt that Louis was an excellent and devoted father, the immaturity and lack of intellectual curiosity that had so troubled Alice was a problem for Victoria as well, as after all she had had the rare good fortune to raise her children for over two decades with the help of the intellectually talented Albert, and she was worried about the effect on his children, who now looked to him alone for guidance. She was especially anxious about his youngest daughter, her great favourite Alix, who was just six years old and therefore particularly vulnerable. 'Alicky... looked very sweet in her long cloak,' she wrote on 2 February after coming back from a walk. 'I feel a constant returning pang in looking at this lovely little child, thinking that her darling mother, who so doted on her, (is) no longer here on earth to watch over her.'[9]

The visit was bittersweet for both Victoria and her grandchildren as although they were able to give each other a great deal of comfort, Alice's absence hung heavily over them and any happiness that they might have felt was naturally inhibited by the fact that she was not there to share it with them. At night, Victoria loved to go up to the nursery and say goodnight to the younger children, Ernie and Alix, when they were tucked up in bed, just as Alice had always done every night. 'It pleases them so and darling Alice always did it,' she wrote in her journal. 'It makes me so sad.'[10] On 18 February, they all left Osborne House and travelled together to Windsor Castle, where the quiet routine of intimate family dinners, bedtime kisses and gentle excursions that seemed to be doing them all so much good continued. To Ernie's great delight, his grandmother had presented him with a splendid Skye terrier puppy that he had taken a shine to in the Osborne stables and the little dog, which was named Charlie, no doubt proved to be an excellent distraction to Louis' two youngest children, both of whom had inherited the family passion for dogs. At Windsor, there were daily visits to the mausoleum at Frogmore, where they laid flowers at the foot of Albert's tomb then spent a few moments in quiet reflection before returning to the castle. The sculptor Boehm was still working on the memorial to Alice and May that Bertie and Victoria had commissioned on the day of her death and although it would not be placed in the chapel for several months, Victoria visited the cast in Boehm's studio on more than one occasion and was able to report that it was 'perfectly beautiful, so like, so touching, so full of grace, so simple and such complete repose. Little May is very like, now too. She lies peacefully, nestling in her dear mother's arms.'[11] For Alice's five surviving children, Windsor Castle was full of memories of their mother and, thanks to Victoria's preoccupation with her dead, portraits, photographs and busts of Alice were on prominent display in every room, alongside those of her father and grandmother, the Duchess of Kent. At some point in February, Victoria even had Alice's four daughters photographed, looking very forlorn in their black mourning dresses, in front of a large photograph and small marble bust of their mother. All four girls look utterly bereft but it is the desolate face of little Alix, who is obviously fighting back tears as she holds another photograph of her mother, that is especially haunting.

The family left England on 28 February, taking with them Alice's youngest brother, twenty-five-year-old Prince Leopold, who was a great favourite with his nieces and nephew and also very close to his brother-in-law Louis who 'dreaded returning to that desolate house'[12] and so had requested his company. Victoria would happily have kept Louis and the children with her forever and wrote in her journal later that she 'felt terribly distressed when the moment came to wish all goodbye… feel the blank so terribly, now they are gone. Never, since my dear husband's time, had I spent such a peaceful family life, such perfect intimacy, and dear Louis, I have always loved so much. He is quite a son to me.'[13] Her youngest daughter Princess Beatrice told her mother's cousin Mary, Duchess of Teck, that 'the parting from dear Louis was very sad… we miss the dear children so much, the house feels quite empty without them'. They arrived back in Darmstadt two days later, after being held up by fog for six long hours along the way. As Louis had predicted, it was a dismal home coming – made all the worse by the fact that Leopold had injured his knee getting out of a railway carriage and was forced to spend almost all of his time resting on a sofa, where he was doubtless ministered to most devotedly by his nieces. However, despite everyone's hopes that he would make a quick recovery, Leopold's condition did not fully improve for quite some time and he was forced to miss the wedding, which had already been postponed due to Alice's death, of his brother Prince Arthur to Princess Louise of Prussia, a cousin of Vicky's husband Fritz, on 13 March.

'What a dreadful return it must have been and how you must miss darling Mama,' Victoria wrote to her eldest granddaughter, Princess Victoria, shortly after their return to Darmstadt. 'I had not an opportunity before you went to say how I hope you will try more and more to be a help and comfort to dear Papa, and try to make his dreary life less desolate and to do all you can to improve in every way.'[14] Princess Victoria turned sixteen on 5 April, the age when their family usually started to think about prospective matches, but there was no question of her marrying any time soon when her bereaved father and siblings needed her at home. Although it was naturally expected that Princess Victoria would shoulder much of the burden in her mother's absence, she had the support of her beloved governess Miss Jackson, who was known within the family as

'Madge', and also Wilhelmine von Grancy, one of her mother's ladies in waiting, who had been with Alice when she died and then remained to support and comfort her children. Meanwhile, Alix was still under the care of the redoubtable Miss Orchard, who did everything in her power to help her small charge recover from the loss of her mother and sister, which had left her depressed and withdrawn. However, thanks to Orchie's devoted care and the resilience of her young age, Alix soon bounced back and although she would never forget the terrible events that had occurred that winter, she would at least be able to enjoy life once again. Although their mother had not been quite so preoccupied with remembering the dead as her own mother was, as evidenced by the fact that she found Victoria's protracted wallowing in misery after Albert's death increasingly annoying, mourning dead loved ones was already a familiar part of life in Darmstadt and at least some of Alix's earliest memories would have involved family visits to mausoleums – either to pay her respects to her grandfather Albert or to her brother Frittie, who had died just a few days before her first birthday. However, whereas she may well have associated visits to her English grandmother with the pall of gloom that still hung over the royal palaces, even almost two decades after Albert's death, the atmosphere in the Neues Palais had never been sombre – in fact Alice, even when she was heartbroken by her own losses, had gone to considerable effort to ensure that her children's surroundings were as cheerful and carefree as possible and, under the aegis of the devoted Orchie, they would eventually once more echo with the laughter of her young charges.

Although Alix and her sisters were gradually starting to recover, the health and wellbeing of their ten-year-old brother Ernie, who had always been considered unusually sensitive, still continued to cause concern. He had been tormented by nightmares ever since the death of his little brother Frittie and was now struggling to cope with the loss of his mother and youngest sister. Thinking that it might do him some good to spend plenty of time outdoors, Victoria invited Ernie and his father to Balmoral for a few weeks of deerstalking, shooting, riding and long, bracing walks. They arrived on 25 September, both looking surprisingly well, although Louis was observed to have tears in his eyes as the carriage they were sharing with Victoria approached the castle, which obviously did not displease his mother-in-law, although it hinted that their stay would be an emotionally trying one. It rained virtually every day at the start of their stay but although Ernie, who had inherited his mother's love for books and art, would much rather have spent his time tucked away cosily in the castle's library, he was a good sport and so gamely and with very little complaint agreed to go out stalking and shooting with his father and uncles Arthur and Leopold. The family party was enlivened by the presence of the still extremely glamorous former Empress Eugénie, who was staying nearby at Albergeldie Castle while she recovered from the death of her only child, the Prince Impérial, who had been killed that June while fighting the Zulus in South Africa – much to the dismay of Victoria's youngest daughter Beatrice, who had taken quite a shine to the handsome Bonaparte prince and even hoped to marry him one day. When the weather brightened, Louis was sent off to slaughter the local game while Ernie accompanied his grandmother and aunt Beatrice on gentle walks and sketching trips in the countryside or was squashed between them in the carriage in order to pay pleasant visits to local dignitaries, all of which exactly suited his downcast mood much more than spending hours tramping through sodden heather and wondering when it was going to rain again. When it was time to leave Balmoral on 20 October, both Louis and Ernie were 'terribly upset' to be leaving, while it made Victoria 'quite sick at heart to think of the saddened home (they) are going back to, the loving wife and tender mother gone'. [15]

While Louis and Ernie were enjoying their stay in Scotland, the girls paid a visit to their great aunt Empress Maria Alexandrovna of Russia and her husband Alexander II, who spent part of every summer at Heiligenberg Castle near Jugenheim, the home of Maria's brother Alexander and his morganatic wife Countess Julia Hauke. Like everyone else in the extended family, Empress Maria had been extremely moved by the circumstances of Alice's premature death and so extended a warm welcome to her children, who were invited to join them and get to know their Russian relatives. Empress Maria had spent much of her childhood at Heiligenberg and so loved these regular, cosy little family gatherings, while her husband relished the more informal atmosphere that prevailed at Alexander's relatively modest court. For the Hesse girls though this was a taste of a very different lifestyle for although they were obviously very much at home amidst the grandeur of Buckingham Palace and Windsor Castle and used to seeing family members arrayed in wonderful jewels and military orders, the Romanovs were in a whole different league. Although their grandmother Victoria had once enjoyed a brief flirtation with Emperor Alexander before he married his Hessian princess, she had since then rather taken against the Russians, whom she thought ostentatious to the point of vulgarity and antagonistic towards the British, although she remained friendly with the ruling house and even had a Russian daughter-in-law, Marie Alexandrovna, who had married her son Prince Alfred in a lavish ceremony in St Petersburg in 1874. 'I hope you will not get all Russian from the visits to Jugenheim,' she wrote to Princess Victoria before the visit, reminding her that Alice 'though loving the language had *such* a horror of Russia and the Russians.'[16] Happily, it seems that on this occasion at least, Princess Victoria was able to reassure her grandmother that she had not been overly impressed by her Romanov relatives, telling her that they were lazy, conceited, ignorant, rude and, perhaps worst of all, hostile to her beloved England, but still Victoria worried that these visits might result in an inconvenient romance. Most of Maria and Alexander's six surviving children were rather older than their Hessian cousins and already married and starting their own families, but the two youngest boys, Grand Dukes Sergei and Paul were just twenty-two and nineteen-years-old and, Victoria feared, imbued with all the charisma, glamour and dashing good looks that had made their father so irresistible all those decades earlier – and that was before one even considered the family's fabulous wealth, which was surely enough to turn any young woman's head, however sensible she might be.

Several months would pass before Victoria and her Hesse grandchildren were reunited and in the meantime they maintained a copious correspondence, with the queen clearly taking her resolution to be another mother to them extremely seriously. She was keen to hear about everything that was happening in their lives and if their own letters were deficient in that respect then she also had regular monthly missives from their governess and tutors to fill in the gaps – although even they could be disappointingly lax when it came to corresponding with the queen, much to her irritation. She took a particular interest in the education of her youngest Hessian granddaughter Alix, who was one of her favourites and considered by everyone in the family to be a most particularly delightful child. Like all of her siblings, Alix had inherited Alice's quick wit, appreciation of art and love of reading and learning for its own sake and to Victoria's pleasure, she proved to be a keen student when she followed in her sisters' footsteps and began to take more arduous lessons with their governess Miss Jackson, who ensured that the girls' education followed the same rigorous system that had been implemented several years earlier by their mother, supported by a new English governess, Miss Pryde, who had been picked by their grandmother Victoria. Even from a young age, Alix's days were long and packed with activity, with lessons beginning at around 7 am after she had got up, breakfasted, dressed herself and then made her own bed and tidied her room. Alice had believed that extensive and varied reading was the basis of any good education and accordingly the Hesse children read a wide and often very challenging range of books, encompassing history, theology, science and philosophy as well as the more usual classical literature, which they read in both English and German. As well as the more formal lessons, Alix also enjoyed learning how to draw, paint and knit, while her piano lessons were the absolute highlight of her day. Every detail of her daily life was passed on to her grandmother Victoria, either via her governess' reports or in her own letters, which she sent with pleasing regularity, often accompanied by a small present, usually either a knitted scarf or a particularly nice painting, that she had proudly made herself for 'the best and dearest of Grandmamas'. Alix was almost certainly aware that Victoria had taken a special interest in her and so made a point of signing off her letters as 'your loving and grateful child', which reinforced the bond between them while they were apart.

After a lengthy separation, Alix and her grandmother were reunited on 30 March 1880, when Victoria paid a brief visit to Darmstadt in order to attend the confirmation of her two eldest granddaughters, Victoria and Ella, this time staying for two nights in the main ducal palace, which gave her an opportunity to spend some time catching up with her grandchildren. Confirmations were highly important occasions within the royal family and quite a crowd of relatives gathered for the occasion, including Victoria's children Beatrice, who was her constant companion, and Bertie, who was accompanied by his wife Alexandra. Sadly, Vicky was unable to attend, but her husband Fritz put in an appearance with their eldest daughter Charlotte, Princess of Saxe-Meiningen, which pleased Victoria very much. After the confirmation ceremony was over, Victoria went with Louis and Beatrice to the Rosenhöhe to see Alice's final resting place, where they saw 'on the floor, close to the door, my darling Alice's coffin, covered with a crimson velvet pall, on which were embroidered my darling child's initials, on which were resting numberless fine wreaths and crosses, including the original ones we had sent,' Victoria remembered later on. 'We knelt down and I felt terribly shaken. It seemed too dreadful!'[17] The pathos of the scene was added to by the presence of Frittie and May's small coffins nearby, also covered in velvet palls and huge quantities of flowers. After this, they went to the Neues Palais, which Victoria had not seen since Alice's death and where she was very much moved to see that Alice's belongings were all still exactly where she had left them in her rooms. Victoria dined *en famille* that evening with Beatrice, Louis and the two newly confirmed girls, Princesses Victoria and Ella, and perhaps she was already beginning to surreptitiously watch how her youngest daughter and widowed son-in-law interacted with each other across the dining table. It was Bertie who had first wondered out loud if it might not be a good idea for Louis and Beatrice to get married in order to provide the poor Hesse children with another mother and their father with a suitable helpmate. However, Parliament had passed a bill in 1835 that explicitly prohibited such a marriage between a man and his former sister-in-law and despite repeated efforts to overturn the ruling, it had not yet been successful. That Victoria and Bertie wholeheartedly lent their support to the Deceased Wife's Sister's Marriage Act is perhaps significant, although if they were hoping for a resolution in time to allow Beatrice to marry Louis, and there is little surviving evidence, perhaps thanks to Beatrice's own work excising large sections of her mother's journal after her death, that Victoria was even seriously hoping for such a thing, then they were doomed to disappointment as it would not successfully pass until 1907, by which time Louis was long since dead.

When Louis and Ernie returned to Balmoral that September, they brought with them the two younger girls Irene and Alix (the two elder girls, Victoria and Ella, had already visited their grandmother at Balmoral earlier in the year). Victoria was thrilled to see them again, especially her beloved Alicky, who was 'looking extremely well' and 'quite beautiful, with her splendid eyes and sweet smile'.[18] While her father amused himself shooting and stalking deer (on one occasion bagging a splendid seventeen-stone stag) in the countryside, Alix went on excursions with her grandmother and aunt Beatrice or played in the gardens with three of her Wales cousins, the daughters of her uncle Bertie, who were staying at nearby Abergeldie Castle. On the evening of 4 October, Alix was allowed to stay up late and accompany the rest of the household to Abergeldie, where Bertie and Alexandra were holding a dance for all of the royal servants and tenants, which was a rare treat. The royal party walked down an avenue lined with torch-bearing Highlanders before dancing reels until the early hours, although Alix almost certainly didn't last that long before she had to be put to bed. As the weather was fine that autumn, there were plenty of opportunities to enjoy the beautiful countryside that surrounded Balmoral and Alix accompanied her grandmother on several excursions to some of the loveliest spots, including Glen Gelder Shiel, where they enjoyed a short walk before taking tea, which was accompanied by freshly caught trout. This idyllic Scottish holiday came to an end on 18 October, much to everyone's regret. 'Dear, excellent Louis was much distressed and the darling children cried bitterly,' Victoria wrote after their sad leave-taking that evening. 'I felt how we should miss them and how piteous to think of the motherless home the children were returning to and the desolate one of poor Louis.'[19] Victoria had loved having her grandchildren around her but hard on their heels was a reproving letter to their eldest sister, Princess Victoria, who was regarded as being in charge of her younger siblings in the absence of a mother. 'I hope you, as the oldest sister, will see that the younger ones are very punctual about their lessons – for I am sorry to say that *all* three tried to evade them when they were here.' [20]

Victoria and her favourite Hesse granddaughter Alix would not be reunited for almost two years but, in the meantime, the flow of letters continued as usual as the queen sought to exert her influence over her granddaughters from afar, always emphasising that she loved them as if they were her own children. Now that Alice was dead, all of her mother's issues with her were forgotten, and instead Victoria reinvented their relationship as one of deep mutual understanding and warmth, telling

Alice's eldest daughter that her 'beloved Mama… was the one of my daughters who felt with me so much'[21] and that therefore she instinctively always knew what Alice's wishes would have been with regard to the upbringing of her children. There was no part of their lives that Victoria was not interested in and her advice ranged across a broad range of topics from general life guidance ('If you are humble minded and loving to all and occupy yourself with serious things, you will succeed. Be always ready to listen to the advice of those whom you know to be truly devoted to you – and *not* to those who will flatter you and wish to do what you may like, but which often may be bad for you'[22]), the folly of having close female friendships ('You are right to be civil and friendly to the young girls you may occasionally meet… but never make friendships; girls' friendships and intimacies are vey bad and often lead to great mischief'[23]) to how to behave more elegantly in public (Princess Victoria was an inveterate chatterbox and her grandmother frequently counselled her to speak less 'and especially not too loud and not across the table'[24]). However, the most pressing topic was naturally their marital prospects, with Victoria being especially keen that the pretty Hesse princesses should not be pressured into marrying too young, as many other German princesses were, and certainly not to Russians – who had, in Victoria's view anyway, become even more unsuitable after the horrifying assassination of Alexander II in March 1881. It troubled Victoria that many young women seemed to 'wish to be married for marrying's sake' and she worried that her own young granddaughters might also do so, especially as they were without a mother to advise and caution them. However, that's not to say that Victoria did not have her own candidates for the hands of her beautiful Hesse granddaughters, especially her favourite Alix, whom she hoped to see permanently settled close to her in England.

On 25 September 1882, to Victoria's great pleasure, Louis, Ernie and Alix arrived at Balmoral Castle for an extended visit after enjoying a large family gathering at Darmstadt earlier in the month for Louis' forty-fifth birthday. Alix was ten years old and even more delightfully pretty than ever with lovely eyes and wavy auburn hair. As always the timetable of entertainments on offer at Balmoral involved sedate walks in order to admire the stunning Aberdeenshire scenery, horse rides, picnics, painting expeditions and visits to the estate tenants and local dignitaries while the men spent their time slaughtering the royal game. Also staying at Balmoral was their aunt Princess Beatrice and uncles Prince Arthur and Prince Leopold with their wives, as well as Bertie and Alexandra's three daughters, who were great favourites with their Hesse cousins as they loved nothing better than romping about in the gardens with the swarm of pet dogs that followed their mother and grandmother everywhere. There was also very little chance that Alix and Ernie were allowed to neglect their lessons as they had done during their last visit and so much of their time would have been spent indoors in the nursery, doubtless much to their annoyance. However, on the plus side, both Alix and Ernie were now considered old enough to join the rest of the family for dinner in the evening, which was a signal honour for the children and on 10 October, they were even allowed to attend the first few hours of a ball in the castle ballroom, which was a huge treat, even for Alix, who was already shy around large groups of people that she didn't know. On 21 October, a local photographer from Ballater was asked to come to the castle to photograph Victoria with Louis, Alix, Ernie as well as Princess Beatrice and Prince Arthur's wife Princess Louise of Prussia, whose splendid baby daughter Margaret had the great honour of being perched on her doting grandmother's knee. Both Alix and Ernie are dressed in the Scottish costumes considered suitable for a stay at Balmoral but although her brother looks cheerful and relaxed, Alix looks uncomfortable and ill at ease and hugs one of Victoria's pet dogs for comfort.

At the beginning of 1883, Victoria was feeling especially concerned about the future marriage prospects of her motherless Hesse granddaughters. Although the eldest girl, Princess Victoria turned twenty that April, like many girls in her situation she was expected to remain at home for a while longer in order to supervise the upbringing of her youngest siblings and also act as a substitute chatelaine for her widowed father. Her younger sister, the famously beautiful Ella, was a quite different matter, however, and Victoria was already busying herself trying to promote a match with Prince Frederick of Baden, eldest son of the Crown Prince of Baden and his vivacious wife, Fritz's sister Princess Louise of Prussia. Frederick was nice looking and looked set to be a dutiful and adoring husband to the gorgeous Ella but to Victoria's great disappointment, her granddaughter showed not the slightest bit of interest in him or indeed in anyone else. However, those convivial Hesse and Romanov family gatherings at Heiligenberg were clearly still preying on Victoria's mind when straight after extolling Prince Frederick's virtues in a letter to Princess Victoria she suddenly changed tack in order to warn her granddaughter that 'Russia, I could not wish for any of you and dear Mama always said she would never hear of it.'[25] Nonetheless, when Ella fell in love with her tall, broodingly handsome but rather formidable Russian cousin Grand Duke Sergei in the spring of 1883, there proved to be very little that anyone could do to change her mind. 'How very unfortunate it is of Ella to refuse good Fritz of Baden so good and steady, with such a safe, happy position and for a *Russian*,' Victoria wrote in March of that year. 'I do deeply regret it.'[26] In an attempt to avert what she saw as a terrible mésalliance, Victoria invited Ella to stay with her at Balmoral that summer, with the intention of somehow talking some sense into her – however, all of her efforts were doomed to failure as her granddaughter remained just as attached to Sergei as ever. Ella no doubt thought it a very welcome distraction indeed when a letter arrived from her father in Darmstadt in the middle of June to inform Victoria that Princess Victoria had agreed to marry her cousin, Prince Louis of Battenberg, the extremely handsome eldest son of her great uncle Prince Alexander of Hesse, whom she had known all her life and who had been a great favourite of her mother Alice. That Prince Louis had been a naturalised British citizen ever since he voluntarily joined the British Navy at the age of fourteen in October 1868 did much to ease Queen Victoria's misgivings about the match and the fact that Louis was always strapped for cash and almost certainly unable to support her granddaughter as lavishly as she deserved. It was unfortunate, of course, that Princess Victoria's marriage would necessitate her leaving her father's house and relinquishing the care of her three youngest siblings, but her grandmother couldn't help but be pleased and relieved that she would be swapping Germany for Britain and would therefore be close at hand – unless she accompanied her husband during his frequent overseas postings.

Despite all of Victoria's efforts to prevent the match, and after almost a year of uncertainty, Ella finally and absolutely agreed to marry Sergei that September, having spent several months wrestling with her own doubts and confusion about the prospect of leaving Germany behind and beginning a whole new life in Russia – although to her relief she discovered that there was no need for her to give up the Lutheran Protestantism that she had grown up with in order to convert to Russian Orthodoxy. When the dreaded news of Ella's engagement arrived at Balmoral Castle, Victoria was incensed and disappointed in equal measure that her lovely granddaughter would be living in a decadent and degenerate society that suffered from a 'total lack of principle from the Grand Dukes onwards'.[27] She could not bring herself to answer Ella's letter announcing the engagement but instead informed her elder sister Princess Victoria that she feared that 'our sweet but undecided and inexperienced Ella, with her lovely face, may be misled and get into difficulties and troubles – which might have painful consequences. Louis will understand what I mean,' Victoria added darkly. 'Russians are *so* unscrupulous.'[28] Hurt by her failure to get Ella to agree to a match of her own choosing, Victoria could not resist lashing out at Sergei, who had never actually done anything to incur her ire – not least because she had never actually met him, saying that even if Ella spent a lot of time outside Russia 'she must not look to being much and often with me – as I could not have a Russian Grand Duke staying with me often or for long. That would be utterly impossible'.[29]

By the time the royal family gathered in Darmstadt in April 1884 for Princess Victoria's wedding, Ella's engagement had been formally announced to the world and the wedding scheduled to take place in St Petersburg that June. The fact that Sergei's father had settled a vast personal fortune on her granddaughter, who would be even wealthier than Victoria after her marriage, and that she had already been showered with a priceless collection of jewels by her infatuated fiancé, who brought it with him to Darmstadt then patiently bedecked Ella with every single glittering, shimmering item, did little to mollify Victoria, who arrived on 17 April with the intention of staying for almost three weeks. Her youngest son, Prince Leopold, who had been a great favourite with his Hesse nieces and nephews, had died suddenly in Cannes on 28 March after suffering a fall, and the family gathering was naturally overshadowed by this tragedy. Although the three eldest Hesse girls had punctiliously written letters of condolence to their grieving grandmother, Victoria had been surprised and dismayed not to hear from Ernie, who would, to be fair, always be a reluctant correspondent, and Alix. 'I thought Ernie and Alicky would write to me,' she admonished their eldest sister. 'Dear Uncle loved them, as he did you all, so much and Alicky was such a pet! I hope they feel what a loss he is to them too?'[30] Although Princess Victoria clearly managed to chivvy her lazy youngest siblings into writing to their grandmother, it was not enough to ameliorate Victoria's hurt feelings for although she was very pleased to be reunited with 'sweet Alicky', she could not help but note in her journal that evening that seeing her 'nearly upset me, when I thought of how darling Leopold loved these nieces'.[31] Once again, visiting Darmstadt aroused sad memories of her daughter Alice, especially as this time, Victoria was given Alice's sitting room – which was just as she had left it, with all of her belongings still lying around. Victoria wrote that evening's lengthy journal entry while lying on Alice's own sofa before taking herself off to bed.

Luckily, there was little likelihood for quite some time of her favourite, little Alicky announcing any unsuitable engagements. Alix was about to turn twelve that June and, as always, delighted her grandmother with her delicate prettiness and winsome manner – the awkwardness over her delayed reaction to Prince Leopold's death having now been smoothed over. She spent a great deal of time with her grandmother during the lengthy visit and Victoria's journal is peppered with references to carriage rides, breakfasts, luncheons, cosy family dinners, goodnight kisses and walks with Alix, who made a most pleasant companion for the elderly queen and was no doubt treated to a lot of advice in the process. Grand Duke Sergei was also in Darmstadt for the wedding and although he made a reasonably favourable impression upon his fiancée's formidable grandmother, who insisted upon having a private chat with him, she almost certainly lost no opportunity to drop unsubtle hints about the unsuitability of the match into the impressionable ears of Ella's youngest sister. On 30 April, Princess Victoria, who was feeling so wretchedly unwell on the day that she could hardly bring herself to get dressed and was still limping as the result of twisting her ankle a few days earlier, got married in a simple Lutheran ceremony attended by a plethora of royal luminaries, including her uncle Bertie, Prince of Wales and aunt Vicky, Crown Princess of Prussia, along with all of their children. It was the first wedding of one of Alice's children and her family were determined to do the right thing and give the bride a proper send off into her new life. Alix, who looked very pretty in a short white dress, had the honour of escorting her grandmother Victoria into the chapel and remained close to her for the rest of the long, exhausting day. However, if Alicky's youthful prettiness drew compliments from her family, it was almost certainly her elder sister Ella, who appeared wearing some of the splendid jewels that Sergei had showered upon her after their engagement, who was, after the bride, the cynosure of all eyes on the day. When Victoria left Darmstadt on 6 May, she took Louis and Ella back to Windsor Castle with her – it having become her custom to enjoy some time alone with each granddaughter just before they embarked on marriage.

The bride-to-be's father was not usually invited along but Louis had disgraced himself in the eyes of Alice's family by unwisely choosing the evening of his daughter's wedding to secretly get married to his recently divorced, Polish-born mistress, Alexandrina Hutten-Czapska, who was just nine years older than his eldest daughter and considered a most unsuitable person to be presiding over his household, living in close proximity to Louis' impressionable children and associating on intimate terms with the royal families of Britain, Prussia and Russia. Victoria was furthermore incensed by what she regarded as an insult to the memory of her daughter and, along with the Emperor of Prussia, who immediately telegraphed to order his son and daughter-in-law and their children to distance themselves from the scandal and return home to Berlin, put enormous pressure on Louis to immediately separate from his new wife and have the match annulled – in the meantime, he was not to be allowed out of her sight lest he stray back to his bride. 'If dear Papa should feel lonely when you three elder are married – I should say nothing (though it must pain me) if he chose to make a morganatic marriage with some nice, quiet, sensible and amiable person who would at any rate command the respect of us all as well as of his country,' Victoria wrote to her eldest granddaughter. 'But to choose a lady of another religion who has just been divorced… would I fear be a terrible mistake and one which he would soon repent of when too late.'[32] It was her eldest son Bertie, himself no stranger to disorderly extra marital affairs and no doubt privately inclined to be sympathetic to his former brother-in-law's plight, who was ordered to act as Victoria's emissary and order Louis to have the marriage annulled – which it duly was just three months later, much to the relief of everyone except Louis and his now banished erstwhile wife, who was quietly pensioned off.

Victoria was exceedingly relieved when the whole affair was at an end – not realising that another romantic secret was quietly brewing right beneath her nose as her youngest daughter Beatrice, whom she intended to keep by her side as a companion for the rest of her life, had fallen passionately in love with Louis of Battenberg's younger brother Henry during the trip to Darmstadt and that the two had agreed to get engaged. Although Victoria had previously been in mild favour of Beatrice marrying either the Prince Impérial or Louis of Hesse, she had been relieved when these prospective matches came to nothing and in fact gave strict instructions that the potentially triggering subject of weddings should never be mentioned in Beatrice's presence lest it spark an interest, only natural in a young woman of her class and era, in becoming a bride herself and potentially leaving her mother. The more perceptive members of the royal family decided to keep Victoria in the dark about this latest unwelcome development for as long as possible but the secret had to come out eventually and after much soul-searching, Beatrice finally broke the news shortly after they returned to England. As predicted, Victoria was furious and if her family expected her to quickly reflect upon the situation and calm down they were to be sorely disappointed for the aging queen did no such thing and even refused to speak to her daughter for seven months, preferring instead to communicate via embarrassed intermediaries or by note, which she would occasionally push across the table herself with her eyes ostentatiously averted from her daughter. Observing this unhappy pantomime during her last visit to England as an unmarried woman, Ella might well have reflected that she had got off lightly. 'I think I know what I am doing and if I am unhappy, which I am sure will never be, it will be all my doing,'[33] she told her grandmother Victoria before her wedding, doubtless echoing the thoughts of her aunt Beatrice, who firmly stuck to her plan to marry, despite her mother's attempts to passive aggressively bully her into dropping them.

Chapter Six

'Darling Alicky who is so lovely.'

1884–1888

On 8 June 1884, Ella and her family arrived at the train station in St Petersburg, where they were warmly welcomed in person by her fiancé's enormously tall, immensely strong and bear-like eldest brother Alexander III, who had succeeded as Tsar after the assassination of their father in March 1881, along with his pretty wife Maria, who was the younger sister of the Princess of Wales and known within the family as 'Minnie', and the rest of the imperial family. Although Victoria was of the opinion that Tsar Alexander, who was just the sort of lumbering, bellowing, scruffy sort of man that she most deplored, was not a 'gentleman', he made a huge effort to welcome her granddaughter to Russia and did everything that he could to ensure that Ella's father and siblings also felt at home – with particular attention no doubt being given to Alix, who was the god-daughter of both the Tsar and Tsarina. That this personal welcome was a huge honour would not have been lost on the Hesse family and even far away in England, Victoria noted it in her journal with some satisfaction. She might never become reconciled to Ella's choice of husband but at least the Romanovs appeared to be giving her granddaughter the respect that she deserved. As for Ella's youngest sister Alix, who had turned twelve two days earlier, this was to be her first glimpse of the Russian royal family at home and she was suitably awed by everything that she saw as they travelled by golden carriages pulled by matching white horses through beautiful St Petersburg to the splendid Peterhof Palace, a favourite Romanov summer residence, which would be their home during their stay and where they would enjoy every possible luxury. Although Alix had grown up in a palace, albeit a relatively modest and newly built ducal one, and was used to her grandmother's grand residences, Peterhof and the other imperial Russian palaces were in a whole different league and she was both awed and overwhelmed by their splendour and size. Peterhof had been built in the eighteenth century as a response to Louis XIV's Versailles and Alix and her sisters would have been free to spend hours wandering through the wonderful gardens with their marble colonnades, fountains and statues in between the series of glittering receptions and parties that had been arranged for the week before Ella's wedding.

The first event was a cosy family dinner in the Peterhof Palace on their first evening, which went very well as everyone was on their best behaviour. To Alix's pleasure, she found herself sitting next to Tsar Alexander's eldest son, the sixteen-year-old Tsesarevich Nicholas, who was very unlike his father and in fact bore a close resemblance to their shared first cousin Prince George of Wales, the second son of Alix's uncle Bertie and Nicholas' aunt Alexandra. Although Nicholas had visited Great Britain only once as a child in the summer of 1873, he had spent a lot of time with his British cousins over the years at the annual family get-togethers organised by Maria and Alexandra's parents, the king and queen of Denmark, and he no doubt had plenty of stories about their escapades to share with Alix, who would have been able to tell him about the fun she had with her Wales cousins at Osborne and Balmoral. If that topic of conversation dried up then they could always move on to chatting about yet another shared group of cousins – the children of Nicholas' aunt Marie Alexandrovna, who was married to Alix's uncle Alfred, Duke of Edinburgh. With so much shared family, it is not surprising that Nicholas and Alix, both of whom were prone to shyness around strangers, should have felt completely comfortable in each other's company and indeed appear to have felt as though they had known each other forever right from the very beginning. 'I sat next to little twelve year old Alix, whom I really liked a lot,'[1] Nicholas noted in his journal that evening before adding that he had liked her sister 'beautiful Ella… even more'.[2] Over the following days, Nicholas' diary is littered with references to romping in the gardens, being sprayed with water by his father, sharing 'secrets', chatting, 'romping' and jumping on a trampoline with 'pretty little Alix',[3] her brother Ernie, whom he also liked a great deal, and his own younger sister Xenia, who was three years younger than Alix. Within just five days of their first meeting, Nicholas was able to write that 'Alix and I wrote our names on the window of the

Princess Alice asleep in the antique German cradle bought by her father shortly before her birth, painted by Landseer in 1843. (*Royal Collection Trust/© Her Majesty Queen Elizabeth II, 2019*)

Princess Alice and Prince Albert Edward 'Bertie', July 1856. Alice and her elder brother were extremely close in childhood and could be counted upon to stand up for each other. (*Royal Collection Trust /© Her Majesty Queen Elizabeth II, 2019*)

Princess Alice, November 1857.
(*Royal Collection Trust /© Her Majesty Queen Elizabeth II, 2019*)

Princess Alice and Prince Louis of Hesse sketched by Queen Victoria on 11 December 1860, shortly after they had become engaged. (*Royal Collection Trust /© Her Majesty Queen Elizabeth II, 2019*)

Princess Alice dressed in mourning for her grandmother, the Duchess of Kent, July 1861. (*Royal Collection Trust/© Her Majesty Queen Elizabeth II, 2019*)

Princess Alice in her wedding ensemble, including the veil that would be worn by all of her daughters at their own weddings, George Koberwein, 1862. (*Royal Collection Trust/© Her Majesty Queen Elizabeth II, 2019*)

The Marriage of Princess Alice, George Housman Thomas, 1862. Alice's wedding, which took place in the dining room of Osborne House, was likened to a funeral by her mother. (*Royal Collection Trust/© Her Majesty Queen Elizabeth II, 2019*)

Princess Alice and her husband Louis dressed in the ensembles that they wore to the wedding of her brother Bertie to Princess Alexandra of Denmark in 1863. (*Royal Collection Trust/© Her Majesty Queen Elizabeth II, 2019*)

Princess Alice, after Heinrich von Angeli, c. 1880–90. (*Royal Collection Trust/© Her Majesty Queen Elizabeth II, 2019*)

The coffins of Princess Alice and her two children, Frittie and Marie, in Darmstadt, Heinrich Reinhard Kroh, 1879. After Alice's death, her brother Bertie made an annual trip to Darmstadt in order to pay his respects at her tomb. (*Royal Collection Trust/© Her Majesty Queen Elizabeth II, 2019*)

Princess Alice and Princess Marie's memorial, Frogmore Mausoleum, painted in 1897. When Alix and her siblings visited Victoria at Windsor Castle they would be expected to regularly visit the memorial to their mother and sister. (*Royal Collection Trust / © Her Majesty Queen Elizabeth II, 2019*)

Princess Alix of Hesse, Benedikt Konig, 1873. This delightful bust of the young Alix had pride of place in Queen Victoria's bedchamber at Osborne House and remains there to this day. (*Royal Collection Trust / © Her Majesty Queen Elizabeth II, 2019*)

Princess Alix of Hesse, March 1873. (*Royal Collection Trust / © Her Majesty Queen Elizabeth II, 2019*)

Princess Alice with her children, July 1873. A very grumpy Alix is on her mother's lap. (*Royal Collection Trust / © Her Majesty Queen Elizabeth II, 2019*)

Princess Alice, Louis and their six children, Windsor, circa 1875. Alix is leaning against her mother, while baby Marie is in her father's arms. (*Royal Collection Trust / © Her Majesty Queen Elizabeth II, 2019*)

Princess Alix of Hesse, drawn by her grandmother Queen Victoria on 9 May 1875. She was a terrible sitter and the queen complained in her journal that Alix was extremely fidgety. (*Royal Collection Trust / © Her Majesty Queen Elizabeth II, 2019*)

Princess Alix of Hesse, drawn by her grandmother Queen Victoria on 2 May 1875. (*Royal Collection Trust / © Her Majesty Queen Elizabeth II, 2019*)

The Neues Palais, Darmstadt, 1867–80. (*Royal Collection Trust / © Her Majesty Queen Elizabeth II, 2019*)

Princess Alix of Hesse photographed in Darmstadt, circa 1877. (*Royal Collection Trust / © Her Majesty Queen Elizabeth II, 2019*)

Princess Alice's sitting room, Neues Palais, Darmstadt, 1878. It was left virtually untouched after her death. (*Royal Collection Trust/© Her Majesty Queen Elizabeth II, 2019*)

Princess Alix and Princess Marie of Hesse, May 1878. (*Royal Collection Trust/© Her Majesty Queen Elizabeth II, 2019*)

The family of the Grand Duke of Hesse, Heinrich von Angeli, 1879. After Alice's death, Victoria insisted that Louis bring this painting, which she had commissioned, to England for her. (*Royal Collection Trust/© Her Majesty Queen Elizabeth II, 2019*)

Alix and her three sisters posing in front of a photograph of their deceased mother, Windsor, February 1879. (*Royal Collection Trust / © Her Majesty Queen Elizabeth II, 2019*)

Queen Victoria with the four daughters of Princess Alice of Hesse, Windsor Castle, February 1879. Alix is holding hands with the queen. (*Royal Collection Trust / © Her Majesty Queen Elizabeth II, 2019*)

Princess Alix of Hesse with her uncle Prince Leopold, February 1879. Alix wore the gold bracelets that Leopold gave her for the rest of her life. (*Royal Collection Trust / © Her Majesty Queen Elizabeth II, 2019*)

Prince Louis of Hesse with his children and the Prince and Princess of Wales, March 1880. Alix is kneeling beside her brother Ernie. (*Royal Collection Trust / © Her Majesty Queen Elizabeth II, 2019*)

Queen Victoria with Louis, Alix, Ernie and other family members, Balmoral, 1882. (*Royal Collection Trust / © Her Majesty Queen Elizabeth II, 2019*)

Alix and Irene as bridesmaids for Princess Beatrice, July 1885. (*Royal Collection Trust / © Her Majesty Queen Elizabeth II, 2019*)

Alix of Hesse with Queen Victoria, Princess Beatrice, Prince Albert Victor and Princess Irene, Balmoral, 1887. (*Royal Collection Trust / © Her Majesty Queen Elizabeth II, 2019*)

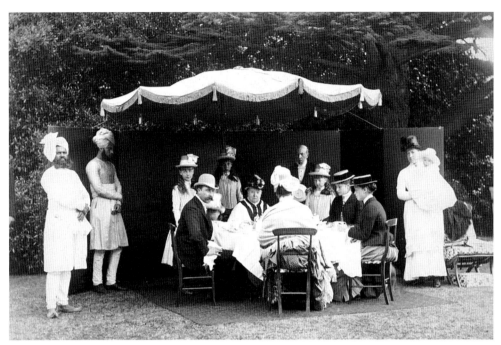

Alix (third from right) breakfasting with Queen Victoria and other family members, Osborne House, May 1887. (*Royal Collection Trust / © Her Majesty Queen Elizabeth II, 2019*)

Alix of Hesse dressed up as a novice nun for one of the Tableau Vivants performed at Balmoral in October 1888. (*Royal Collection Trust / © Her Majesty Queen Elizabeth II, 2019*)

Queen Victoria with members of her family, including Alix, who is back left, Balmoral, June 1891. (*Royal Collection Trust / © Her Majesty Queen Elizabeth II, 2019*)

Grand Duchess Elizabeth Feodorovna and her husband, Sergei, March 1884. They were determined that Elizabeth's sister Alix should marry Nicholas instead of one of her British cousins. (*Royal Collection Trust / © Her Majesty Queen Elizabeth II, 2019*)

Tsesarevich Nicholas and Prince George, Duke of York (the future George V) photographed together while Nicholas was in London for George's wedding in July 1893. It didn't take long before Nicholas was thoroughly sick of being told how much they looked alike. (*Royal Collection Trust / © Her Majesty Queen Elizabeth II, 2019*)

Queen Victoria with her descendants, Coburg, April 1894. The family were gathered together for the wedding of Alix's brother Ernie to their first cousin Princess Victoria Melita. Alix almost stole the show by getting engaged to Nicholas the day after the wedding. (*Royal Collection Trust / © Her Majesty Queen Elizabeth II, 2019*)

Princess Alix of Hesse and Tsesarevich Nicholas photographed shortly after their engagement, while staying at Osborne House on the Isle of Wight, August 1894. (*Royal Collection Trust / © Her Majesty Queen Elizabeth II, 2019*)

The marriage of Princess Alix of Hesse and Nicholas II, Laurits Tuxen, 1895-6. Queen Victoria was unable to attend Alix's wedding in St Petersburg but commissioned this monumental work from Tuxen as the next best thing. (*Royal Collection Trust / © Her Majesty Queen Elizabeth II, 2019*)

Empress Alexandra Feodorovna, signed 'To my beloved grandmama', 1895. After her marriage, Alix continued to write regularly to her grandmother Queen Victoria and enclosed several photographs, such as this one. (*Royal Collection Trust / © Her Majesty Queen Elizabeth II, 2019*)

The arrival of Empress Alexandra Feodorovna and Nicholas II at Balmoral, September 1896, painted by John Percival Gülich, 1896. (*Royal Collection Trust/ © Her Majesty Queen Elizabeth II, 2019*)

Queen Victoria greeting her granddaughter Empress Alexandra Feodorovna and Nicholas II to Balmoral Castle in September 1896, painted by Amadée Forestier in 1896. (*Royal Collection Trust/ © Her Majesty Queen Elizabeth II, 2019*)

Queen Victoria with Empress Alexandra
Feodorovna, Nicholas II, Grand Duchess
Olga and the Prince of Wales, Balmoral,
September 1896. (*Royal Collection Trust /
© Her Majesty Queen Elizabeth II, 2019*)

Empress Alexandra Feodorovna, Heinrich von Angeli,
1897. Alix posed for this sumptuous portrait while
staying with her grandmother at Balmoral Castle
in September 1896. (*Royal Collection Trust / © Her
Majesty Queen Elizabeth II, 2019*)

Queen Victoria, Robert Milne,
June 1899. (*Royal Collection
Trust / © Her Majesty Queen
Elizabeth II, 2019*)

Italian House (we love each other)[4] and they grew increasingly attached as the days went by. However, Alix had clearly heard enough over the years to know that her grandmother Victoria would not appreciate her budding romance and so there was no mention of 'Nicky' when she wrote to her – instead she glossed over his presence, writing that 'I have been much with little Xenia and her brothers' and adding that 'it is very pretty here and I enjoy myself very much,'[5] leaving Victoria to draw her own conclusions about what was *really* going on around the magnificent fountains and marble colonnades at the Peterhof.

On 15 June, Ella and Sergei were married in an opulent ceremony in the Winter Palace, watched by an immense crowd of royal guests from all across Europe. As was traditional for all Romanov brides, including those who were marrying into the family, Ella walked in a procession up the stately marble Jordan Staircase of the palace before dressing for her wedding in the justly celebrated Malachite Drawing Room. Alix watched from the sidelines as her sister was laced into her ornate wedding gown, which was cut in the distinctive style favoured at the Russian court and spangled with several thousand roubles worth of diamonds and pearls. As was traditional, Ella wore the Romanov wedding jewels, which comprised a splendid kokoshnik diamond tiara, a diamond nuptial crown, a diamond riviére necklace and a pair of enormously heavy diamond girandole earrings. Along with all this dazzling Romanov finery, with all of its historical significance, Ella also wore her mother's Honiton lace wedding veil, which had been preserved along with her other precious possessions in Darmstadt and would be worn by all of her daughters on their wedding days. When she was ready, Ella was escorted next door to the Arabian Drawing Room, where Sergei and the rest of the wedding party awaited her. The Tsesarevich Nicholas was acting as one of his uncle's four best men, who would have the job of holding the heavy wedding crowns over the couple's heads as they said their vows, and he and Alix, who was looking very pretty indeed in white muslin with roses pinned into her auburn hair, no doubt exchanged shy smiles as the party processed down the stairs and through almost a quarter of a mile of state rooms, all lined with thousands of courtiers, to the chapel where the ceremony was to be held. It was Alix's first experience of a Russian Orthodox wedding and she was completely captivated by the mysterious beauty of the ceremony, which was so different from the much less flamboyant manner with which weddings were celebrated in the Lutheran church. The smoky, incense-scented air, soft chanting of the priests and the flickering taper candles held throughout the lengthy ceremony by the bride and groom all impressed her enormously and although, as a devout Lutheran German girl, she had no desire whatsoever to convert, she couldn't help but feel inspired and stirred by the ancient mysticism of the Russian Orthodox Church. After the wedding ceremony, there was a grand banquet followed by a polonaise ball, after which all of the family guests drove in state to Ella's new home, the Beloselsky-Belozersky Palace, where the newly married couple hosted an intimate dinner party for their relatives.

The beautiful idyll in Russia came to an end all too quickly after Ella's wedding when Alix and her family took their leave of their Russian relatives and returned home to Darmstadt. 'I am very very sad that the Darmstadts are going tomorrow and even more so that dearest Alix is leaving me,'[6] Nicholas sadly confided to his journal. He secretly presented her with a pretty brooch, which she initially accepted before quickly returning it, having had second thoughts about the propriety of accepting gifts from him. At twelve, Alix was old enough to be aware of the fuss that had surrounded her elder sister's decision to marry into the Russian royal family and how greatly their grandmother Victoria, of whom they were all at least a little bit afraid, disapproved of the match – even though she warmly returned Nicholas' adolescent regard, she would have known right from the very beginning that such a match would not be looked upon with favour and may even have believed that her father and grandmother would be able to outright forbid it. Ella had stood firm in the face of their disapproval and all of Victoria's attempts, both subtle and blatant, to prevent her engagement to Sergei – would Alix also be capable of such defiance if matters came to a head between herself and Nicholas? Although Victoria greatly enjoyed hearing the Hesse girls' excited descriptions of the magnificence of St Petersburg and Ella's wedding, she was still not a little worried about the effect that the enormous wealth and, as she saw it, vulgar self-indulgence of the Romanovs would have upon her impressionable granddaughters. 'Everything seems to have gone off uncommonly well and been most splendid,' she wrote to Princess Victoria, 'but I hope that Darling Ella won't be spoilt by all this admiration and adulation and all this glitter of jewellery and grandeur etc?'[7] To Victoria's relief, despite all of her new wealth, huge palaces and dazzling jewels, Ella seemed to remain as unspoilt as ever and never assumed the airs that her grandmother associated with the other Romanov princesses, such as her daughter-in-law Marie, who made herself unpopular at court by flaunting her fabulous Russian jewels and insisting upon taking precedence.

Victoria had an opportunity to judge Ella's appearance and demeanour for herself in April 1885, when she revisited Darmstadt in order to attend the christening of Princess Victoria's first child, Alice, who had been born in Windsor Castle in February, and Ernie's confirmation on 25 April, which would have been Princess Alice's forty-second birthday. Victoria arrived two days before the joint ceremony and noted that Ella 'looked lovely, but very thin'[8] when she met her at the train station but was still 'just the same sweet gentle creature as ever'.[9] She was reunited with Alix at luncheon, after which they drove out to Braunshardt, an eighteenth-century rococo mansion, one of several residences that had been inherited by Louis when he became Grand Duke and which Victoria described as 'a colourful chocolate box'. On the 25th, Ernie's confirmation took place in the morning and was followed by a family luncheon, after which they all trooped back into the chapel for baby Alice's christening, at which Victoria and Ella were amongst the godparents. By the end of 1884, Victoria had become begrudgingly reconciled to her youngest daughter Beatrice's determination to marry Prince Henry of Battenberg and gave her consent to the match taking place on the understanding that the couple would make their home permanently with her. 'I am becoming more reconciled to the possibility of this event' she wrote to Alix's eldest sister. 'Of course it remains a shock to me and there will be things very difficult to get over with my feelings – still as he is so amiable and prepared to do what I wish, I hope all may be for the best and may turn out well.'[10] As a younger son with few prospects and not much cash, Henry, who was known within the family as 'Liko', had absolutely no problem whatsoever with this and was more than happy to reside in Britain at Victoria's expense forever, which did much to endear him to her. The couple were both guests at the family celebration in Darmstadt, which gave Victoria the chance to closely observe them. The sight of them both praying together in the chapel gave her a rather unwelcome jolt but she was also 'strangely moved' and pleased by their evident sincere love for each other, which boded well for their future happiness when they were all living together after the wedding. She had also, no doubt very begrudgingly, become reconciled to Ella's Russian Grand Duke after spending a lot of time with him in Darmstadt – on 30 April, she even felt able to write in her journal that 'at luncheon, Serge sat near me several times and we get on very well'.[11]

Once all of the practical details of the match had been determined, Victoria began to plan Beatrice's wedding with an unexpected but most welcome gusto. Like Princess Alice, she was to be married on the Isle of Wight, but instead of a dining room turned into a makeshift chapel, her wedding was to take place in pretty St Mildred's Church in the tiny village of Whippingham, where the royal family worshipped during their stays on the island. Both Albert and, to a lesser extent, Victoria had had a hand in the remodelling of the church shortly after their purchase of Osborne House, giving it a distinctly Germanic appearance with a large square central tower that can still be seen for miles around. There was also a private external door, surmounted with Victoria and Albert's intertwined initials, which led directly to the royal pew, where there were beautiful marble memorials to Albert, Princess Alice, Prince Leopold and Princes Sigismund and Waldemar of Prussia – Vicky's two little boys who had died in childhood. It might not have been as grand as St George's Chapel in Windsor Castle, where her sister Louise and most of her brothers had got married, but it was pretty and full of family memories and so Beatrice was satisfied. One of the benefits of being the last of Victoria's children to marry was that Beatrice had a bevy of nieces to pick from when it came to choosing bridesmaids – which also came with the drawback of not wanting to cause offence by leaving anyone out, with the result that she ended up with ten bridesmaids on her big day. As perhaps the prettiest of Victoria's unmarried granddaughters, the now thirteen-year-old Alix of Hesse was naturally a shoo in, along with her elder sister Irene; Princesses Victoria, Louise and Maud of Wales; Princesses Marie, Victoria Melita and Alexandra of Edinburgh, the daughters of Prince Alfred and Marie Alexandrovna; and Princesses Helena Victoria and Marie Louise of Schleswig-Holstein, the daughters of Princess Helena and her husband Christian, who were amongst Alix's closest friends as they often visited

Darmstadt. Absent were the three unmarried daughters of Vicky and Fritz, who were not invited to the wedding thanks to the Prussian royal family's frank disapproval of Beatrice's unimpressive choice of husband, and the daughters of Prince Arthur and Prince Leopold, who were considered too young to be part of the ceremony.

Alix arrived on the Isle of Wight on 20 July as part of a large family group, which included the groom and his parents, which had been picked up from the port of Flushing by the Royal Yacht *Victoria and Albert*. The crossing had been stormy and wild and several of the party, including the groom, had suffered terribly from sea sickness and continued to look alarmingly unwell after arriving at Osborne House. Not so Alix who was 'looking lovelier than ever'[12] and also, along with her brother Ernie 'immensely grown'[13] since Victoria had last seen them in Darmstadt in May 1884. It was swelteringly hot that summer and as was her custom, Victoria ordered that most of her meals, including a formal family dinner, should be taken in a large marquee erected on the lawn, which could be a torture for everyone as it was poorly ventilated and stuffy. Alix was still considered too young to attend such events and so spent most of her time romping in the gardens or on the royal private beach with her other younger cousins while the grown-ups prepared for the wedding, which took place on 23 July. Dressed in a flounced white dress with a small bunch of red and white carnations pinned to her chest, Alix was waiting with her uncle Bertie and the other nine bridesmaids at the church gate when Beatrice, wearing her mother's Honiton lace wedding veil for the occasion, arrived for her wedding with Victoria, who was to lead her up the aisle with Bertie walking on her other side. Alix walked beside her cousin Maud of Wales in the procession and Victoria noted later how pretty the bridesmaids looked as they knelt behind their aunt during the lengthy ceremony. When the wedding was over, Alix had the great honour, along with her sister Irene and cousin Louise of Wales, of riding back to Osborne in Victoria's carriage, which reminded the queen of Alice, 'their darling mother, who had been married here, also on the same month'.[14] They were the first of the guests to arrive back at Osborne and there was much tiresome hanging about while they waited for the register to be signed, before they could go out to luncheon, which was to be held in the dreaded marquee on the lawn. Once again, Alix was not considered old enough to attend that evening's formal dinner, which took place after the newly married couple had left for their honeymoon, but she was allowed to make a brief appearance afterwards in the drawing room with her cousins. After the splendours of Ella's wedding in St Petersburg, Beatrice's relatively modest nuptials at Osborne House must have seemed very homely indeed – however, although Alix had undoubtedly enjoyed her brief taste of extravagant Romanov hospitality, she almost certainly much preferred the low-key charm of her aunt's wedding on the Isle of Wight. Alix stayed on at Osborne House for almost a month after the wedding, which gave her an opportunity to enjoy the celebrated Cowes Regatta, which began on 4 August. There was also the usual round of entertainment at Osborne, which included a concert by a Siamese band, which Victoria described as 'peculiar and wild' but with 'a certain amount of melody' and going out on her uncle Bertie's yacht, the *Aline*. It was a perfect balmy summer and when Alix and her family reluctantly said their goodbyes on 21 August, Victoria admitted in her journal that she was 'so sorry to part with them'.[15]

Almost two years were to pass before Alix returned to her grandmother. She was originally supposed to accompany her father and Irene when they visited Balmoral in September 1886, but her slow recovery from a bout of scarlet fever led to fears that she might still be infectious and so she was left at home to recover. Her father adored Balmoral, which did much to endear him to his mother-in-law as she was well aware that none of her children or their spouses were keen on the place. Louis, however, saw nothing wrong with the gloomy 'Scottish' decor with its profusions of tartan, antlers and dark wood and he liked nothing better than spending the entire day out on the estate, stalking deer or shooting grouse. Alix was fully recovered by the following summer though and so was able to accompany the rest of her family to London for the grand celebrations that were held for Victoria's Golden Jubilee, which marked the fiftieth anniversary of her accession on 20 June 1837. On 21 June 1887, along with several other female members of Victoria's immediate family, Alix rode in a splendid procession of carriages that wound through the cheerfully decorated London streets, which were lined with guardsmen and vast cheering crowds, from Buckingham Palace to Westminster Abbey where they alighted in order to attend a splendid service of thanksgiving, at the end of which each of Victoria's descendants and their spouses stepped forward, bowed or curtseyed and then kissed her hand, after which she 'embraced them warmly'.[16] Alix was a shy and awkward teenager and already hated such grand public ceremonies, but even so she must have felt deeply honoured to participate in an event of such significance, not just to the nation but also to her family and she would wear with pride the special Jubilee brooch that Victoria presented to her after they returned, thoroughly exhausted, to the palace that afternoon. The following day, Alix and her family accompanied Victoria to Windsor Castle, where they were serenaded after dinner by the boys of nearby Eton school, which pleased the old queen very much. During their stay at Windsor, Alix was one of her grandmother's most constant companions and breakfasted, took tea and drove out with her every day, which included the usual visits to Frogmore mausoleum, where Boehm's beautiful memorial to Princess Alice and little May was now in place.

At fifteen, Alix was now old enough to accompany her grandmother to the various celebratory events that had been arranged for her around Windsor, including a trip to Dutton on 28 June, the anniversary of Victoria's coronation, where they were serenaded by school children and presented with flowers. The following day, Alix accompanied Victoria on the train back to London and then rode with her in her carriage from Paddington to Buckingham Palace, where they were to attend Victoria's Jubilee garden party, with a nostalgic stop at Kensington Palace along the way. When Frederick Sargent painted his huge painting of that day's garden party, which included several portraits of notable guests and members of the royal family, he did not think to include a likeness of Princess Alix of Hesse but she was there nonetheless, dressed in a pretty dress and spending most of her time with Ella and Sergei, who were due to return to Russia that evening. Although many people mistook his shyness for aloofness and therefore found him rather formidable, Alix always got on very well with Sergei, whose reserved disposition almost exactly matched her own. Although she is missing from the painting of the royal garden party, Alix can be glimpsed in Tuxen's epic painting of Queen Victoria and her family gathered together in the green drawing room at Windsor Castle, which commemorates the great gathering of the clan that occurred for her Golden Jubilee. Alix and her sisters were amongst the long line of royal family members who trooped through Tuxen's studio in order to pose for this monumental work, which carefully placed the most significant family members in the foreground, while at the same time kept feuding relatives tactfully apart. Tuxen was especially struck by the graceful loveliness of Ella and Alix, both of whom do indeed look especially beautiful – Alix is depicted chatting to her cousin Princess Maud of Wales while her brother Ernie stands just behind her, while Ella has a more prominent position towards the front.

By the start of July, the large family party began to break up as everyone returned home again, but Alix remained with her grandmother until 15 September. On 13 July, she accompanied Victoria on a visit to Hatfield House, the ancestral home of the Prime Minister, Lord Salisbury, where the royal party were very lavishly entertained before driving back to the station along a route lined with wildly cheering crowds. The following day, Alix once again formed part of a group of royal ladies who accompanied Victoria to Smith's Lawn in Windsor Park, where she was to lay the foundation stone of a new equestrian statue of Prince Albert, which had been donated by the women and girls of the nation. Several photographs were taken that day and in one, one can clearly discern Alix's unmistakeable profile as she smiles across at her grandmother, who is being helped down from her carriage. Although she was one of the youngest royal ladies present, she was also one of the tallest, towering over her diminutive aunts and the petite Princess of Wales, which made her seem rather older than she actually was. On 19 July, she went with the rest of the family party to Osborne House, where Victoria intended to recuperate from what had been a most gruelling few weeks, in between excursions into the nearby towns of Ryde and Cowes, which Alix often participated in. On 30 July, the enigmatic and extremely beautiful Empress Elisabeth of Austria came for luncheon at Osborne House, which must have been a huge treat for Alix and the younger members of the party, who would have heard a lot about the glamorous, eccentric Empress, who was widely known as 'Sissi', but had very few opportunities to actually see her in the flesh, as she usually eschewed royal gatherings in favour of travelling incognito. Just over a month later, Alix would have found herself in the company of yet another Empress: Eugénie of France, who joined them at Balmoral after the royal party left

Osborne House for Scotland on 24 August. At Balmoral they enjoyed the usual round of long walks, carriage rides, picnics, painting excursions and intimate family dinners in the stuffy, tartan decorated dining room. As Alix was still not yet considered old enough to join the adults in the evening, she was not usually allowed to attend dinner with the rest of the family (although on one occasion at Osborne, she was asked to come down and join everyone else when they realised that there was an unlucky thirteen people at dinner that evening) but at Balmoral, 'darling Alicky who is so lovely'[17] was able to join everyone else, much to her pleasure.

Earlier that year, in February 1887, Victoria had been appalled to learn that Alix's elder sister Irene had fallen in love with her first cousin Prince Henry of Prussia, the second son of their aunt Vicky. Victoria's relationship with her eldest daughter's Prussian family was rather frosty at this point and so she was less than pleased to learn that one of her beloved Hesse granddaughters, about whom she had always taken such a close and particular interest, was planning to become a princess of Prussia. 'I am so deeply hurt at Irene's conduct towards me,' she wrote to Irene's eldest sister Princess Victoria, shortly after the news broke, 'which is neither kind, grateful or straightforward… How can I trust her again after such conduct? Loving her as I do, treating her and you all as my own children and having to a great extent acted a mother's part to you all and been so very intimate with her, this want of openness has hurt me deeply.'[18] Ever since Princess Alice's death, Victoria had ceaselessly encouraged the four Hesse girls to regard her as a surrogate mother, had overseen their education and made a point of including them in family holidays and celebrations – however, in return she had expected complete loyalty and obedience and therefore quickly became incensed when they asserted their own preferences and defied her. This became especially obvious when it came to the question of their marriages – a matter in which Victoria naturally expected to exert her influence and even, to some degree, have the final say.

Although the Hesse princesses were relatively penniless, especially when compared to their British and Prussian cousins who would bring their husbands large fortunes, they were still highly eligible thanks to their close relationship with Victoria, impeccable breeding and, last but not least, reputation of being the most beautiful princesses in Europe.

However, not everyone agreed – Prince Henry's grandmother, the Empress of Prussia, who was already a thorn in the side of both her daughter-in-law Vicky and Queen Victoria, was also furious when she heard about the match, which she considered completely inappropriate and insufficiently grand for one of her grandsons. Luckily for Irene though, the Empress' spiteful nastiness about the situation did much to bring her grandmother Victoria, who was naturally thoroughly offended that the Prussians did not approve of her own much-loved granddaughters, on to her side, although some time would pass before she became properly reconciled to the marriage. 'I dare hardly hope for better things for lovely Alicky,' Victoria wrote at the height of the crisis. 'Although I still have lingering hopes left there!'[19] Now that Irene was engaged, only Alix was left and although she was not expected to marry for quite some time, Victoria had clearly started to make some plans for her future. 'I must tell you… that my heart and mind are bent on securing dear Alicky for either Eddie or Georgie,' she wrote to Alix's eldest sister in spring 1887. 'You must prevent *further* Russians or other people coming to snap her up.'[20] When Alix attended her grandmother's Jubilee celebrations, Victoria watched her interactions with her cousins Prince Albert Victor (who would be created Duke of Clarence in May 1890), and Prince George of Wales, the two sons of the Prince of Wales, very closely to see if there were any decided preferences between them. The elder, Albert Victor, who was known within the family as 'Eddy', was already twenty-three years old but as heir to both the British throne and the Empire, obviously a far better match than his younger brother, twenty-two-year-old George. At fifteen, Alix was entrancingly pretty and, in the view of most of her family at least, becoming ever-more lovely with each passing year and, to Victoria's pleasure, it seemed as though her male cousins were just as captivated by her as everyone else. Unfortunately, Victoria was not able to contrive for one of them to lead Alix in to the special celebratory luncheon in the dining room of Buckingham Palace on 20 June, an honour that fell to the sombre Prince Friedrich of Saxe-Meiningen, and as she was not yet out in society, Alix was not able to attend the grand dinner parties held that evening and the next, but there would have been ample other opportunities to observe them together during her long stay that summer. Certainly, by the end of the year, Victoria had decided that her beloved Alicky would make a perfect bride for her cousin Eddy and had resolved to do whatever she could to bring the match about.

Alix had known Eddy all her life and had almost certainly never had any romantic interest in him, although both he and his younger brother George bore a superficial resemblance to their cousin Nicholas, the Tsesarevich, the son of their mother's sister, in whom she very definitely took an interest. Both Eddy and George had been sent away to train as Royal Navy cadets in 1877 and subsequently were not at home as often as their sisters, with whom Alix was far more familiar as they were frequently around when she stayed with her grandmother at Balmoral and Osborne. By early 1888, when Victoria's vague plan to marry him to Alix of Hesse had crystallised into a hardened resolve, Eddy was in his mid-twenties and already had a certain louche reputation with it being rumoured that he regularly frequented homosexual brothels, had contracted a sexually transmitted disease, fathered an illegitimate child and had kept at least two Gaiety Girl mistresses – none of which can be absolutely proven even now, although the more serious rumour, that Eddy was in fact Jack the Ripper, can definitely be disproved as complete nonsense. Within his family, who knew him best, Eddy was very well liked, especially by his mother, who adored him, and his siblings, who appreciated his generous good nature and kind heart. Beyond this close knit family circle, however, the young prince was considered stupid to the point of retardation, lazy and ineffectual and there were many who wondered what sort of king he would one day make. Although she loved him and appreciated his many good qualities, his grandmother Victoria was under no illusions about Eddy's shortcomings and had long ago perceived that it was of the upmost importance to select the perfect wife for him as the success of his future reign might very well depend on the calibre of the woman who ruled beside him – and who could be more suitable for such a weighty task than her favourite granddaughter Alix of Hesse? If Eddy was not personally good enough for the pretty, intelligent and virtuous Alix then Victoria certainly did not allow this to deter her – as far as she was concerned, the fact that he was one of the most eligible bachelors in the world and would one day rule over an Empire definitely compensated for any personal, intellectual and moral deficiencies that he may have had.

On 31 July 1888, Alix and her brother Ernie returned to Osborne House for another long visit to their grandmother. She was now sixteen years old and strikingly pretty with long auburn hair and beautiful blue eyes. Her grandmother noted approvingly in her journal that evening that Alix looked 'so tall and lovely'[21] and as she had been confirmed and officially come 'out' into society earlier in the year and was now able to join the adults for dinner, Victoria now had even more opportunities to observe her and assess her suitability to take on the weighty task of marrying Eddy. Since Victoria had last seen her, Alix had, at her grandmother's request, been given her very own lady-in-waiting, an old friend Gretchen von Fabrice, and made her first visit to Berlin to act as bridesmaid for her sister Irene when she married Henry of Prussia in the glorious Baroque chapel of the Charlottenburg Palace on 24 May. Although there was some lingering hostility to the match, the Prussian royal family had nonetheless insisted that the wedding take place in Berlin and had treated Irene and her family with great courtesy, which did much to mollify Victoria and ease the bad feeling between the families. Even Vicky's ailing husband Fritz, who had succeeded his father as Emperor in March of that year, made a brief appearance even though he was terminally ill with cancer and would indeed pass away in the middle of June, to the great sorrow of all of his family who had always feared what would happen when his unstable eldest son Wilhelm took power and had prayed that it would not happen for many more years. Alix and her siblings had never liked Wilhelm, who was a bully, and like everyone else they had no illusions about what sort of Emperor he would be and rather feared the repercussions both in their family and all of Europe. Fritz's death, which Victoria had described as an 'awful misfortune', and the unwelcome succession of Wilhelm and his spiteful and equally much disliked wife Dona, would have been much discussed at Osborne House that summer, with Victoria no doubt keen to expand at length on her view that 'it is too dreadful for us all to think of Willie and Bismark and Dona being the supreme head of all now! Two so unfit and one so wicked.'[22] The day after their arrival, Victoria took Ernie and Alix with her when she visited Empress Eugénie who was staying at Osborne Cottage with her two nieces. Eugénie had been great friends with Victoria ever since she first visited England with her husband Napoléon III in April 1855 and everyone loved spending time with her, especially when she was in the mood to reminisce about the decadent imperial court that she had once presided over in Paris, before she was forced to flee to England in 1870. A week later, Eugénie and her nieces spent the evening at Osborne and after dinner the two younger ladies performed Spanish dances for the other guests while Alix and her aunt Beatrice accompanied them on the piano.

Once again, Alix was to be Victoria's almost constant companion during this visit, this time ably assisted by her brother Ernie, who was just the sort of handsome, clever and charming young man that Victoria most liked and no doubt reminded her of her beloved Albert at the same age thanks to his passionate love of books, art and history. It was stifling hot that summer and Victoria's journals convey much of the lethargy that the party felt as they sweltered and tried to get comfortable in the heat. In between taking daily carriage rides and enjoying sedate meals taken either in the summer house or in the tent that had as usual been set up on the Osborne House lawn, Alix and her brother would have spent hours lazing about the gardens, reading in hammocks slung between trees or paddling in the cooling waters of the Solent at the family's private beach. Like her brother, Alix was a voracious reader and never went anywhere without a pile of books, including a much treasured German edition of her mother's letters, which had been published in 1883 and into which she had inscribed her own name. Despite the heat, royal obligations nonetheless continued and on 8 August, Alix accompanied her grandmother and aunt Princess Beatrice on a visit to a local alms house, where they spent some time chatting to the residents – a task that Alix, who was painfully shy, did not especially enjoy, even if, like her mother, she was inclined to take her responsibilities as a benefactor to the less fortunate very seriously. On 21 August, Alix and Ernie accompanied their grandmother to Scotland, along with their father Louis, who had joined them all a day previously. Before going on to Balmoral, the party stopped in Glasgow, in order to visit the International Exhibition in Kelvingrove Park, which Alix especially enjoyed, as evidenced by the notes that she made on the catalogue, which she kept as a souvenir of the event. While Ernie and Louis stayed on the Royal Yacht *Victoria and Albert*, in which they had also made the journey from the Isle of Wight to Scotland, Alix stayed with the other royal ladies in Blythswood House, a neoclassical mansion in Renfrew. On the second day of their visit, they visited Paisley, where Victoria was very intrigued by the tombs of various Stuart ancestors, including Marjorie, eldest daughter of Robert the Bruce, from whom the Stuart royal house was descended. Victoria had never lost her fascination with her glamorous, tragic Stuart ancestors and still never missed an opportunity to reverently view any places or artefacts that were associated with them, no matter how tenuously.

The royal party, this time without Ernie, arrived at Balmoral Castle on the morning of 25 August, having travelled by overnight train from Renfrew, which was a surprisingly comfortable journey thanks to the luxuriousness of Victoria's private train, which boasted saloons lavishly upholstered in blue silk and lined with gilded teak and walnut panelling. There were two single beds in Victoria's elegant night compartment, one of which would usually have been occupied by her constant companion Princess Beatrice, although as a special favour Alix may also have been invited to share a room with her grandmother on the long trip up north to Scotland. Once at Balmoral, Alix continued to be Victoria's most constant companion, alongside her long-suffering aunt Beatrice, whose intrepid husband had gone off on a yachting trip, leaving her to bear the burden of her demanding mother and two small children on her own. As always, there were excursions every day, including one after tea time on 29 August, when Alix and her grandmother drove in a carriage up Glen Gelder and then around to Bowman's Moss, both of which were favourite scenic spots of the aging queen. On other days they visited such beauty spots as the Falls of Garavalt, Corrie Mulzie and the Danzig Shiel, usually taking their tea there and doing some sketching before returning to the castle, where they would rest before getting ready for dinner, which was usually a simple family affair except for the rare occasions when they had guests. Alix was still shy and reserved around people that she did not know but was very different when surrounded by family and friends and would become quite animated, although she lacked the sparkling vivacity of other female family members such as her uncle Bertie's sister-in-law, the Empress of Russia. On 7 September, Alix's father returned to Darmstadt but she remained behind at Balmoral, where they were joined by Eddy a few days later. He had already been carefully prepared in advance by his grandmother, who extolled Alix's virtues at length and made it clear that she would be most displeased if he did not make an effort to endear himself to his pretty cousin.

Although he would much rather have been going out shooting and hunting every day, Eddy manfully did his duty and remained close to his grandmother and Alix during his stay, accompanying them on their walks and doing his best to amuse his cousin after dinner. It could be extremely dull at Balmoral which, of course, is exactly how Victoria liked it, but that season, everyone was kept relatively busy preparing for a theatrical performance that was to be held on 5 October and which would involve a series of elaborate tableaux vivants designed to celebrate the birthday of Beatrice's husband Henry. Rather ambitiously, each tableaux, which would be enacted by members of the royal family and household, would relate to every letter of Henry's name 'Henry Maurice'. For days before the performance, everyone pitched in to prepare, with even Victoria deigning to wield a brush and paint some scenery. On 27 September, the family party was increased when Eddy's mother Alexandra, with her three daughters in tow, descended on the Balmoral estate, where they stayed as usual at Abergeldie, all no doubt agog to find out how their brother's courtship of Alix was progressing. The day after their arrival, Victoria and Alix visited them for tea, which gave the Princess of Wales an opportunity to assess the situation – she had, of course, known Alix ever since she was born but had only recently been required to consider her as a potential daughter-in-law and it was not a match that she particularly approved of, mainly because she didn't really want her precious Eddy marrying anyone. However, as her husband Bertie was all in favour of a match between their son and the daughter of his favourite sister, Alexandra, who obeyed him in all things, was obliged to go along with the plan regardless of her own feelings.

By the 1st October, the ballroom had been prepared for the tableaux and rehearsals began for the performance a few days later. Predictably, and to their great embarrassment, Eddy and Alix were called upon to perform together in the first piece, which had a 'Harvest' theme, although to their relief even Victoria balked at getting them onstage as bride and groom in the wedding scene enacted for 'Union' – in the end Princess Louise played the part of bride to Eddy's distinctly unhappy groom, while Alix played the part of a Hessian peasant girl. Alix looked particularly lovely dressed as a novice nun in one of the tableaux, during which she knelt on a prayer chair and gazed mournfully down at a book, presumably in prayer while her distant cousin Princess Frederica of Hanover, known within the family as 'Lily', pretended to cut her long loose hair. Afterwards, Victoria singled this particular tableaux out for praise, calling it 'really beautiful'. Whether the sight of Alix with her hair down and dressed in virginal white inspired amorous feelings in her cousin's breast remained to be seen but certainly the signs augured well for the pair, with Eddy confiding to his brother George that Alix was 'a lovely girl now and everything that is nice, and I have got my eye on her; you know what that means,'[23] while he wrote to her brother-in-law Louis of Battenberg that she was 'looking prettier than ever, and will I am sure be very handsome when she grows up'.[24] However, when Alix finally left Balmoral on 10 October, there was still no sign of any declaration from the bashful Eddy and when Alix wrote to her grandmother from Buckingham Palace, where she stayed for the night on her way to the coast, there was no mention of him in her letter. She may have kept her thoughts about Eddy close to her chest, where her grandmother was concerned anyway, but Alix could not have failed to be impressed by the glorious future that would be hers if she agreed to be his wife.

As Queen Victoria's favourite granddaughter, she was naturally already very well acquainted with the splendid royal residences, jewels and splendour that her grandmother enjoyed but had probably never before imagined what it would be like to own all of this wealth herself. The thought of living in Britain, which she had been visiting since childhood, was also a very appealing one, especially as it meant seeing more of her family there, particularly her grandmother and various uncles and aunts. She would also have been aware of the fact that her mother had never ceased longing for home even many years after she had moved to Germany – to the extent that she had done everything possible to replicate a perfect British upbringing for her own children, complete with English nannies, seaside holidays and traditional stodgy nursery food. The thought of raising her own family in Britain would therefore have been immensely appealing to Alix, who had recently witnessed for herself how happy and contented her eldest sister Victoria was there, even though her husband was frequently overseas. It could all have been so perfect – if it wasn't for the fact that the key to all of this glittering largesse was the unappealing prospect of marriage to poor Prince Eddy.

Chapter Seven

'What fancy has she got in her head?'

1889–1892

Thousands of miles away in her huge palace in St Petersburg, Alix's elder sister Ella watched the events unfolding in Scotland with horror, kept abreast of the latest developments by a flurry of family letters that made Queen Victoria's intentions for Alix and Eddy all too plain. She was just as fond of the unfortunate Prince Eddy as everyone else but was keen for Alix to understand that there was a huge difference between enjoying his genial company very occasionally at a family event and spending the rest of her life with him as his wife and constant companion. 'He does not look over strong and is too stupid,' she wrote in exasperation to her brother Ernie. 'You would see that clever girl turn into a flirt as she is so pretty and England with a stupid husband is not at all the place for her.'[1] Although Alix herself had done her best to reassure Ella that she had no intention of marrying Eddy, her sister was not convinced and believed that if Victoria applied enough pressure then Alix would almost certainly capitulate and marry him, if only to avoid another distressing family drama such as the ones that had followed the engagements of her sister Irene and aunt Beatrice. As the youngest surviving Hesse princess, Alix had spent the longest time under Victoria's protection after the premature death of her mother and was therefore the most vulnerable to her domineering grandmother's passive aggressive coercions and blandishments, especially as they came with a hefty side helping of reminders of the duty that she owed to Victoria in exchange for the interest that she had taken in her family over the years. It was all 'quite dreadful' as far as Ella was concerned, not least because she had already long since decided that she wanted Alix to settle close to her in Russia, rather than even further away in England.

Although Ella's marriage to Sergei was going well and she professed herself to be extremely happy with the husband that she had chosen for herself, she was still feeling lonely and homesick in Russia. Ella would almost certainly have felt much less cut off if she had children to care for but as she and Sergei remained childless while her sisters and cousins all started their own families, she quickly started to feel increasingly isolated and left out while her family felt even further away than ever. While most of her relatives envied Ella's fabulous wealth and the luxurious lifestyle that it enabled her to enjoy, those closest to her knew that she felt herself to be living in a gilded cage and would have given up a great deal just to see more of her family, especially her sisters. Although Ella did everything that she could to see as much as possible of her father and siblings, the expense and logistical difficulties of travelling to and from Russia meant that these precious visits were frustratingly rare. It's hardly surprising therefore that Ella decided to promote a match between her youngest sister Alix and the Tsesarevich Nicholas, encouraged by the budding romance that had begun to blossom between the pair during her wedding celebrations almost five years earlier in the spring of 1884. Although they had not set eyes on each other since Alix's return to Darmstadt after the wedding, Nicholas had never forgotten his pretty German cousin while Alix still treasured her memories of the all-too-brief time that they had spent frolicking together at Peterhof. Five years was a long time though and both Nicholas and Alix had changed a great deal since they had last met – who knew what they would make of each other now? Luckily, Ella's husband Sergei wholeheartedly approved of the scheme, probably because he was equally keen for her to have at least one family member within visiting range, and so he was more than happy to issue an invitation for Alix, her father Louis and brother, Ernie, to visit them in St Petersburg at the start of 1889.

On a freezing cold and windy day at the end of January 1889, Ella and Sergei were waiting at Tsarskoe Selo station in order to join the Hesse party for the last leg of their journey to St Petersburg, where they were to be met by the Tsar, his son, the Tsesarevich and various other members of the Russian royal family at Varshavsky station. Although Alix made no mention of how he looked in her journal, she could not fail to have been impressed by the sight of Nicholas, who had spent the morning ice skating before he hastily donned his military uniform in order to meet her. In contrast, Nicholas noted in his journal that evening that Alix 'has grown up a lot and become prettier'[2] after the family party had spent several hours at the Anichkov Palace taking tea in the apartments of his mother Empress Maria, who was naturally very curious to have another close look at her goddaughter Alix, who had not only captured her own son's heart, but was currently the favourite candidate to marry her nephew Eddy. Doubtless Nicholas, who had spent a great deal of time with his British cousins over the years and knew both Eddy and his brother George very well, was also fully aware of Victoria's plan to marry Alix to the elder of the two, but clearly he did not allow the fact that he might potentially be putting his cousin's nose out of joint to influence his own behaviour as he gazed longingly across at the enchantingly pretty Hesse princess. The conversation that day was dominated by the shocking news that had just arrived from Austria of the murder-suicide that morning of the Crown Prince Rudolf and his seventeen-year-old mistress Baroness Mary Vetsera at his hunting lodge in Mayerling. As Rudolf was the only son and heir of Emperor Franz Josef and his enigmatic wife Empress Elisabeth, his sudden death would have been of enormous interest to the Russian royal family even without the mysterious circumstances that surrounded it and they spent a great deal of time picking over the few known details, which became increasingly salacious as more information was gradually revealed despite the Emperor's initial efforts to convince the world that his son had died of natural causes. At first, Nicholas feared that he would be packed off to Vienna in order to attend the funeral, which would mean missing some of Alix's visit, but luckily he was spared the ordeal and could remain in Russia. There was also some concern that an upcoming court ball at the Winter Palace would have to be cancelled due to the Crown Prince's death – until Empress Maria fortuitously recalled that the Austrian royal family had insulted the Russians by going ahead with a ball shortly after the death of a Romanov prince, at which point it was decided that the ball should become an extremely chic *bal noir,* with all of the guests required to wear black.

St Petersburg in the winter, when the velvety dark nights are long and pristine white snow sparkles like diamonds in the sunlight, is like the beautiful backdrop to a romantic fairy tale and to Ella and Sergei's great delight, Alix and Nicholas became increasingly captivated with each other over the next six weeks. Alix's trip started badly with a cold so troublesome that she was forced to have breakfast in bed on her second morning after which, to her disappointment, she was judged to still not be well enough to accompany everyone else to dinner at the Anichkov Palace, which was followed by a trip to the circus. Instead, while her brother and father were spending the evening with Nicholas, she sadly played a little piano and then had an early night. Fortunately, she was feeling much better the next day and was reunited with Nicholas at dinner, during which he sat opposite her, after which they went to a party hosted by the Vorontsov family, which went on until the early hours of the morning. As the weeks passed in a seemingly endless round of parties, concerts, frolicking in the snow in the gardens of the Anichkov Palace and convivial trips to the ice-skating rink, Alix grew increasingly close to the handsome heir to the Russian throne, who thanks to his resemblance to her Wales cousins seemed so familiar and yet was different to anyone else that she had ever met. On 9 February, she attended the *bal noir* in the splendid ballroom of the Winter Palace, where she dazzled Nicholas in a black gown worn with diamonds, white flowers and a sash and danced a sedate cotillion with him before partnering her brother-in-law Sergei for a mazurka. Thanks to the enormous wealth and generosity of her hosts, Alix was seeing Russian society at its very best and would leave St Petersburg in March with a lasting impression of stately snow-covered streets glimpsed from within the warm comfort of a well-upholstered carriage, opulent candlelit dinners and pleasant evenings spent amidst the splendour of the Romanov palaces. It was all extremely seductive and for a time at least, Alix allowed her head to be turned – until she remembered that she would be required to give up her Lutheran faith and adopt Russian Orthodoxy in order to be able to marry Nicholas. Although her sister Ella had not been expected to convert in order to marry Sergei, who was a younger brother of the Tsar, who had three sons of his own, and therefore not expected to ever inherit the throne, it was a very different matter for anyone who intended to marry the Tsesarevich and one day rule alongside him.

Queen Victoria spent that spring enjoying some much-needed sunshine in Biarritz, where she was discomforted to hear reports of the romance that was blossoming between her granddaughter and the Tsesarevich. Although all of Alix's siblings were in on the secret, they still hastened to deny all knowledge of the affair to their grandmother, with even poor Ernie coming under pressure to write and assure his 'darling Grandmama' that 'all what is written in the newspapers is simply nonsense'[3] and that he was sure that Nicholas had no serious interest in Alix anyway. If Victoria had known that in St Petersburg Ella was not only praying for the marriage to come about, but also enjoying long intimate chats with Nicholas about his love for her sister, then she would almost certainly have been apoplectic. 'And now let me say a word about Alicky,' Victoria wrote to Alix's eldest sister from the South of France at the end of March. 'Is there no hope about [Eddy]? She…should be made to reflect seriously on the folly of throwing away the chance of a very good husband, kind, affectionate and steady and of entering a united happy family and a very good position which is second to none in the world! Dear Uncle and Aunt wish it so much and poor E is so unhappy at the thought of losing her also! Can you and Ernie not do any good? What fancy has she got in her head?'[4] This last statement must surely have been a rhetorical question for Victoria, who had herself once long ago been waltzed around a candlelit ballroom by a dashing young Tsesarevich, almost certainly knew all too well just who was on Alix's mind.

Deeply troubled by the prospect of losing another granddaughter to Russia, Victoria invited Alix to visit her in August that year, although she admitted to Princess Victoria shortly before their arrival that although she was delighted to be seeing them again, she was worried about the indecisiveness of 'poor Eddy (who is so devoted to Alicky)'[5] and feared that if he did not act and propose to her then she would almost certainly look elsewhere. When Alix arrived at Osborne House on 13 August, she had no idea that she was entering into an ambush orchestrated by her grandmother, and for the first part of her visit everything was indeed as normal, with the usual round of sedate tea parties on the lawn, visits to the local towns and gentle carriage rides with Victoria and her aunt Beatrice. On 22 August, she accompanied Victoria on the royal train to Palé Hall in Gwynedd, North Wales, where they stayed for four nights and very much enjoyed their excursions into the local countryside, which included a visit to a coal mine, before it was time to once again board the night train to Aberdeenshire. When they stopped for breakfast in Aberdeen, it was to find Alix's brother, Ernie, waiting for them and he accompanied them on to Balmoral, where they were to stay until the beginning of October. Alix and Ernie had always been very close but in recent years he had become one of her most trusted confidantes and a chief ally when it came to the thorny task of handling their domineering grandmother.

While Alix was innocently accompanying her grandmother on her daily walks and carriage rides to Dal Doulie, Invercauld and Lochnagar, half-heartedly sketching the scenery and making polite conversation with her aunt Beatrice across the tea table, her unfortunate cousin Eddy was mentally limbering up for the hideous ordeal of courting her in front of an assembled audience of several members of their family. Encouraged by Victoria to believe himself in love with Alix, he confided to her brother-in-law Prince Louis on 6 September that he was afraid that Victoria might have already ruined things by letting Alix know that he was planning to propose. 'I fear that she or someone else may have told Alicky, which was I think a great mistake, and as you say relations can only spoil my chance by mixing themselves up in the affair,' he wrote anxiously. 'I guessed that myself last year, and therefore was very careful how I approached Alicky and did not give her the slightest sign that I loved her.'[6] Although his cousin Nicholas' infatuation with Alix was well-known within her family, it had perhaps not reached Eddy's ears for he went on to affirm his intention of proposing to Alix himself, assuring Louis that he would 'do all I can to persuade Alicky that I love her for herself and for herself only and that my parents and relations have had nothing whatever to do with it as far as I myself am concerned… I can't tell you what a happy creature I shall be if it only comes off right, for I do indeed know what a prize there is to be won.'[7] The unfortunate prince made his first appearance at Balmoral a few days later, dropping in for luncheon on his way to Mar Lodge, where he and the rest of his family were staying with his sister Princess Louise and her new husband, the Duke of Fife, whom she had married in July that year. Eddy may not have planned to propose to Alix on this occasion but he certainly arrived at Balmoral with every intention of singling her out and making himself agreeable to her, with a view to proposing marriage later on when he was more certain of her feelings. Alix's famous reserve, which made many people think her cold, unfriendly and snobbish, once more worked against her on this occasion as her cousin, and indeed most of their family, had literally no idea what she thought of him, so deeply hidden and inscrutable were her thoughts. However, before Eddy could make his move, Ernie, who had doubtless been persuaded to do so by his mortified sister, swooped in and took him aside for a private chat, during which he revealed that contrary to whatever their grandmother had been saying, Alix was not interested in receiving a proposal of marriage from Eddy and would be very upset if he did so. The embarrassed prince had no idea what to think, especially as Ernie could give him no clue as to why precisely Alix found the prospect so unappealing. Worried that he might have upset Alix in some way, Eddy even asked her brother if he had done something to offend her but to his disappointment, Ernie could not, or would not, say.

Eddy left Balmoral feeling absolutely crushed by this serious blow – however, some small lingering hope still remained for on the following day, his father Bertie arrived at Balmoral in order to talk of 'various things', which doubtless included his son's ardent pursuit of Alix, with Victoria. The next day, Alix accompanied her grandmother on a visit to the Wales family gathering at Mar Lodge, where she once again encountered Eddy, this time emboldened by the presence of his family. On the way to Mar, Alix rode in a carriage with her aunt Beatrice, who may have seized this opportunity to discreetly question her young niece about her feelings for her cousin and perhaps offer some advice. Over the next few days, Victoria quizzed Alix as well, still determined to bring the much-wanted match about even though it was becoming increasingly clear that Eddy's feelings for his Hesse cousin were not reciprocated. At first, the embarrassed Alix did all that she could to evade the most unwelcome topic but in the end she was forced to give in and admit that, as Eddy's brother George put it in a letter to her brother-in-law Louis, 'she does not care about him sufficiently to marry him but is very fond of him as a cousin'[8] although she half-heartedly suggested that if it really meant so much to Victoria then she would marry Eddy even though she was sure that they would both be miserable together. Although Eddy did his best to hide his hurt feelings in public, in private he was feeling humiliated, affronted and seriously upset and confided to Prince Louis that 'I can't really believe Alicky knows how much I really love her, or she would not I think have treated me quite so cruelly. For I can't help considering it so, as she apparently gives me no chance at all, and little or no hope; although I shall continue loving her, and in the hope that someday she may think better of what she has said, and give me the chance of being one of the happiest beings in the world.'⁹ Nonetheless, despite this faint show of bravado, Eddy knew that it was all over and within less than a year of being turned down by Alix, he was ardently pursuing a very different match, with the pretty and vivacious Princesse Hélène d'Orléans, daughter of the Comte de Paris, head of the deposed Orléanist pretenders to the now defunct French throne. Unlike Alix, whose chilly reserve had always kept him at a distance, Hélène made no secret of her feelings for him and before too long, all romantic thoughts of his Hesse cousin were consigned to the past – although, unfortunately for Eddy, this courtship was also doomed to failure thanks to the fact that the lovely Hélène was a Roman Catholic and thus, when permission to convert was not forthcoming from her father or Pope Leo XIII, unable to marry the heir to the British throne.

While Eddy was dealing with his great disappointment, Queen Victoria was both astounded by Alix's self-assured and stubborn refusal to go along with her grandmother's plans for her future and also rather impressed by her will power. 'It is most sad about Alicky and Eddy,' she wrote to Alix's eldest sister. 'We still have a faint lingering hope that she may – if he remains unmarried, after all when she comes to reflect and see what a sad and serious thing it is to throw away such a marriage with such a position and in such an amiable family in her Mother's country, where she would be received with open arms.'¹⁰ It was completely inconceivable to Victoria, who wholeheartedly and with much justification believed that there was no better position in the world than her own, that anyone in their right mind would ever turn down the opportunity to become queen of Great Britain, especially when that person was her own granddaughter, who had been given every chance to experience the riches and prestige that came with the title. The fact that, to her mind at least, Alix owed her grateful obedience for all the interest that she had taken in her over the years just added to her sense of insulted injustice. Although outwardly things continued as always at Balmoral, with Alix in almost constant attendance upon her grandmother, relations between the two were distinctly cool as Victoria mulled over this latest disappointment and her granddaughter did her best to evade any further discussions about the painful topic of Eddy. After Alix and Ernie left Balmoral on 2 October they went on to London, where they spent two nights in Buckingham Palace before heading to the coast for the next leg of their journey home to Darmstadt. If this was a last-ditch attempt by Victoria to remind Alix of the splendours that would be hers if she agreed to marry Eddy, then it failed for the princess remained imperturbable and after spending a couple of days enjoying some sightseeing with her brother, sailed off to Germany with hardly a care in the world. However, she must have felt some disquiet about the fact that both of her suitors were due to head to Greece later that month to attend the wedding of her cousin, Princess Sophia of Prussia, one of the daughters of Alix's aunt Vicky, to Crown Prince Constantine of Greece, a first cousin of both Eddy and Tsesarevich Nicholas, who were due to play prominent parts in the ceremony. No unseemly drama ensued at the family gathering in Athens, but the awkwardness of the overall situation almost certainly led many senior royals to conclude that it would be best for everyone if the question of the dangerously lovely Alix's marriage was settled sooner rather than later.

'We have just a faint lingering hope that Alicky might in time look to see what a pleasant home and what a useful position she will lose if she ultimately persists in not yielding to Eddy's really earnest wishes,' Victoria wrote to Alix's eldest sister at the end of October 1889. 'There are so few for her to marry and Eddie is very good.'[11] It was hopeless though – Alix's mind was quite made up and besides, despite what her grandmother might think, there were several other potential candidates for her hand, not least the handsome Tsesarevich, with whom she had exchanged several rather decorous and polite letters since their last meeting in spring 1889. Victoria would not have another opportunity to discuss the matter in person with Alix until April 1890, when she arrived in Darmstadt for a week-long visit, during which the Neues Palais would also be filled with Prussian relatives, including Alix's aunt Vicky and overbearing cousin, Wilhelm II who was, luckily for everyone, in a markedly good mood during his stay, which meant that he was not, for once, inclined to bully his cousins or make anyone cry. It would have been Princess Alice's forty-seventh birthday two days after her mother's arrival in Darmstadt and so Victoria, Alix and other family members duly paid a visit to the Rosenhöhe mausoleum in order to place wreaths beside her tomb. As usual, Alix spent a lot of time with Victoria during this visit, and they doubtless had much to talk about during their daily carriage rides and excursions around Darmstadt, which included braving the rain in order to take a day trip to the lovely Prinz Emil Garten and then a pretty old schloss at Secheim. Victoria was naturally keen to know if Alix had changed her mind about Eddy but probably wasn't very surprised when her granddaughter reaffirmed that she had absolutely no desire to marry her cousin. Certainly, it seems as though the matter was dropped after this visit as whatever Alix said to Victoria during their snatched private chats in the gardens of the Neues Palais or while trotting around Secheim, made such a strong impression upon the queen that she now resolved to make an entirely different plan for her precious granddaughter. The fact that Alix was planning to visit her sister Ella in Russia that summer only added further impetus to Victoria's desire to see her suitably married off as quickly as possible before her attachment to Nicholas had an opportunity to become more serious.

On 6 June 1890, Alix turned eighteen – an age when most of her sisters and cousins were either already married and working on producing the next generation of Queen Victoria's descendants or at least seriously thinking about finding a suitably eligible prince and settling down. Thanks to her reputation as one of the most beautiful princesses in Europe, there was a great deal of interest in Alix's matrimonial plans, although her lack of wealth meant that she was never considered to be amongst the top tier of eligible princesses, which included the four extremely pretty daughters of the fabulously wealthy Comte de Paris, who were highly sought after thanks to a winning combination of French chic, good looks and large quantities of cold, hard cash. Nonetheless, her close relationship to several crowned heads and descent from Queen Victoria, did much to compensate for her lack of money and assets and it was generally assumed that she would at least make a good if not brilliant match. Now that it was clear that Alix was never going to agree to marry Eddy, Victoria began to look about for an alternative and settled upon the wealthy and intelligent twenty-three-year-old Prince Maximilian of Baden, who was a nephew of Victoria's sister-in-law Princess Alexandrine, Duchess of Saxe-Coburg Gotha, while his mother Princess Maria of Leuchtenberg was a granddaughter of both Tsar Nicholas I and Eugène de Beauharnais, son of Empress Joséphine. Victoria was already inclined to favour Maximilian as he bore a close resemblance to his cousin, Napoléon III, whose looks she very much admired and so it is hardly surprising that she began to think of matching him with one of her granddaughters. Her initial plan had been to marry him to Princess Maud of Wales, the youngest daughter of Bertie and Alexandra, but when it got back to her that Maximilian had announced that he did not want to marry one of the English princesses, she turned her attention instead to Alix, who might be more acceptable, while mentally allocating Maud to her cousin Ernie instead. As always with Victoria, once an idea had occurred to her, she did not like to waste any time before making it a reality and so Maximilian was ordered to pay a visit to Darmstadt, where he was to make himself agreeable to Princess Alix – much to her horror for she had absolutely no desire to marry him.

Alix spent that summer at her sister's enormous and very grand country estate, Ilinskoe, near Moscow, which gave her a decided taste for the simple, rustic pleasures of the Russian countryside that would remain with her for the rest of her life. To her disappointment, Nicholas was too busy with official functions and preparations for his upcoming tour of the East, which would take him to China, Japan and India, to be able to visit Ilinskoe, but in his absence, Sergei and Ella did all that they could to promote him to Alix. It seems strange that Nicholas would miss an opportunity to spend time with the girl that he had resolved to one day marry but he was also deeply disappointed not to be able to see her and confided in his journal: 'Oh, Lord, how I want to go to Ilinskoe… otherwise if I do not see her now, I shall have to wait a whole year and that will be hard.'[12] He was almost certainly wrestling with his feelings for Alix at this time too, even writing in his journal in 1891 that 'for a long time I resisted my feelings and tried to deceive myself about the impossibility of achieving my most cherished wish!'[13] Nicholas was well aware that Alix's grandmother Victoria was keen for her to marry his cousin Eddy and if that wasn't discouraging enough, his own parents had expressed their disapproval of the match, which they considered insufficiently illustrious, while Alix's own extremely reserved and aloof personality was, they believed, quite inappropriate for the demanding role of Empress. If she had been more vivacious and outgoing then perhaps they might have overlooked everything else if it made their son happy, but the fact of the matter was that both Alexander III and his wife Maria believed that marrying Alix would be a mistake for both Nicholas and his future success as Tsar. Instead, they preferred the enchanting Princesse Hélène d'Orléans, despite the fact that she was entangled in a hopeless romance with his cousin Eddy.

Both Ella and Sergei were well aware of Alexander and Maria's disapproval but persisted nonetheless with their promotion of the match, rather selfishly encouraged as always by the fact that it would bring Alix to Russia, where she could be a companion for her sister. In England, Victoria had also caught wind of the situation and, as always, felt compelled to write in very strong terms to Alix's eldest sister, Princess Victoria, whom she felt ought to have more influence and authority over her rebellious younger siblings. Victoria had naturally been most annoyed to hear about Alix's trip to Russia, although she claimed that her displeasure was more due to the unwelcome rumours and press speculation about an engagement between Alix and Nicholas that it might cause, rather than a fear that the pair might throw caution to the wind during the visit and pledge their love to each other. 'I did not mean anything about Niki as he is away and besides it would not do on account of the religion and I know moreover Minnie does not wish it,'[14] she wrote, referring to the great dislike that Empress Maria (known within the family as 'Minnie') had for the match. 'But there are many other Grand Dukes and Princes and I heard that Ella was determined to try and get a marriage with another Russian and this… would grievously hurt Uncle Bertie and Aunt Alix as well as me… If you take care and tell Ella that no marriage for Alicky in Russia would be allowed, then there will be an end of it.'[15] The fact that Ella had recently made the decision to convert to the Russian Orthodox Church and was becoming increasingly full of zeal for her new religion, only made Victoria, who was otherwise extremely supportive of Ella's decision, more anxious as she quickly perceived that once Ella was converted, she would doubtless do her best to impress upon Alix the similarities between Lutheranism and the Orthodox Church and how easy the transition between the two would be for her. 'I hope I was right in telling Uncle Bertie that I knew there was no question of a marriage for her in Russia and that you have brought her back safe and free?'[16]

Victoria wrote to Princess Victoria in October 1890 after the latter had returned from Russia accompanied by Alix, who would be going on to Malta with her for another long visit. 'Uncle Bertie says that he knows Ella will move Heaven and Earth to get her to marry a Grand Duke!'[17]

On 29 December 1890, Victoria felt sufficiently moved about the situation to once more write at length about it to Alix's eldest sister, Princess Victoria. 'I had your assurance that nothing was to be feared in that quarter, but I know it for certain, that in spite of all your (Papa's, Ernie's and your) objections and still more contrary to the positive wish of his parents who do not wish him to marry A as they feel, as everyone must do, for the youngest sister to marry the son of the Emperor would never answer and lead to no happiness,'[18] she wrote, clearly very disturbed by the possibility that Alix and Nicholas were considering going against the wishes of his parents. 'Well in spite of all this, behind all your backs, Ella and S do all they can to bring it about, encouraging and even urging the boy to do it.'[19] The source for all of this disquieting information was her daughter-in-law Princess Alexandra, the Russian Empress' sister, who had passed it all on to Victoria in the strictest confidence. 'This must not be allowed to go on,' Victoria ordered her granddaughter. 'Papa must put his foot down and there must be no more visits of Alicky to Russia – and he must and you and Ernie must insist on a stop being put to the whole affair.'[20] One can easily imagine Princess Victoria's despair upon reading the letter, knowing full well that her tender-hearted, easy-going father and brother could absolutely not be relied upon to put a stop to anything that Alix wanted to do, even if she herself might have the fortitude to at least try to reason with her self-willed youngest sister. However, although Princess Victoria very much enjoyed her visits to Ella's residences in St Petersburg and the countryside, she could not help but agree with her grandmother's assessment that 'the state of Russia is so bad, so rotten that at any moment something dreadful might happen and though it may not signify to Ella, the wife of the Thronfolger (heir to the throne) is in a most difficult and precarious position.'[21] The shocking assassination of Nicholas' grandfather, Alexander II, the aftermath of which he had witnessed with his own eyes, hung like a dank cloud over the entire Romanov family and there was no doubt in anyone's minds, least of all their own, that it was only a matter of time before the nation's many political dissidents, who were constantly hatching new murderous plots, succeeded again. Victoria had no love for the Russians, whom she believed had behaved shamefully during the Crimean War, but in this instance she was motivated by genuine fear for Alix's safety should she marry Nicholas, who would always be a potential target for assassins, and take up residence in Russia. She would have been furious if she had known that Alix's sister Ella airily dismissed Victoria's fears as the ignorant and ill-informed result of 'all the idiotic trash in the newspapers'.[22]

To her great disappointment, Victoria had no opportunity to discuss the matter with Alix in person until 23 May 1891, when the princess arrived at Balmoral Castle with her eldest sister Victoria and their father Louis – just in time to celebrate the queen's seventy-second birthday the following day. In the distant, much happier past, Victoria's birthdays had always been held at Osborne House but after her beloved Albert's death, they were more usually spent at Balmoral Castle, which aroused rather less painful memories of those who were no longer there to celebrate with her. That morning, she was visited in her rooms by the faithful Princess Beatrice and her three young children, who presented Victoria with flowers. Alix and the rest of the family had their opportunity to wish Victoria a happy birthday in her sitting room, where all of her presents were, as usual, laid out on a specially decorated birthday table. As it was a Sunday, the whole family went to church after breakfast, after which Victoria set about reading and replying to the 101 telegrams and forty-three letters that arrived throughout the day, many of which were from far flung relatives, who knew that they would never hear the end of it if they neglected to send birthday greetings on this most auspicious day. Alix was part of the family party that took luncheon with the queen when she finally emerged from her sitting room and then later in the day she joined her on a trip to her beloved Danzig Shiel, where they all had tea while enjoying the breathtakingly beautiful and wild scenery that Victoria loved to paint over and over again. To the queen's great satisfaction, there were eighteen people, including her granddaughter Alix, at dinner that night, which involved her son-in-law Louis, now completely forgiven for his unpropitious and mercifully short lived second marriage, proposing a toast to her health. During the next few weeks, Alix was as always one of the queen's most favourite companions, along with her aunt Princess

Beatrice, who had very little time to herself, which made her an object of some pity within the royal family. The day after Victoria's birthday celebrations, Alix and Beatrice accompanied Victoria on two drives – the first to the residence of her personal physician Dr Profeit, who lived in Craig Gowan House on the Balmoral estate, where Victoria liked to sketch, and the second to Birkhall, one of the royal houses on the estate, where they took tea, although it was uncomfortably cold.

On 6 June, Alix celebrated her nineteenth birthday. It was the first time that she'd spent the day with her grandmother Victoria and so the queen felt obliged to make a great deal of fuss of her. As was traditional, the day began with an inspection of Alix's birthday table, which was set up in the castle's breakfast room, after which she was allowed some time to herself, while her sister Princess Victoria accompanied their grandmother on her morning drive. In honour of the special occasion, Princess Beatrice's two eldest children, Alexander and Victoria Eugenie (known within the family as 'Ena' and later destined to become Queen of Spain), were allowed to join the older members of the family at luncheon as a special treat, after which Victoria, Louis and Alix departed on a carriage ride through Braemar and around a scenic spot known as the Lion's Head before returning to Balmoral for a special birthday dinner. After dinner, the whole party trooped down to the ballroom, which was already full of the royal servants and tenants, who had been invited to join the family while they watched two small theatrical pieces, 'Domestic Economy' and 'A Night on the Hills', which were being performed in Alix's honour. In the interval between the two acts, Alix and her aunt Beatrice played a march and also a selection of tunes from Gilbert and Sullivan's *The Gondoliers*, which 'delighted the people' according to Victoria.

After a delightful few weeks, which involved visiting all of their favourite haunts, the royal party departed Balmoral on 19 June in order to return to Windsor Castle. It was stiflingly hot on the royal train, which made the trip very uncomfortable, although they were all distracted from their discomfort when the train went over the new Tay Bridge and then the Forth Bridge, which Victoria declared to be 'quite stupendous and a marvellous piece of construction'.[23] They arrived at Windsor Castle at nine o' clock the next morning, upon which Victoria immediately had breakfast before changing out of her travelling clothes. In the afternoon,

Alix accompanied her on the daily pilgrimage to Frogmore, where they had tea and enjoyed the beautiful evening sunshine before returning for dinner. The Windsor estate was especially lovely that summer, with the rhododendrons in full bloom and the castle gardens looking more beautiful than ever. On 20 June, they all tore themselves away in order to go to London for the wedding of Alberta 'Betty' Ponsonby, daughter of Victoria's Private Secretary and a great favourite with the royal family, to Colonel William Montgomery, which took place in the Guard's Chapel at Wellington Barracks, but by evening they were back in Frogmore again, enjoying tea under the trees. When Alix, her sister and father left Windsor on 27 June, it was with much sadness and regret on both sides, with Victoria feeling as always particularly unhappy to see them go, especially as, like many other grandmothers, she felt as though their visits were becoming less frequent as they grew older and became busier with their own lives. At the end of the year, she was greatly cheered up when Alix's former suitor Eddy became engaged to Princess May of Teck (her name was 'Victoria Mary' but she was informally known as 'May'), the daughter of her cousin Princess Mary Adelaide, Duchess of Cambridge, who had grown up on the fringes of the royal family, but the family celebration, tinged with much relief that Eddy had at last found a suitable bride who was willing to take him on, came to an abrupt and shocking end on 14 January 1892 when the unfortunate prince died of pneumonia at Sandringham House at the age of just twenty-eight.

At home in Darmstadt, Alix continued to act as her father's hostess and as the leading lady in the province – a role that she had naturally assumed as the only remaining unmarried daughter still living at home. Her entry into Hesse society had been marked by a very grand ball organised by her sister Ella, who came all the way from Russia in order to oversee the arrangements and ensure that Alix looked her very best for the occasion, which she attended in a silk and tulle gown, simply decorated with fragrant lilies of the valley, which she also wore pinned in her hair. A delightful photograph of Ella and Alix preparing for the ball in front of a mirror still survives, Ella turns towards the viewer as she hands a rather quizzical looking Alix a spray of lilies, while the princess' much-loved English nanny Miss Orchard sternly pins another bunch into Alix's auburn hair. Another photograph, taken shortly afterwards, shows both sisters together, looking beautiful and ready for the evening ahead – this time, Ella gazes distractedly to the side while Alix frowns heavily into the distance. Visible on the wrists of both princesses are the thin gold bracelets given to them as children by their uncle Prince Leopold, which they were now completely unable to remove and would remain in situ for the rests of their lives. Although sixteen-year-old Alix didn't seem especially thrilled by the prospect of her first ball, parties were a regular part of life at even the relatively modest Darmstadt court and as the first lady, it was her job to organise and oversee the festivities, which she did with some success, with her costume balls being especially notable. Thankfully, her brother Ernie adored parties and dancing and when he was able to be present, which he usually was, things were much less awkward for her as he always did his very best to ensure that she enjoyed herself and shielded her from the crowds. Far more to her taste were the quieter, more intimate tea parties and dinner parties, attended by favoured courtiers and local nobility, that she regularly presided over in the familiar surroundings of the Neues Palais and which did not require her to assume a vivacity that did not come naturally to her.

On 4 March 1892, Alix was hosting a luncheon party for her father when to everyone's shock, the Grand Duke suddenly collapsed at the table. He had been diagnosed with heart problems some time earlier but as he had not had any severe symptoms and appeared to be reasonably healthy for his age, which was fifty-four, this sudden collapse, apparently as the result of a stroke, took everyone by surprise. At first, the prognosis was good as it seemed as though his speech and mental abilities had not been affected, but by the following day, Louis' condition had deteriorated so much that his children were sent for, with even Ella and Sergei immediately leaving Moscow and travelling without stopping in order to attend his bedside, arriving on 9 March. Despite the best efforts of the physicians, Louis fell into a coma on 12 March and by evening his children were forced to accept the terrible fact that he was fading fast and would probably not live through the night. They were all at his bedside when at quarter past one in the morning, Louis passed peacefully away. At Windsor Castle, Victoria received the terrible news from Princess Beatrice as she was dressing for breakfast. 'Darling Louis, whom I loved so dearly, who was so devoted to me and I to him for more than thirty years, it is too dreadful to lose him too!'[24] she wrote in her journal that evening, obviously very much distressed. 'He was so devoted to England and it was his greatest happiness to be with us... How he was adored by his children, now indeed orphans! Poor darling Ernie how he is to be pitied with his great youth burdened now with responsibilities and poor sweet Alicky without a parent... It is too awful and I am quite crushed and broken hearted.' [25]

Chapter Eight

'To hurt one that one loves is fearful.'

1892–1894

Louis, Grand Duke of Hesse was laid to rest alongside his wife Princess Alice in the Rosenhöhe Mausoleum on Thursday, 17 March 1892, with all of his children in attendance along with his brothers-in-law Prince Alfred and Prince Arthur, who obediently sent full reports of the event back to their mother, informing her that it was 'very impressive, touching and mournful'[1] and had been attended by large crowds. At Victoria's request, at precisely the same time, a memorial service took place in the royal chapel at Windsor Castle, which was attended by the royal household and was, according to the queen, 'very beautiful, simple and impressive'.[2] Afterwards, she drove down to the Frogmore Mausoleum with her daughters Princess Louise and Princess Beatrice, in order to lay wreaths at Alice's memorial while reflecting on the fact that she and Louis were now almost certainly reunited in Heaven. However, deep although her own personal sorrow undoubtedly was, Victoria never stopped thinking about her unfortunate grandchildren, in particular, the youngest, Alix, whom she felt especially sorry for. 'What must your grief be, you who were so devoted to that beloved father, who was father and mother to you,' she wrote to Princess Victoria. 'It adds to my quite overwhelming grief to think of your distress and of poor dear Ernie and Alicky alone – orphans! It is awful. But I am still there and while I live, Alicky, till she is married, will be more than ever my own child – as you all are.'[3]

Shortly after the funeral, Victoria rather unwillingly departed on her annual holiday, this time to the Grand Hotel de Costebelle in Hyères in the South of France, where she spent the weeks brooding on all of her various losses and the sad bereavement of her Hesse grandchildren, about whom she thought constantly. On 22 March, Prince Arthur, who had travelled down from Darmstadt after the funeral, gave Victoria a most melancholy packet of letters from the Hesse princesses, including a 'distracting'[4] one from Alix, who was absolutely distraught. There was also a letter from Ernie, who had succeeded as Grand Duke, begging her to visit them in Darmstadt on her way back to England, which she immediately agreed to do even though it would undoubtedly be 'a dreadful trial'.[5] Victoria arrived in Darmstadt on 26 April, the day after what would have been Princess Alice's forty-ninth birthday, which just added to the miserable atmosphere as the queen, swathed as always in black, descended from her train carriage on to the station platform, where Victoria, Irene and Alix were waiting for her in 'deepest mourning with long veils'[6] beside their brother Ernie, who was dressed in plain clothes. In the past, her son-in-law Louis had always been so thrilled to see her that he had tended to jump without any ceremony into her carriage to greet her – this time there was none of this and Victoria's heart ached as she embraced her pale and unhappy grandchildren. As Victoria had predicted, the visit was to be a deeply gloomy one, thanks to the obvious absence of the loud and cheerful Louis at the Neues Palais and the subdued manner of his children, who missed him terribly. After a very sombre luncheon, during which Ernie sat beside her in what had formerly been his father's place, Victoria went on a long carriage ride through the surrounding countryside with Irene and Alix, after which they had tea, using Princess Alice's gold tea set, which had been a present from her bridesmaids in 1862. The following day, the two princesses accompanied their grandmother to the Rosenhöhe, where they viewed their father's casket, which lay on the floor, covered by a crimson and gold pall and surrounded by heaps of floral wreaths, to which the queen and Princess Beatrice added two more. Later that day, Victoria had a private conversation with Alix's old nanny, Miss Orchard who told her in confidence that 'dear Alicky's grief was terrible... for it was a silent grief, which she locked up within her',[7] becoming even more reserved and withdrawn than before, which very much upset her grandmother, who could already see for herself how thin and unwell Alix looked after over a month of crying, sleepless nights and eating very little.

Now that her brother had become Grand Duke, it became more imperative than ever that Alix marry as soon as possible for her position, which was currently very pleasant, would quickly become much less enjoyable when Ernie inevitably married and his wife took over the reins as first lady in Darmstadt, forcing her into second place and the irksome position of unmarried sister and third wheel. Victoria was already busying herself with plans for Ernie's future, even consulting the eminent physician Sir William Jenner about the advisability of first cousin marriages and the potential future threat of haemophilia should Ernie marry his first cousin Princess Victoria Melita, one of the four vivacious daughters of Prince Alfred, Duke of Edinburgh, who was also closely related to the Russian royal family thanks to her mother Marie Alexandrovna. Although Dr Jenner had advised that it would be a bad idea for Ernie to marry his cousin Princess Maud of Wales due to her 'weakness',[8] he thought that it would be perfectly acceptable for him to instead marry one of the Edinburgh girls as they were 'so strong and healthy'[9] and took after their famously robust mother, who could only be described as the epitome of rude health, which Jenner believed would lead to even greater strength and health for their offspring. Reassured by Jenner, Victoria immediately fired off a letter to Ernie, recommending that he consider marrying Victoria Melita, whom she believed would be an excellent wife and chatelaine of his household. Ernie was not totally opposed to the idea but Alix, who had drawn even closer to her brother since the death of their father and had a tendency to be possessive, was horrified by the prospect of being lorded over by one of the bumptious, extrovert Edinburgh princesses, whose self-assertive personalities were so very different to her own. However, Ernie was only twenty-three when their father died and was able to reassure his sister that he had no intention of marrying for at least a few more years.

There was plenty of time for the Hesse siblings to discuss their future plans with their grandmother when they paid a visit to Balmoral Castle in the autumn of 1892, arriving on 21 September. 'It was a sad return here for them and poor dear Alicky had tears in her eyes,'[10] Victoria wrote in her journal that evening. Balmoral had been one of the most favourite places in all the world of both of their parents and to be there without Louis, who had especially enjoyed the many delights that it offered, was deeply painful to both of them. They were barely given time to rest after their journey before Victoria whisked them off on her daily carriage ride, this time taking them just past lovely Invercauld Castle, where they stopped to have tea. The weather was extremely cold and frosty that September, which made the queen's daily excursions rather less pleasant than usual, but there was no way that anyone could get out of them without incurring her severe displeasure and so Ernie and Alix both gamely climbed into the carriage, piled as many blankets as they could find over themselves and hoped for the best. Staying nearby at Mar Lodge were Princess Alexandra and her daughters, all of whom were still mourning the unfortunate Prince Eddy, which made for rather melancholy conversations around the tea table as they all lamented the losses that 1892 had dealt to them. Visits to Balmoral had always been a little dull but on this occasion it was positively miserable, made worse by the freezing cold weather which swathed the surrounding countryside in a thick and gloomy fog every morning. Always very sensitive to her surroundings, Alix found it all particularly trying and within less than a week of her arrival, her concerned grandmother was noting in her journal how 'dreadfully sad and thin'[11] she looked. Her mood lightened on 4 October though when she braved the pouring rain in order to make the short trip to Ballater station in order to meet her sister Irene, who arrived with her husband Henry and their three-year-old son Waldemar, who was known in the family as 'Toddy' and apparently looked 'delightful' in his miniature kilt. To the despair of his parents, Waldemar had inherited the family curse of haemophilia and was therefore very much cosseted and protected by the family, particularly his uncle Ernie, who had never forgotten the horror of that terrible day in 1870 when his younger brother Frittie had died before his very eyes and his mother's screams had echoed through the palace corridors.

When Ernie and Alix left on 10 October, they were both very sad to be leaving the side of their grandmother, while she was very moved to see them leave and to 'think of their returning to their lonely home, without father or mother'.[12] Whereas in the past they had been able to stay with Victoria for well over a month, Ernie's new duties as Grand Duke of Hesse and Alix's desire to always be at his side meant that they were no longer at liberty to leave Germany for more than a few weeks at a time. Alix's poor health was also a concern – as her grandmother had noted in Scotland, she was really not herself and was looking particularly thin and ill as she battled the depression that had engulfed her in the wake of her father's death. Throwing herself into her role of right-hand woman to her brother did much to distract her from the deep and apparently endless sadness that enveloped her, but even so she suffered and hardly knew what to do with herself when she was not busying herself with organising tea parties, overseeing menus and making sure that Ernie felt properly cared for and supported as he shouldered the burden of his new position. On 25 January 1893, Alix went with her brother to Berlin for the wedding of their cousin Princess Margaret of Prussia to Prince Frederick of Hesse-Kassel, which was a very grand affair, attended by royal personages from all over Europe. Although Ernie had been keen for Alix to accompany him, she hated such events and confided to Victoria beforehand that 'I dread it terribly, as I have a great dislike of such large festivities and especially now, that I have lost my own sweet darling papa, but it must be and I pray God may give the strength to do my duty.'[13] However, it was not all terrible for to Alix's great happiness, Tsesarevich Nicholas was also to be there, although she had no way of knowing that his primary reason for travelling all the way to Berlin was not to attend the wedding, but actually in order to find out if their feelings for each other had changed since the last time that they met in 1889.

After several fruitless attempts to encourage him to marry someone else, including Princess Margaret of Prussia and one of the Edinburgh girls, his parents had finally given up and informed him that if his heart was really and truly set on Alix of Hesse then they would give their permission for the match to go ahead. Nicholas was overjoyed by this turnabout but troubled by the fact that he had recently become romantically involved with a ballerina, Mathilde Kschessinska, who had caught his eye while performing with the Imperial Ballet at the Mariinsky Theatre. 'I have noticed something very strange within myself,'[14] Nicholas confided to his journal while trying to reconcile his love for Alix with the passion that he felt for Mathilde, his 'little K'. 'I never thought that two similar feelings, two loves could co-exist at one time within one heart.'[15] However, although Nicholas did his best to spend some time with Alix in Berlin, he found it impossible to do so thanks to the strict etiquette enforced at the Prussian court and the endless formal ceremonies that somehow contrived to keep them apart. Confused and worried that Alix, who gave him no encouragement to approach her and was now apparently even more reserved and remote than ever, did not share his feelings, Nicholas decided not to force the issue during his stay in Berlin and left the German capital feeling disappointed and even more bewildered than ever – which resulted in his immediately hurrying off to spend the night with his ballerina as soon as he got back to St Petersburg. However, although he consoled himself with another woman, Nicholas had certainly not forgotten Alix. 'Berlin and all those ceremonies and functions… where we generally used to be about half a mile off from each other, cannot be called a pleasant meeting,'[16] he wrote to her that October, still clearly regretting the wasted opportunity to spend some time with her many months later.

While in Berlin, Alix managed to develop an ear infection that lingered on for weeks and made her feel even more wretchedly down spirited than ever. It was clear that she urgently needed a break and so in the spring of 1893, she and Ernie left Germany in order to make a much-longed-for trip to the sunnier climes of Italy, where they followed in the footsteps of their mother Princess Alice, who had so much enjoyed her own Italian adventure in 1873, and their elder sisters Victoria, Ella and Irene, who spent three weeks touring Milan, Venice and Florence in October 1882. On Friday, 14 April, Princess Beatrice's thirty-sixth birthday, Ernie and Alix arrived in Florence and immediately went to visit their grandmother Victoria, who was staying at the Villa Palmieri on the outskirts of the city. The pair stayed for luncheon before returning to their own lodgings in Florence, where they planned to spend the next few weeks wandering the streets and visiting all of the major galleries and most important churches. Although Alix was a bit less excited by art than her brother, who was a passionate devotee of art history, she still very much enjoyed their visits to the Uffizi and Pitti Palace, where she was so entranced by a Botticelli Madonna that she bought a print that she hung in pride of place on her sitting room wall when they returned to Darmstadt. Although they had plenty of time to themselves, they were still required to visit their grandmother almost daily, usually staying for tea on the beautiful terrace, or dinner, and accompanying her on excursions, including one on 16 April to the Medici Villa La Petraia, which enjoyed a wonderful view towards Florence from one of the terraces and where they enjoyed tea, braved the gathering storm clouds overhead in order to stroll around the gardens and bought copious amounts of flowers to take back with them. On 18 April, they accompanied Victoria to Fiesole and the imposing Castello di Vincigliata before returning to have tea on the terrace, while a few days later they joined her on the balcony of the Palazzo Riccardi in order to watch a special procession organised to celebrate the silver wedding anniversary of the king and queen of Italy. The royal wedding anniversary was properly celebrated on 22 April with illuminations and fireworks in the city, after which Alix joined her grandmother for a carriage ride through the streets of Florence so that they could enjoy the festivities, which went on for most of the night with even Victoria staying out until past ten as she was enjoying herself so much.

While they were together in Italy, Victoria had personally invited both Alix and her brother to the wedding of their cousin Prince George of Wales to Princess May of Teck, who had been briefly engaged to his elder brother Eddy before his sudden and unexpected death. However, upon reflection, Alix decided that although her brother Ernie was planning to attend, she herself could not afford to do so. 'It is too kind of you asking me to come to the wedding, but I fear it is impossible, as we have been about so much this year already, and as Ernie cannot stop very long in England, the journey would be scarcely worth the while for me, would it, and then it is so expensive also,' she wrote to Victoria on 2 June. 'A gentleman does not need so much luggage and really our journey to Italy and Ernie's official ones and Berlin were very expensive. Excuse my writing so openly, but I thought it was only right you should know the reason of my not accepting your awfully kind invitation and hope you will not mind it, and let me come perhaps next year with Ernie.'[17] Victoria was deeply disappointed that Alix would not be at the wedding, which was to be one of the highlights of the royal family's year, but she accepted her decision and also, significantly, respected Alix's pride by not offering to fund the trip. Her sangfroid could also be explained by the fact that the handsome Tsesarevich Nicholas had unexpectedly accepted his invitation to the wedding and was expected to arrive in London, where he would be staying with his aunt Alexandra and her family at Marlborough House, at the end of June. It would be the first time since the summer of 1873, when he had accompanied his parents on a long visit to England, that Victoria set eyes upon Nicholas and she was naturally desperately curious to see what he was like now, having heard so much about him from her granddaughters and his Wales cousins, who usually saw him every year at the annual family gathering in Denmark. Fate decreed that their first meeting should take place at Windsor Castle on 1 July, the anniversary of Alix's parents wedding at Osborne thirty-one years earlier, and although Victoria was naturally very nervous beforehand, she was quickly charmed by the personable young Russian prince as well as being instantly put at ease by his close resemblance to his cousin Prince George. When Nicholas, who was feeling relaxed and jaunty after a long carriage ride around a boiling-hot London with his cousin George, arrived just after two, Victoria, whom he described rather rudely in his journal as 'a round ball on unsteady legs',[18] was waiting for him at the top of the castle's grand stone staircase. 'All were in uniform to do him honour and to show him every possible civility,'[19] she wrote that evening, clearly still very much impressed by him. 'He is charming and wonderfully like Georgie. He always speaks English... he is very simple and unaffected',[20] while Nicholas for his part noted only that she was 'remarkably kind'[21] to him. After luncheon, they went to the relatively intimate Audience Room, where to Nicholas' great surprise, Victoria ceremoniously invested him with the Order of the Garter, after which they parted on excellent terms, each feeling like they had suitably impressed the other.

It was Nicholas' second visit to England, the land where his beloved Alix had spent many of her childhood holidays and to which she felt enormously attached. Windsor Castle, where she had spent so many summers, was of particular interest to him and he enjoyed looking around after Victoria had once again escaped to the privacy of Frogmore, even visiting the chapel where his cousin Eddy's body had been interred. That evening, Nicholas went with his Wales relatives to see the Comédie Française perform *Les Effrontés* and then accompanied his uncle Bertie, of whom he was very fond, to the Marlborough Club, to which he had newly been elected a member – which resulted in a terrible hangover, made worse by the dreadful and oppressive heat, the following morning. Although Nicholas was very much enjoying his visit to London, there were two significant annoyances to contend with – namely the absence of Alix of Hesse, whose brother Ernie arrived without her on 4 July, and the fact that everyone he met felt compelled to comment on his great resemblance to his cousin George and even, on occasion, mistook one for the other. 'I am getting quite tired of hearing the same thing all the time,'[22] Nicholas noted tersely in his diary, although he was obviously not entirely displeased with the comparison for the very next morning he gamely posed for photographs with George in the gardens of Marlborough House, before he set off for another long carriage ride around London, this time taking in Westminster Abbey, St Paul's Cathedral, the Tower of London and, finally, St James' Palace, which would be George and May's home after their wedding and which Nicholas, deeply unimpressed, likened to a 'prison'.[23] The evening before the wedding, Nicholas attended a state banquet at Buckingham Palace, where he was guest of honour, sitting beside Victoria who once again described him as 'charming' and delightedly recorded that 'his great likeness to Georgie leads to no end of funny mistakes, the one being taken for the other!'[24] Also present that evening was Ernie of Hesse, who was sitting in between the Princess of Wales and Victoria Melita's formidable mother Marie, his prospective mother-in-law, which must have been quite an ordeal for him. After dinner, the party went on to the palace's Blue Drawing Room, where Nicholas and Ernie would no doubt have made a beeline for each other in order to talk about Alix. Certainly, Nicholas, who had naturally expected her to be present, was deeply disappointed not to find her there.

The following day, Nicholas rode with his aunt Alexandra and grandparents, the king and queen of Denmark in the procession to St James' Palace, where he escorted his grandmother to their position close to the altar. Victoria, who entered and left with Alix's brother, Ernie, had the place of honour, where she spent the ceremony vividly recalling her own wedding, which had taken place on the same spot fifty-three years earlier, and that of her eldest daughter Vicky. After the ceremony, everyone returned to Buckingham Palace, where they made an appearance on the famous balcony before the private celebrations began with a rather late luncheon. The royal guests were seated at two tables in the palace's state dining room, with the newly married couple in the places of honour on one and the Prince of Wales and his mother-in-law, the queen of Denmark heading the other, at which Nicholas sat. He made little comment about Buckingham Palace in his journal, other than to comment that the ballroom was 'magnificent',[25] but like other Russian visitors, he no doubt thought it rather unimpressive and even a little shabby in comparison with the splendid Romanov palaces in St Petersburg. However, he couldn't help but be deeply struck and impressed by the tremendous popularity that Victoria and her family enjoyed with the people, who came out in their thousands to cheer them on the royal wedding day and although there had been more than one unsuccessful attempt on Victoria's life, there was remarkably little security to be seen around the queen and her family, which was a marked contrast to the way that Nicholas' family had lived since the assassination of his grandfather. Once the newly married couple had departed for their honeymoon, Nicholas and most of his fellow guests, including Ernie of Hesse, headed off for a dinner party at Marlborough House, where they no doubt toasted George and May several times before celebrating into the small hours.

The following day was uncomfortably hot, and Nicholas returned with his uncle Bertie to Buckingham Palace in order to take his leave of Victoria, who was returning to Windsor Castle that afternoon, very happy indeed to be escaping some of the heat. Poor Nicholas was less fortunate though as it was his fate to endure a luncheon party in the frock coat that he had worn in order to visit Victoria, after which he noted that he was 'left soaked through'[26] and forced to change before he visited the House of Lords and House of Commons, where he was fortunate enough to hear the Prime Minister, Lord Gladstone speak. The last few days of his visit were filled with the same round of family gatherings, sightseeing and official functions, including one in the City, where he nervously gave his very first speech in English to a gathering that comprised over 700 aldermen and the Lord Mayor of London. Luckily for Nicholas, although the food was terrible, there had already been several toasts so his words were greeted with enormous enthusiasm by the assembled company, who cheered and pounded the tables with their cutlery when he finished speaking. When Nicholas left England two days later, it was with much regret and sadness. Although he had been raised to view the British and their queen with politely hostile suspicion, he had nonetheless very much enjoyed his visit and had even felt strangely at home, thanks to the warm welcome that he had received and also the presence of so many much-loved family members. There had been one notable absence, however, and as he left England behind, his heart ached for the lost opportunity to spend some much-longed-for time with his beloved Alix, although it had been wonderful to see people and places that were familiar to her, including her much-loved grandmother, whose approval he was keen to court. He almost certainly knew, thanks to Ella and the gossip relayed back to Russia by his aunt Alexandra, that Victoria was very definitely not in favour of his romance with Alix and so he did all that he could to endear himself to her, doubtless much heartened by the fact that Victoria hadn't been very keen on Sergei either at first but had quickly changed her opinion after meeting him. However, although he knew that Victoria exerted a powerful influence over Alix, he was also aware that she had still been unable to persuade her into marrying her cousin Eddy even though she very much wished it and this, coupled with the fact that his parents had finally become reconciled to the inevitability of his marriage to Alix, would have strengthened his resolve to make the woman that he had loved for almost a decade his wife.

Now that George was successfully married to the eminently suitable May of Teck and the future of the dynasty appeared secure in their hands, Victoria turned her attention once again to the issue of Alix's brother Ernie, who turned twenty-five in November 1893 and as Grand Duke of Hesse was, in her view, in urgent need of a wife. Following the advice of Dr Jenner, Victoria had resolved to make a match between Ernie and his first cousin, Princess Victoria Melita, and set about encouraging her hesitant grandson to seal the deal. 'I have written twice to Ernie about the necessity of his showing some attention and interest', Victoria wrote in some exasperation to Ernie's eldest sister Princess Victoria. 'Pray tell him and say he must answer me. Aunt Marie fears he no longer wishes it, which I am sure is not the case.'[27] The fact of the matter was that although Ernie was keen to do everything that he could to oblige his grandmother, of whom he was not a little afraid, he did not agree that there was any pressing need for him to marry quite so quickly and was furthermore unsure that Victoria Melita was the right bride for him as although they were well matched in some ways, even sharing a birthday, he did not feel that they were compatible enough for marriage. It was useless to resist Victoria when her mind was made up though and despite his half-hearted efforts to postpone making a decision about the matter,

Ernie was soon forced to give in and on 9 January 1894, duly proposed to Victoria Melita and was accepted, to the great delight of her father and their shared grandmother. In fact, the only person who wasn't crowing over the news was Alix, who disliked Victoria Melita and was horrified by the prospect of seeing her installed as chatelaine of her family home in Darmstadt, where she herself was used to being in charge and being her brother's constant companion. The fact that she was not without suitors of her own was naturally some consolation, but at this point marriage seemed a very long way off, especially as she had recently informed Nicholas that there was no way that she could consider marrying him, thanks to her unwillingness to convert to his religion.

Poor Nicholas had spent four months brooding about Alix's non-appearance at George's wedding and the distance, both geographical and emotional, that yawned between them, before finally deciding to open communications between them by writing to request that she send him a photograph of herself as he would be 'so happy to have one near me'.[28] If Nicholas had hoped that she would respond with the warmth and affection that he craved then he was to be sorely disappointed by Alix's response, which effectively dashed all of the hopes and dreams that he had harboured for almost a decade. 'I have tried to look at it in every light that is possible, but I always return to one thing', Alix wrote. 'You, dear Nicky, who have also such a strong belief will understand me that I think it is a sin to change my belief, and I should be miserable all the days of my life, knowing that I had done a wrongful thing... What happiness can come from a marriage which begins without the real blessing of God?'[29] After writing about the importance of her faith and her certainty that it would be wrong to change religion, she concluded with her certain assurance that he would 'understand this clearly and see as I do, that we are not only torturing ourselves, about something impossible and it would not be a kindness to let you go on having vain hopes, which will never be realised. And now goodbye, my darling Nicky, and may God bless and protect you.'[30] At the same time, Alix also wrote a letter to Nicholas' sister Xenia, reiterating her decision and asking that she 'not believe that my love is less…that has made it so far more hard and difficult to me and I have been torturing myself. To hurt one that one loves is fearful, and yet I don't want him to go on hoping, as I can never change my religion… I feel too upset to write any more.'[31] When her letter arrived nine days later, Nicholas, who had been warned by Ella not to expect a happy resolution, could not bring himself to open it straight away and left it on his table overnight before finally working up the nerve to open it the following morning. 'I learned that everything is over between us,' he wrote miserably in his journal later that day. 'It is impossible for her to change religion, and all my hopes are shattered by this implacable obstacle, my best dreams and my most cherishes wishes for the future… All day I went about in a daze, it is terribly difficult to appear calm and carefree when the question affecting your whole future life is suddenly decided in this way!'[32]

It took over a month, punctuated by moping and drinking, before the devastated Nicholas felt able to respond to Alix's letter. 'I could not write to you all these days on account of the sad state of mind I was in. Now that my restlessness has passed I feel more calm and am able to answer your letter quietly. Let me thank you first of all for the frank and open way in which you spoke to me in that letter! There is nothing worse in the world than things misunderstood and not brought to the point. I knew from the beginning what an obstacle there rose between us and I felt so deeply for you all these years, knowing perfectly the great difficulties you would have had to overcome… I cannot deny the reasons you give me, dear Alix; but I have got one which is also true: you hardly know the depth of our religion. If you only could have learnt it with somebody who knows it… perhaps then, it would not have troubled you in the same way as it does now!'[33] Desperate to change her mind, Nicholas tried to persuade Alix that if she only studied his religion then perhaps she might see that it was not so very different to her own Lutheran faith, before returning to the undeniable bond between them. 'Don't you think, dearest, that the five years, since we know each other, have passed in vain and with no result? Certainly not – for me at least. And how am I to change my feelings after waiting and wishing for so long, even now after that sad letter you sent me?… Do not say 'no' directly, my dearest Alix, do not ruin my life already! Do you think there can exist any happiness in the whole world without you!'[34]

In England, Victoria was being kept appraised of these promising developments by Alix's sisters and Nicholas' aunt, Alexandra, who told her that he was 'miserable' to have his hopes so soundly dashed and agreed that the whole mess was at least partially Ella's fault for she had 'always encouraged him instead of doing the reverse.'[35] For her part, Ella may have been ordered by Alix to let the matter drop, but she still remained optimistic that her youngest sister would eventually come to her senses and change her mind about marrying Nicholas, writing to Victoria that: 'The best is to leave her alone as of course it is a very very sore heart one touches – well all is in God's hands and dearest Grandmama, if ever she accepts – your motherly love will be what she longs for most.'[36] One can imagine Victoria's mounting incredulity as she read Ella's letter, in which she tried to convince her grandmother that Alix need have no fears about marrying into the Russian royal family and living in Russia, for 'much is exaggerated'[37] while at the same time airily dismissing Victoria's fears that Alix might be targeted by terrorists by reminding her that 'may we not all die suddenly?'[38] It was all in vain though, for Victoria remained resolutely unimpressed and continued to express her relief that Alix had rejected Nicholas. There could be no doubt that Victoria approved of Nicholas on a personal level for he was both handsome and extremely charming, but as ruler of a vast empire herself, she was no doubt curious about what sort of ruler he would one day make and after fifty-six years on the throne, during which time she had seen several world leaders come and go, she would almost certainly have noted the shallow, apathetic weakness that lay beneath Nicholas' agreeable, good-humoured façade and hoped that he had many years ahead of him in which to grow and mature before he was called upon to rule over Russia.

Victoria invited Alix and Ernie to visit her at the end of the year but was disappointed when her granddaughter politely made their excuses, evidently keen to avoid any face-to-face discussions about Nicholas and her future prospects. However, she could not remain aloof forever and in February 1894, the two Hesse siblings travelled to London, although when Ernie took the train down to visit Victoria on the Isle of Wight two days after their arrival, Alix, surprisingly, did not accompany him but instead remained behind in the capital, where she was happily enjoying a spot of sightseeing and shopping. When Victoria returned to Windsor Castle on 22 February, Ernie and Alix joined her there for the usual round of daily visits to the Mausoleum, tea in the grounds of Frogmore and insipid evenings in the state apartments before they accompanied their grandmother to Buckingham Palace four days later in order to attend the first Drawing Room of the season, a most exhausting and boring affair for all concerned. During their stay, the conversation was naturally dominated by discussions about Ernie's upcoming wedding to Victoria Melita, which was scheduled to take place in Coburg that April, her father having succeeded as Duke of Saxe-Coburg Gotha after the death of his uncle Ernest, who had been Prince Albert's only brother. Although Victoria had missed numerous family weddings over the past few years, she was determined to travel to Coburg for this one, feeling that the absence of both of Ernie's parents made her presence especially necessary. As for Alix, she participated in the preparations for her brother's wedding, but she found it difficult to feign excitement about the event, knowing that it would mark a serious change in her own circumstances once Victoria Melita was living in Darmstadt with them. She was also still struggling to recover from the death of her father, which was naturally uppermost in her thoughts as Ernie's wedding approached. 'I long for my precious one more than ever', she wrote to Victoria at the end of 1893. 'How happy he would have been to see Ernie happy, and what a comfort it would have been to me, as life indeed will be very different for me, as I shall be feeling myself *de trop*.'[39]

In April 1894, a large group of European royalty gathered in Coburg, once a relatively obscure little German town that had been elevated to celebrity status by a series of high- profile marriages over the last century, for the wedding of Ernie and Victoria Melita. Shortly before she left for Coburg with her brother, Alix received a letter from Nicholas' sister Xenia, delicately trying to discover if her feelings had changed. 'Darling, why did you speak about that subject, which we never wanted to mention again?' Alix responded. 'It is cruel as you know it never can be – all along I have said so, do you think it is not already hard enough, to know you are hurting first the person whom of all others you would long to please. But it cannot be – he knows it – and so do not, I pray you, speak of it again. I know Ella will begin again, but what is the good of it, and it is cruel always to say I am ruining his life – can I help it, when to make him happy I should be committing a sin in my conscience.'[40] Alix's terse and apparently definitive response arrived on the very day that Nicholas was due to leave for Coburg and made him so upset, when Xenia helpfully relayed its contents to him, that he refused to go, until his mother convinced him that it would be rude to cancel at such short notice. She also recommended that he approach Alix's grandmother Victoria for help, believing that when it came to it, the prestige of a match between her granddaughter and the heir to the Russian throne would ultimately outweigh all other considerations that she might have. Two days later, Nicholas arrived in Coburg, after a train journey that had taken him over 1,200 miles from St Petersburg. With him was his uncle Sergei and his wife Ella, who was undaunted by Alix's repeated assertions that she could not and would not marry Nicholas, and arrived confident that she would be able to talk her sister into changing her mind. The Romanov party, exhausted after their long journey, were greeted on the platform of Coburg station by a large group of royal relatives, which included Alix herself, no doubt feeling very awkward to be reunited with Nicholas in front of such an intimidating crowd of interested relatives. The couple did not get a chance to speak until the following day, when Ernie and Ella contrived to bring them together in the latter's rooms in the Schloss Ehrenburg, with Alix looking, as the besotted Nicholas later wrote in his journal, 'noticeably prettier, but... extremely sad'.[41] Left alone, the pair talked all morning while Alix 'cried a lot, poor thing'[42] as she insisted over and over again that although she loved Nicholas deeply, she was not prepared to change her religion for him. Nicholas was upset but still determined not to give up, now that the much-longed-for prize seemed to be within his grasp at last.

Queen Victoria, relaxed and cheerful after another successful Italian holiday, arrived in Coburg in great state later that day. Although Nicholas was amongst the throng of royal guests that gathered to greet her in one of the schloss' rococo saloons, Alix, clearly still upset by that morning's painful conversation, was absent, even though she would have had her brother and all of her sisters on hand to support her. Due to the size of the family party, it was divided into two for mealtimes, with one group headed by Queen Victoria, acting as the mother of the groom, and the other by Nicholas' aunt, Marie, the mother of the bride. Both Nicholas and Alix were in the latter group, which gave them the opportunity to spend a little more time together that evening, although there would be no further opportunities for serious conversation until the following morning, when they met again after breakfast to talk about the future. Meanwhile, Victoria remained completely oblivious to the drama that was unfolding beneath the same roof – as expected, returning to Coburg, the childhood home of her beloved Albert, had awoken painful memories of happier times and their life together and her mood swiftly took a melancholy nosedive. The rest of the family party was beginning to realise that something was going on between the Russian heir and the lovely Princess Alix, who was generally held to be the current reigning beauty of the family. Although Alix was always reserved, she was even more aloof and silent than ever, while her eyes were unmistakably reddened by crying. As for Nicholas, he was doing his best to appear as genial and cheerful as usual but it was obvious that there was something on his mind as he smiled and chatted to his gathered royal relatives at the family dinner party that was held the night before the wedding. In the end, it was Alix's cousin Emperor Wilhelm who decided that enough was enough and decided to intervene, having decided that having a German cousin on the Russian throne might one day be of use to him as he furthered his own territorial ambitions in Europe. Rejecting the gentle persuasions of her sister Ella, for whom he still carried a torch, he instead forcefully lectured her at some length about how ridiculous and unnecessary it was for her to reject Nicholas on the grounds of religion, when there was really hardly any difference between the Russian Orthodox Church and Lutheranism. This was, of course, not quite correct but when Ella joined her voice to his and reminded her sister how easy she had found the transition between the two, Alix began to waver and wonder if perhaps she could after all follow in her sister's footsteps. Naturally, neither sister felt able to remind Wilhelm that the differences between Lutheranism and Orthodoxy had apparently mattered a great deal when his sister Sophia had converted to the Orthodox Church after her marriage to the Crown Prince of Greece – a move that had infuriated her brother so much that he had caused a family rift by banning her from Germany for three years.

On Thursday, 19 April, Ernie and Victoria Melita, who wore Princess Alice's lace wedding veil, were married in the chapel of the Schloss Ehrenburg in front of a huge crowd of royal guests. Alix was seated with her sisters, while Nicholas was seated between her aunt Vicky and uncle Bertie, which must have been rather nerve-racking, as both almost certainly knew that he had spent the past two days trying in vain to persuade their niece to marry him. 'The pastor gave a splendid sermon, which surprisingly went straight to the heart of my own problem', Nicholas wrote in his diary that evening. 'At that moment, I terribly wanted to be able to look into Alix's soul!'[43] At the wedding breakfast, he was seated in the place of honour beside Victoria, who once again found him to be 'a dear, charming boy,' and opposite the newly married pair, who left afterwards for their wedding night in Kranichstein, which would be followed the next morning by their official entrance into Darmstadt as Grand Duke and Duchess. As he was embracing Nicholas before their departure, Ernie delivered a whispered exhortation not to give up hope, which did much to boost the young Tsesarevich's spirits. Alix would not be present at Victoria Melita's triumph but instead remained behind in Coburg, where she attended a quiet family dinner party that evening, while Nicholas attended a dinner hosted by his aunt Marie, which was rather uncomfortable as all the men were forced to wear uniform because of the presence of Wilhelm, who was never seen out of it. The following morning, his resolve stiffened by his own wearingly strident lecture from Wilhelm, who now sat in the room next door awaiting an update, Nicholas once again met with Alix, although he was feeling distinctly pessimistic about his prospects, having become convinced that the kind attentions of her family over the past few days were due to well-meaning pity because they knew that there was no chance of her accepting his proposal. He was therefore astonished and thrilled when she informed him that she had changed her mind and was now willing to do whatever was required of her in order to become his wife, at which point both of them burst into tears. 'God, what a mountain has fallen from my shoulders; with what joy have I been able to delight dear Papa and Mama!' Nicholas wrote in his journal later that day. 'I spent the whole day in a daze, not quite knowing what had happened to me!'[44]

Chapter Nine

'My own precious Nicky darling.'

April 1894–November 1894

Queen Victoria had just finished having breakfast with her daughter Beatrice when the 'much agitated'[1] Ella came in with the unbelievable news that Alix and Nicholas had just that minute got engaged. 'I was quite thunderstruck, as though I knew Nicky much wished it, I thought Alicky was not sure of her mind,' the elderly queen wrote later on. 'Saw them both. Alicky had tears in her eyes but looked very bright and I kissed them both.'[2] Nicholas endeared himself to Victoria by saying that Alix was 'much too good'[3] for him and then promising to make the religious issue as easy as possible for her, but even so her fears for her granddaughter's future were not assuaged and she noted in her journal that the engagement 'has the drawback that Russia is so far, the position a difficult one, as well as the question of the religion'.[4] However, she concluded without enthusiasm that 'as her brother is married now and they are really attached to one another, it is perhaps better so'.[5] The rest of their relatives reacted with delight to the news, which would not just bring together two much-liked members of the extended family but also create a new union between the royal houses of Germany, Russia and Britain. Not that Alix and her betrothed cared very much about that as they spent the first day of their engagement accepting the excited congratulations of their relatives, marvelling at the enormous pile of telegrams that was already piling up in Nicholas' room and taking a long romantic walk through the grounds of Prince Albert's birthplace and childhood home, Schloss Rosenau. In the evening, they enjoyed the illuminations for Ernie's wedding, which had been postponed by bad weather, before attending a concert performed by the Bavarian regimental string orchestra, who 'played brilliantly' according to Nicholas, who thought that everything was wonderful and amazing in the wake of his engagement. 'I still cannot believe that I have a bride,'[6] he wrote, wonderingly, in his journal after spending the rest of the evening sitting alone in his little sitting room with his fiancée who, now that the terrible strain of the last few days was in the past, was finally every bit as warm, affectionate and loving as he could ever have wished.

Victoria had another opportunity to observe them together the following morning when they had breakfast with her. The pair impressed her with their obvious love for each other and she felt able to comment on how 'simple, natural and kind'[7] Nicholas was as he talked about their plans for the future. Later that day, the family posed for photographs in the garden with Queen Victoria proudly positioned at the very heart of the group, enjoying her position as 'Grandmother of Europe', flanked by Wilhelm II and his mother, her eldest daughter, Vicky. Behind them, together at last, stand Nicholas and Alix, their sombre expressions hiding the deep and joyous delight that had overwhelmed them since becoming engaged. Amongst the ever growing mountain of letters and telegrams on Nicholas' desk was a heartfelt letter from their mutual cousin George, Duke of York. 'I am indeed delighted to think that everything is settled at last and that the great wish of your heart is at last accomplished, as I well know that for some years you have loved Alix and wished to marry her,' he wrote with obvious pleasure at the good news, which would draw their family even closer together. 'I am quite certain that she will make you an excellent wife and she is charming, lovely and accomplished. I am also so glad that your engagement has taken place at Coburg and I know it will have given Grandmama the greatest possible pleasure to be present on this happy occasion, she is very fond of Alix and has always told me how much she hoped that some day she would marry you.'[8] This latter point may not have been entirely true, but the happiness felt by Alix's British relatives was genuine as they prepared to see the last of Alice's daughters happily settled at last. In Russia, Nicholas' parents were also thrilled by the news, their lingering doubts about the suitability of Alix to eventually don the mantle of Tsarina, tempered by their great relief that their son was finally to be married – a relief that was entirely shared by their people, who had been anxiously awaiting news of their Tsesarevich's engagement for several years. Nicholas' mother was disappointed not to have been present for this important event in her son's life though. 'How envious and *furious* I am that the uncles and aunts were present while *Papa* and *myself* who are *closest* to you were excluded!' she wrote to Nicholas. 'It's horribly sad and hard for us.'[9]

The rest of Alix's stay in Coburg passed in a haze of happiness as she spent every possible moment with Nicholas, enjoying the fact that as an engaged couple they were finally able to spend time alone together, either driving around the countryside, visiting lovely Rosenau where they picked armfuls of flowers or simply sitting together in her pretty little sitting room. They had breakfast with Victoria nearly every day, with the queen becoming so charmed by Nicholas that she insisted that from now on he was to call her 'granny'. On 26 April, the young Tsesarevich wrested himself away from his fiancée and visited Victoria in her rooms, where they spent a few hours discussing Alix's future in Russia, which Nicholas had promised to make as happy and safe as possible. 'He is so sensible and nice,'[10] Victoria wrote later, adding that he had expressed a hope that he would be allowed to visit Alix in England at the end of June. Victoria had already long since decided to invite her granddaughter for a long visit so that Ernie and Victoria Melita could have some time alone together in Darmstadt and the news of her engagement had only made her more determined to do so for she feared, rightly as it turned out, that she would hardly see Alix once she married and settled in Russia. Fearful that Nicholas' parents would not allow him to visit her in England, Alix added her own pleas to his mother Empress Maria, whom she knew was desperate to have him back home again in St Petersburg. 'You will let him come to England this summer, won't you, because it would be so hard to be parted so long, and Grandmama is looking forward to his visit so much,' she wrote to her future mother-in-law. 'He has quite won her heart, as he has of all those who know him.'[11]

Fortunately for Alix, she was not expected to accompany Victoria when she left Coburg on 28 April, but was instead able to remain with Nicholas for two precious days longer, which gave them an opportunity to pay a quiet visit to Ernie and Victoria Melita in Darmstadt, where they seemed extremely happy and content together – for now at least. It was Nicholas' first visit to her family home in Darmstadt and he was delighted to finally see for himself the prettily decorated, bright and airy English-style rooms where his beloved Alix had grown up and which would one day be replicated by them both for their own children. However, as it is often wont to do, the time for parting arrived all too quickly and on 2 May, Nicholas accompanied Alix to the station so that she could catch the train back to Darmstadt, where she was to spend the night before leaving for England the following day. 'It was too awful saying goodbye like that, with a lot of people looking on from all sides,' Nicholas wrote to her that night. 'I shall never forget the sweet, sad and yet smiling expression of your angelic face looking out of the window as the train was beginning to move!'[12] For her part, Alix, was equally distressed to be parted from her love. 'My own precious Nicky darling, I am lying in bed but cannot go to sleep before I have written to you, as speak alas, we cannot,' she wrote from Darmstadt that night. 'Oh, how I miss you, it is not to be described and I long for the two hours all alone with you. No goodnight kiss and blessing, it is hard. But our thoughts will meet, won't they?'[13]

A few days before her granddaughter was due to arrive in England, Queen Victoria sat down at her writing desk in Windsor Castle and picked up her pen to write her first ever letter to the Tsesarevich Nicholas. After thanking him for thoughtfully sending her a present, she launched into the main crux of the letter. 'I need not say how much my thoughts (have) been with you and my sweet Alicky since we left dearest Coburg and I am sure the parting from her will have been very painful for both. We are looking forward with such pleasure to her arrival on Friday and I shall watch over her most anxiously and carefully that she should get some rest and quiet and do all to get strong which she has not been for some time. While she is here, alone without you, I think she ought to go about and out as little as possible as she would be stared at and made an object of curiosity, which in her present position as your bride would be most unpleasant and improper. As she has no parents, I feel I am the only person who can really be answerable for her. All her dear sisters after their beloved mother's death looked to me as their second mother, but *they* had still their dear father. Now poor dear Alicky is an orphan and has no one but me at all in that position… I am so sorry not to be able to take her to Balmoral, which is the finest air in the world, but it was rather too bracing for her two years ago. I hope in the autumn she might be able to do so. Believe me with true affection, dear Nicky, your devoted (future) Grandmama.'[14] Nicholas was thoroughly charmed to receive this letter from his fiancée's grandmother, which he described to Alix as 'very kind', although 'not knowing her handwriting, it took me a good deal of trouble to decipher it'.[15] To Nicholas' despair, he never quite managed to work out Victoria's handwriting and replying to her letters would become a severe trial to him. 'I must again answer a letter from Granny, if you knew what trouble they give me', he wrote to Alix later in the month. 'Of course I try to write in a very grand and old fashioned like style – had you seen one of them you would be quite upset. But her letters are so awfully difficult to read, she has got a way of shortening her sentences and words in such a manner that I could not make out for a long time.'[16]

Although Alix was very glad to be reunited with her grandmother, being at Windsor Castle reminded her not just of Coburg, where she had been so happy with Nicholas, but also her last visit to England with her brother Ernie, without whom she was feeling 'quite lost'. A letter from Nicholas, along with flowers that he had picked in their favourite spot at Rosenau were waiting for her in her room in the castle and they now took pride of place on her desk, while the rest of the bedroom was filled with photographs of him. 'All your photos are looking at me with their beautiful big eyes,' she wrote to him that evening. 'Oh, were you but here. I could press you to my heart.'[17] Now that she had Alix to herself, Victoria was keen to hear everything about her relationship with Nicholas and on 4 May decided to question her closely while they went out driving alone together, much to her granddaughter's discomfort. 'She began by asking me so many questions, when, how, and where, and what had made me change my decision and so on, till I no longer knew what to say,' she wrote to Nicholas afterwards. 'She is very fond of you, my love, as you know. Then she dropped off to sleep and I admired the beautiful nature. Windsor Castle through the dark trees in the distance, with sunshine on it and brighter blue shades – like a beautiful vision.'[18] Although Alix's stay at Windsor Castle passed with the usual round of daily carriage rides with 'Granny', visits to the mausoleum, sedate family dinners, piano duets with aunt Beatrice (always a torment for Alix, who hated playing piano in public) and early nights, this time it was enlivened by letters and telegrams from her beloved Nicky, which arrived almost daily. She was also taking Russian lessons with a young German Russian lady, Catherine Schneider, whom she presented to her grandmother on 19 May. That same evening, the royal family and court gathered in the

Waterloo Gallery where they were treated to a performance of one of Victoria's favourite operas, *Faust* by Charles Gounod, with the celebrated Canadian soprano Emma Albani performing the role of 'Marguerite'. It was to be Alix's last night at Windsor, for the following evening she went to stay with her aunt Princess Helena at her home Cumberland Lodge, in the Windsor Great Park, while Queen Victoria went up to Balmoral without her, having decided that the climate there was too harsh for her delicate granddaughter. Instead, Alix was going to be spending a month recuperating in the Yorkshire spa town of Harrogate, where the sulphur-rich waters were believed to be especially efficacious for nervous and muscular complaints. She had been complaining of mysterious pains in her legs for several years, which her eldest sister believed were symptoms of sciatica, but had never been properly diagnosed. By the spring of 1894, Victoria was concerned enough about Alix's health to insist that she take the waters instead of accompanying her to Scotland.

While in Harrogate, Alix stayed at Cathcart House, which was run by the Allen family and said to be the best hotel in the town. Although Alix had hoped to evade unwelcome attention by using the alias of Baroness Starkenburg, the news that she had arrived in the area spread like wildfire and she would quickly find herself being followed and mobbed whenever she went outdoors – an experience that she, who was so notoriously reserved and private, found extremely unpleasant. 'When I go into a shop to buy flowers, girls stand and stare in at the window,' she wrote to Nicholas during her stay in Harrogate. 'The chemist told Madeleine that he had sent in a petition that a policeman should stand near the house to keep people off, as he saw how they stared. Most kind, but it makes no difference.'[19] She was also feeling lonely, especially as her birthday was approaching and she had no family with her to celebrate with, and as a result her thoughts began to take a melancholy turn. 'Not only do I miss you but I long also for Ernie, who used to be always running into my room at every hour of the day,' Alix wrote to Nicholas on 23 May. 'A kinder, dearer brother never was… And beloved Papa, oh, it is terrible to know that I shall never more see him in this world. I miss him more and more especially now that through you my heart is so full. Tomorrow my little sister May would have been twenty… quite grown up. Sweet little child that she was.'[20] Luckily, her grandmother took family birthdays very seriously and was already determined that Alix would not be left to celebrate alone in Harrogate. 'For her dear birthday, she must *not* be left quite alone and you really must go and spend it with her,' she wrote to Alix's eldest sister Princess Victoria on 25 May. 'It is probably her last unmarried birthday and she really *must* not be left alone. Do promise that you will go to her.'[21]

Naturally, the dutiful and affectionate Princess Victoria could not resist such a heartfelt plea and so she travelled up to Harrogate, accompanied by her daughters Alice and Louise, for Alix's birthday, which passed very merrily indeed with plenty of gifts and a drive out to the countryside, although Queen Victoria's present of a pretty tea basket and photograph of herself with her son Bertie was much overshadowed by Nicholas' offering of a magnificent bracelet, which was yet another taste of the splendid jewels that would be coming Alix's way after her marriage. Nonetheless, she was conscious of her grandmother's kindness in arranging for her sister to visit her in Harrogate and wrote to thank her a few days later. 'Victoria being here for my birthday was a great pleasure, as it would have been too sad to have spent my birthday without one relation. I have never been away like this without one before.'[22] After explaining that her lack of letters was due to the fact that the sulphur baths left her completely exhausted and discussing arrangements for Nicholas' much-longed-for return to England the following month, Alix addressed her grandmother's concerns about her future. 'Yes, darling Grandmama, the new position I am sure will be full of trials and difficulties, but with God's help and that of a loving husband it will be easier that we now picture it to ourselves. The distance is great, but yet in three days one can get to England. I am sure his parents will often allow us to come over to you. Why, I could not bear the idea of not seeing you again, after the kind angel you have been to me, ever since dear Mama died, and I cling to you more than ever, now that I am quite an orphan. God bless you for all your kindness to me, beloved Grandmama dear. I have no words to thank you enough for all. Please do not think that my marrying will make a difference in my love to you – certainly it will not, and when I am far away, I shall long to think that there is one, the dearest and kindest woman alive, who loves me a little bit.'[23]

Taking her responsibilities as Alix's only living grandparent and self-appointed guardian very seriously, Victoria, her thoughts clearly fixed on her granddaughter, sat down to write once more to Nicholas on 6 June. 'I write to you on this dear day, our darling Alicky's birthday, which I am sure must be very dear to you and I also wish you many happy returns. Thank you for your very kind letter of the 20 May, for my birthday… The accounts of dear Alicky are upon the whole satisfactory, but she requires great quiet and rest and I send you a copy of a letter from the doctor at Harrogate who is [a] very clever, nice man. She keeps a strict regime of life as well as diet. She has to lie down a great deal. This ought to have been done long ago… Her dear father's death, her anxiety about her brother and the struggle about her future have all tried her nerves very much. You will, I hope, therefore not hurry on the marriage as she ought, for your as well as her sake, to be strong and well before that.'[24] Clearly, although Victoria had resigned herself to the match, she was in no hurry to see it actually happen, even if it was clear that Nicholas was understandably keen for their engagement to be as short as possible. Victoria was able to be far more frank with Alix's eldest sister, Princess Victoria of Battenberg, who often found herself lumbered with the unenviable task of acting as family peacemaker, particularly when it came to her sisters and their occasionally unsatisfactory behaviour. 'Darling Victoria, the more I think of sweet Alicky's marriage, the more unhappy I am!' Victoria wrote from Balmoral on 25 May. 'Not as to the personality, for I like him very much but on account of the country, the policy and the differences with us and the awful insecurity to which that sweet child will be exposed. To think she is learning Russian and will have probably to talk to a priest – my whole nature rises up against it – in spite of my efforts to be satisfied. But I will try and bear it and make the best of it. Still, the feeling that I had laboured so hard to prevent it and that I felt at last there was no longer any danger and all in one night – everything was changed. Ella should never have encouraged it originally as she did.'[25]

On 15 June 1894, Nicholas left Russia for England and his much longed-for reunion with his beloved Alix. To his delight and relief, his father agreed to let him borrow the imperial yacht *Polar Star* for the journey, which would take two days longer than travelling by train but meant that the Tsesarevich could avoid Berlin, which he loathed. Victoria had originally intended for Nicholas and Alix to join her at Balmoral but the pair decided instead to spend a few days together at Elm Grove in Walton-on-Thames, a lovely Georgian house rented by Alix's sister Victoria and her family, before moving on to Windsor Castle to stay with the queen when she had returned from Scotland. Nicholas arrived on 18 June and was reunited with Alix that same day, much to their joy. The following morning, Nicholas woke up overjoyed to finally be under the same roof as his fiancée and after spending the morning taking a carriage ride around the area, accompanied by Alix's two nieces, Alice and Louise, who 'jumped around terribly',[26] the pair were finally able to spend some quiet time together before the family party set out en masse for a boat trip along the Thames, which the Tsesarevich enjoyed very much. 'The trip was wonderful, the banks remarkably beautiful,' he wrote in his journal that night. 'We met a mass of other boaters, mostly ladies. I loved all the buildings along the river bank.'[27] The following day passed in much the same way, with the happy pair spending the morning sitting together on an old rug in the gardens before luncheon, after which they all took another boat trip down the Thames before finding a suitably picturesque and secluded spot to have a picnic. 'Another wonderful, peaceful day like yesterday; in truth, what blissful existence!'[28] Nicholas noted rapturously in his journal. The quiet, easy-going pace of life at Walton-on-Thames suited him perfectly and he would have been happy to remain there forever with Alix at his side – sadly, however, they were forced to pack up their belongings and head to Windsor Castle the following day, where they were in for a very different daily routine, revolving around the habits and whims of Alix's grandmother.

Now that he was nearly part of the family, Nicholas' arrival no longer required any fanfare or pageantry and instead he and Alix quietly drove to Frogmore House, where they had tea with Victoria before walking up to the castle, where they were delighted to discover that their rooms were close together and that Victoria had thoughtfully arranged for a copy of Angeli's beautiful portrait of his mother to be hung in his bedchamber. Although he missed the peaceful solitude of Walton-on-Thames, Nicholas still found much to enjoy about his stay at Windsor Castle, which he found very impressive and quite different to any of the imperial residences in Russia. It amused him to wear the Windsor uniform, which involved a navy tailcoat with scarlet collar and cuffs, although he was less thrilled by the stockings and pumps, which rubbed his feet raw, that he had to wear with it. The regime at Windsor that June followed the same pattern as always with the usual round of carriage rides, visits to the Mausoleum at Frogmore, family dinners and musical interludes – for Alix, however, this dull timetable of activities that she had been familiar with since childhood, was now given an extra fillip by the presence of Nicholas, who was intrigued and rather charmed by the private life of Queen Victoria, whom he now cheerfully referred to as 'Granny' in his journal and letters. Although Alix was expected to attend her grandmother just as she had always done, they were still able to spend plenty of time alone together, either in their sitting rooms or outside in the beautiful grounds of Windsor Castle and Frogmore House where, on one occasion, Nicholas managed to lock himself into a lavatory for over half an hour until his fiancée was able to free him. On 23 June, there was cause for celebration when his cousin George, Duke of York and his wife May had their first child, Edward (the future Edward VIII) which, according to Nicholas, provoked 'general happiness and rejoicing'[29] at Windsor and on the following day Nicholas and Alix went by train to White Lodge in Richmond Park, the Duchess of York's family home, in order to see the new baby and congratulate his proud parents. They returned again a few days later, this time with Queen Victoria, who was naturally keen to meet the new third in line to the throne, whom she deemed to be a 'fine, strong looking child'.[30]

When Nicholas went to stay at Sandringham for the night on 28 June, Alix was bereft without him. 'I feel low he is gone, only they begged so hard he should come, so off he went,' she wrote to his sister Xenia before adding that: 'It is such unutterable joy having the dear boy here and he is so awfully good and kind.'[31] In faraway Norfolk, Nicholas was also pining for his beloved – to the extent that he wrote her a long letter that evening even though they would be seeing each other again the following afternoon. 'My sweet darling! I love you, I love you – is all that I can say!!!!!! I miss you now in the evening so dreadfully, when the others are gone to bed.'[32] He arrived back in Windsor in time for a grand dinner held in honour of the Archduke Franz Ferdinand of Austria, whose assassination in 1914 would be the catalyst for the First World

War. Nicholas, sweltering in full dress uniform, led Victoria into dinner and sat beside her, with Alix who, according to Victoria, 'looked lovely as always',[33] a few places away. Nicholas rarely strayed from Alix's side for the rest of their visit, even though this meant seeing a great deal of 'Granny', who took a decided shine to him as the weeks went by. 'It seems funny to me, all this life here and the extent to which I have become part of the English family,' Nicholas boasted to his brother George. 'I have become almost as indispensable to my future grandmother as her two Indians and her Scotsman; I am, as it were, attached to her and the best thing is that she does not like me to leave her side.'[34] Certainly, Victoria's journal is littered with references to carriage rides, lunches and teas taken in the company of Alix and her fiancé, who delighted her with his cheerful, straightforward manner and obvious passionate love for her granddaughter. On 5 July, she missed them very much when they went, chaperoned by members of their households, into London, where they spent time with relatives and visited the theatre before spending the night at Marlborough House. This was a delightful treat for them both but for Nicholas, one of the undoubted highlights of his visit occurred later on when they accompanied Victoria on a visit to Aldershot Garrison in Hampshire, the home of the British Army, which Nicholas, who loved all things military, was most keen to see for himself. As for Victoria, she had quite another treat in store for her at the formal dinner that evening in the Aldershot Royal Pavilion, where they were all staying. 'For dinner, I am going to put on a red Circassian coat, which will absolutely drive Granny wild,' Nicholas wrote to his sister Xenia from Aldershot. 'She has already asked me several times when I am going to wear a cossack uniform, and so for dinner I shall appear in it.'[35]

On 16 July, Alix and Nicholas went with Victoria to White Lodge for the christening of George and May's new baby, Edward. To his great pleasure, Nicholas was asked to be one of the godfathers and observed the ceremony with great interest, although he was rather surprised by the fact that the baby was to have seven names in total, which was quite unlike the Russian practice. 'Instead of immersing him, the Archbishop wet his fingers and touched the baby's head,'[36] he wrote in his journal that evening, noting also that the now iconic photograph of Victoria with her great-grandson Edward on her lap while flanked by her son Bertie and grandson George, the 'four generations' of the royal family, was taken that afternoon in the long gallery of White Lodge. The chequered history of the Romanov family, which had involved more than its fair share of violent premature death as well as embittered feuding, had ensured that such a photo had rarely been possible for them, not least because the various generations of his ancestors had heartily loathed each other and would rather have died than pose for a picture together, and Nicholas was therefore suitably impressed by the dignity and longevity of the British royal family, headed by the formidable but benevolent 'Granny'. Although Nicholas still found Victoria faintly ludicrous, he had also become very fond of her, not least because of her love for his beloved Alix, who remained her favourite granddaughter. He was very pleased therefore when they accompanied Victoria to Osborne House on 19 July, although this pleasure was tinged with sadness for the removal to the Isle of Wight marked the end of his month-long sojourn in England. Osborne had been the setting for many of Alix's happiest childhood memories and he was naturally keen to see it for himself, from the nursery where she had slept as a child to the Swiss Cottage where she and her cousins had played for hours on long, hot summer days. 'Granny's life here is the same, transposed from Windsor,' he noted with amusement in his journal during their stay. 'But not for us, as the sea is near.'[37] Although they were occasionally thwarted by the weather, Alix and Nicholas spent as much time as possible outdoors, enjoying the private beach at Osborne, which commands a view across the Solent towards the mainland. On 22 July, the Russian sailors from the *Polar Star*, which was moored at Trinity Pier, trooped up to the house where they were greeted by Victoria, upon which they called out to her in Russian. 'Nicky then told them I was pleased to see them and they answered and then marched off,' she wrote in her journal. 'They were fine looking, tall men.'[38]

Nicholas very reluctantly left England the following day after what had perhaps been the happiest month of his life, during which he had been encouraged to feel truly at home and had been able to spend a great deal of time with Alix, who, he believed, looked lovelier with every passing day. The only disappointment was that Victoria's plan to have the engaged couple's portraits painted by Angeli was thwarted by the lack of time, although later Nicholas would tell Alex that he was very relieved to have avoided the lengthy sittings that the work would have necessitated. 'Nicky gave us some lovely presents,' Victoria wrote in her journal on his last day. 'Then took a last drive with him and Alicky… At a little before 11, Nicky went to dress, having taken leave of all the ladies and gentlemen. He soon returned and took leave of me in hall, thanking me much for all of my kindness and kissing me very affectionately. Alicky, who looked very sad, accompanied him with Beatrice and Liko to Trinity Pier. The band played the Russian anthem as he drove away.'[39] As if to echo the sombre, depressed mood of both Alix and Nicholas, the heavens opened after lunch and it began to pour with rain, which was then replaced by a heavy mist. 'I became sadder and sadder as the hour of our separation approached!' Nicholas wrote in his journal when he was safely aboard the *Polar Star* that evening. 'I did not leave my sweet dear bride for a single moment… I changed into the uniform of the Guard Corps and after saying goodbye to dear Granny, I went to the landing stage with Alix. After parting from my darling bride, I boarded the cutter… Was exhausted from sadness and longing.'[40] Nicholas looked at Alix for as long as he could as his launch moved away, but was forced to give up when 'such a lump came up in my throat that I had to turn away and I sobbed in the boat like I did this afternoon.'[41] Waiting for him in his cabin was a letter from Alix, who had written it the previous evening while fretting about his departure and the separation that would follow. 'Oh sweety love, what shall I do without you, I am so accustomed now to have you always near me, that I shall feel quite lost… Could I but slip into your pocket instead of the thermometer, what unspeakable joy, to be ever near you, and to watch for every little wish to try and fulfil it… With what passion I love you, like a fire burning and consuming me, and to feel this love returned. What bliss could be greater?'[42]

Left behind at Osborne, Alix did her best to hide her despair and once again resumed her usual routine of accompanying Victoria on her daily carriage rides, which occurred no matter what the weather might be, and acting as her grandmother's constant companion, with very little time to herself, although she managed to have at least one swimming lesson in the Osborne floating pool, which she found frightening at first but quickly began to enjoy. 'I have just returned from a solitary drive with Granny,' she wrote to Nicholas after one excursion with Victoria. 'She was talkative until a dreadful spasm of pain came on, which made her pale, and cry. She says she can't help it, it gets on her nerves when the pain is so great. I rubbed her leg for a quarter of an hour and then it got better by degrees. Poor dear, it is horrid seeing her suffer so. I am young so it does not matter so, suffering pain. I daresay it is even good to have to bear pain – but she, an old lady, that is hard, and it makes one sad to see it, and it frightens me… Granny dictated her diary to me this afternoon, she wanted me to do it so much again… She makes notes every day, but so indistinctly that she can scarcely read them herself.'[43] Although her wedding date had not yet been set and looked to be several months away, it would have occurred to both of them that this might well be the last such visit and that the next time they met, Alix would be a married woman with a rank and status that made it no longer appropriate for her to be at her grandmother's beck and call while Victoria's pre-eminent position in her life as guardian, protector and advisor would be taken by Nicholas. When Alix finally returned to Darmstadt on the last day of July, both were deeply upset by this parting, which might be the last time they saw each other for quite some time. 'Took leave with the greatest regret of Alicky, whom I had watched over ever since May,'[44] Victoria wrote in her journal that evening after Alix had taken her leave with her sister Princess Victoria and her husband Louis on the royal yacht *Victoria and Albert*, which was to take them directly to Flushing in the Netherlands.

It was a strange homecoming for Alix as Victoria Melita was now not only fully installed as the new Grand Duchess, but she was also pregnant with her first child. However, now that Alix was engaged and would not have to live with her brother and his wife for very long, she was able to put her dislike of her sister-in-law aside and the pair got along very well. The trio spent that summer at the family's country residence, Schloss Wolfsgarten, near Frankfurt, which had been a great favourite with Alix and Ernie since they were children. There, they played tennis, went for walks in the lovely gardens or simply lazed about reading books either alone or to each other. Seeing Ernie and Victoria Melita together made Alix miss Nicholas and the happy times that they had shared in England desperately though. 'It does one good to see how they love each other, but it makes me greedily long for you,'[45] she wrote on 4 August. Two days later, Nicholas' sister Xenia married Grand Duke Alexander

Mikhailovich (known by everyone as 'Sandro') in the chapel of the Peterhof Palace. Nicholas had hoped that Alix would be able to attend the opulent ceremony but unfortunately she was not able to be there, although her aunt Alexandra, Princess of Wales, who was also aunt of the bride, made the trip to Russia for the occasion and provoked great admiration from Nicholas' cousin Grand Duke Konstantin, who wrote in his diary that 'she is fifty one years old but looks thirty'.[46] The wedding day was a great success but the groom and more than one guest could not help but notice how tired and unwell the Emperor, usually the very epitome of rude good health and vigour, looked. 'Poor Papa is in very low spirits having to give himself up into the hands of the doctors, which is of itself a bore, not always, alas, to be avoided,' Nicholas wrote to Alix a few days later. 'He feels it more than the others do, having been ill only twice in his life – twenty two years ago, and this winter!'[47] Although at first everyone was optimistic that the Emperor would make a swift recovery, by the end of September it had become increasingly clear that he was gravely ill. His family hoped that moving him to the more temperate climate of the Crimea would help him regain his strength but to their dismay, he collapsed shortly after arriving at Livadia Palace there, worn out by the exertion of travelling, and his condition deteriorated even more than ever.

Nicholas had hoped to visit Alix in Darmstadt that autumn but after much internal wrangling decided instead to accompany his parents to the Livadia Palace. 'You will understand that I could not do otherwise than to sacrifice my own happiness for some time,' he wrote to Alix once the decision had been made, clearly miserable not to be seeing her as quickly as he had hoped. 'Of course, it is too hard, not to be able to fly over to you. I could not do otherwise than this, my decision that I had taken after a whole day's violent struggle, as a devoted son and my father's first faithful servant – I have to be with him wherever he needs me.'[48] Although the Tsar's family publicly made light of the situation, the fact that Nicholas had cancelled his plans to visit Alix alerted Victoria to the fact that matters might well have taken a serious turn, although at the same time she dismissed newspaper accounts of Alexander's illness as 'exaggerated'.[49] However, as the days went by and the Emperor's condition steadily worsened, everyone was forced to accept the fact that he might very well not recover. By 17 October, the situation had become so grave that Nicholas' parents gave permission for him to send for Alix so that she could support him and receive Alexander's blessing before he passed away. At first it was decided that Ernie would take his sister to Odessa, where she would be met by Ella, but then the plan changed and it was decided that her sister Victoria would take her to Warsaw instead. In faraway Balmoral, Victoria was kept fully up to date with developments and was filled with anxiety about Alix, who set out on her epic journey from Darmstadt to the Crimea on 18 October. 'If only the long journey and great (emotional stress) do not hurt poor darling Alicky, who already has had so much to go through and it will be so trying besides the fatigue,' she wrote to Princess Victoria. 'It makes me very anxious and unhappy! All my fears about her future marriage now show themselves so strongly and my blood runs cold when I think of her *so* young most likely placed on that very unsafe throne, her dear life and above all her husband's constantly threatened and unable to see her but rarely; it is a great additional anxiety in my declining years! Oh, how I wish it was not to be that I should lose my sweet Alicky. All I most earnestly ask now is that nothing should be settled for her future without my being told before. She has no parents and I am her only grandparent and feel I have a claim on her! She is like my own child as you all are my dear children but she and he are orphans... Do explain what I have said to Nicky and also to both that I do pray that (at any time) she will come to see me once more before she marries. Do, do that. I feel as if she was being carried off already.'[50]

When Alix arrived in the Crimea, she was immediately taken to see the dying Tsar, who had insisted upon struggling out of bed and dressing in full uniform in order to greet her, although the effort completely exhausted him. For the next few days there was little that they could do but wait and send daily telegrams to Victoria, who was anxiously waiting for news in Scotland. On 30 October, she was 'much startled at getting a telegram from Bertie saying that the news being worse from Livadia and Minnie having earnestly entreated them to come, they were starting tomorrow morning at eight... Heard from Nicky and Alice that the poor Emperor had slept less and was weaker.'[51] They set out for the Crimea the following morning, but it was too late for Alexander III passed away on

1 November. 'He died as he lived, a bitter enemy of resounding phrases, a confirmed hater of melodrama,' his new son-in-law Sandro recalled in his memoirs. 'Just muttered a short prayer and kissed his wife.'[52] Nicholas' terrible grief was mixed with horror as it dawned upon him that the great responsibilities that his father had so unwillingly and yet capably shouldered had now fallen upon him. He was just twenty-six years old and was now ruler of one of the greatest empires that the world had ever seen, comprising around 14 million square miles and containing over 125 million people. 'My God, my God, what a day,' he wrote in his journal that evening. 'The Lord has called unto Him our adored, dearly beloved Papa. My head is going round, I cannot believe it – it seems inconceivable, a terrible reality.'[53] His brother-in-law Sandro later recalled in his memoirs that after the Tsar's death, Nicholas, overwhelmed by the enormity of what had happened, wept terribly. 'He could not collect his thoughts,' he wrote in his memoirs. 'He knew he was the Emperor now and the weight of this terrifying fact crushed him. "Sandro, what am I going to do," he exclaimed pathetically. "What is going to happen to me, to you, to Xenia, to Alix, to mother, to all of Russia? I am not prepared to be a Tsar. I never wanted to become one. I know nothing of the business of ruling. I have no idea of even how to talk to the ministers.'[54]

The news arrived at Balmoral while Victoria was having her daily carriage ride around the estate. 'Though it was to be expected for some time past that the illness must terminate fatally, the news seemed almost incredible and very sad,' she wrote in her journal that evening. 'Almost directly afterwards had a telegram from Alicky and Nicky, as follows: "Dearest beloved father has been taken from us. He gently went to sleep." Poor Minny, how my heart bleeds for her and poor dear Nicky and darling Alicky. May God help them all! What a terrible load of responsibility and anxiety has been laid upon the poor children! I had hoped and trusted they would have many years of comparative quiet and happiness before ascending this thorny throne.'[55]

Chapter Ten

'Tomorrow, poor Alicky's fate will be sealed.'

1894–1896

The day after Alexander's death, Alix was formally received into the Russian Orthodox Church in a quiet ceremony in the Livadia Palace chapel and would be known by the name Alexandra Feodorovna from this point onward. The couple had hoped to marry quietly in Livadia before making the journey back to St Petersburg but were persuaded out of it by Nicholas' uncles, Sergei and Vladimir, who convinced him that it would be better to wait until after his father's funeral. 'To me this seems quite unfitting!'[1] Nicholas privately protested in his journal but he nonetheless acquiesced. Alix's affectionate and caring presence was a great comfort but even so he was preoccupied with his grief and dread of what the future held. His father had postponed teaching him statecraft until it was too late and now he had absolutely no idea what to do. He was not exaggerating when he told Sandro that he didn't even have any idea how to speak to his own ministers and he could not help but feel apprehensive about what his new duties would entail. Although, like virtually everyone else, he heartily disliked Alix's overbearing cousin Wilhelm, he was nonetheless one of the very few people who could appreciate some of Nicholas' feelings in the aftermath of his father's death and his letter of condolence, which offered friendship and support, must have been a comfort to the young Tsar. 'The heavy and responsible task for which Providence has destined you has come upon you with the suddenness of a surprise, through the unexpected and untimely death of your dear lamented father,' Wilhelm wrote. 'These lines are to express my fullest and warmest sympathy with you and your Alix and your poor distressed mother. I can well understand the feelings which must have agitated your heart in witnessing the ebbing away of the life of your father, as his illness and sudden passing away were so very like my own dear Papa's… My prayers to God for you and your happiness are unceasing. May Heaven comfort you in your grief and give you strength for your heavy duties, and may a long and peaceful reign give you the opportunity of looking after the welfare of your subjects... As for me, you will always find me the same in undiminished friendship and love to you.'[2]

The other person who could appreciate the unique difficulties that faced Nicholas was Alix's grandmother, Victoria. She too had come to the throne at a young age and had felt completely unprepared for the task ahead, although unlike Nicholas she had also had to battle against chauvinistic prejudice against her gender. 'They wish to treat me like a little girl but I will show them that I am Queen of England,' Victoria had declared shortly after succeeding to the throne in 1839 and it was this self-assurance and courage that had triumphantly carried her through the many crisis that had marred the early years of her reign. Nicholas' problem was not just that he had not been blessed with an abundance of either of these qualities, but that everyone else around him knew it and felt just as apprehensive about the future. Like her grandson Wilhelm, Victoria wasted very little time before writing to offer her condolences to Nicholas. 'I can hardly express all my feelings in writing to you my dearest (future) grandson. The best I can find are comprised in "God bless you",' she wrote from Balmoral Castle. 'May He indeed bless, protect and guide you in your very responsible and very high position in which it has pleased Him to place you when still so young! May our two countries ever be friends, and may you be as great a lover of peace as your dear father was! What terribly sad scenes you must have gone through, loving your father as I know you did! I am thankful, darling Alicky was with you through this trying time of sorrow, tho' I can't help fearing she will feel the reaction afterwards... You *will* understand, I am sure, how very much disappointed and distressed I am not to see beloved Alicky, who is like my own child, once more before she marries, but I feel it could not be otherwise; and I hope and trust we may meet next year.'[3] It had long been Victoria's custom to spend time with each of her granddaughters before their marriage and naturally, as Alix was such a favourite, she had been especially keen to have her all to herself for a few weeks that winter before she embarked on married life. The news, which arrived via telegrams from Alix and Ella, that Alix and Nicholas intended to marry before the end of the month rather than waiting until the following spring as she had hoped, therefore distressed her very much. 'When I heard it by telegraph… it gave me a dreadful shock for tho' I dreaded it would be so I hoped against hope,' she complained to Alix's eldest sister Victoria. 'I cannot deny that it is impossible it should be otherwise and that it is best for darling Alicky – she would fret and worry away from Nicky – and her position at home or with us would be very difficult. And lastly it is a great advantage for her that she should begin her life there quietly and the wedding be very quiet. Still the disappointment of not seeing her again as my *sweet* innocent *gentle* Alicky is *very very great* – for alas I am sure it will be then as a *mighty Empress*!! And *cela me revolte* to feel she has been taken *possession* of and carried away as it were by these Russians. I wish she had *not* gone to Livadia and yet that was also impossible!'[4]

Although Victoria would always have taken a great interest in the passing of the ruler of Russia, the fact that his successor was engaged to her granddaughter and therefore very nearly a part of her own family, naturally made her feel personally involved. Alix was constantly on her mind in the aftermath of Alexander's death and she sent daily telegrams to the stunned and bewildered young couple, offering condolences, advice and affection. Nicholas was particularly touched by the queen's solicitude and kindness towards him and sat down to write a letter of thanks as soon as he had the opportunity. 'Dearest Grandmama, I am deeply grieved that it is impossible for Alicky to come and say goodbye before our wedding, to you – but, as Mama is probably going south soon the marriage has to be hastened with,' he added, aware that Victoria was deeply upset by the fact that they were due to marry so quickly. 'But be sure that as soon as we can find any possibility of crossing over to England to see you – we shall do it. God grant that day may come very soon… The one great comfort I have got in my utter misery – is my darling Alicky's deep love, that I return her fully.'[5]

On 8 November, Alix and the Imperial family accompanied the body of Alexander III on its final doleful journey back to St Petersburg, stopping in Moscow along the way. Travelling with them were the Prince and Princess of Wales, who had arrived a few days earlier, and who were proving to be a valuable source of support for both Alix and also Nicholas' mother, who was completely distraught. Once they were back in St Petersburg, Alix was disappointed to find that Nicholas now had barely any time spare to spend with her and that often they were only able to spend an hour or so together thanks to his royal duties and the preparations for his father's funeral. Alix was also kept busy preparing for her wedding, which necessitated an elaborate trousseau, including a magnificent wedding dress, which had to be made in record time in order to be ready. She was also spending a lot of time with her future mother-in-law Maria and although the two women had little in common, they grew temporarily close during this harrowing time – united by their grief and shared concern for Nicholas. Victoria had hoped to send Princess Beatrice to Russia to act as her representative at the wedding but the haste with which the ceremony was being planned precluded this, much to their disappointment. However, although Alix felt somewhat neglected by Nicholas in the weeks before her wedding, she had the support of Ella and Ernie, who had rushed from Darmstadt to be at her side. Also present was their mutual cousin George, Duke of York as well as Alix's uncle Prince Alfred, Duke of Saxe-Coburg Gotha, whose wife Marie was Nicholas' aunt – Marie could be difficult, snobbish and overbearing but she came into her own at times like this and was a great support to her deeply upset female relatives, who hardly knew what to do with themselves.

When Alexander III was laid to rest on 19 November, Victoria attended a memorial service at Windsor Castle, which was scheduled to begin at the exact same time as the funeral. 'The music was beautiful and a fine Russian hymn always sung at funerals throughout the Greek Church was sung without accompaniment and was very impressive,'[6] she wrote in her journal later on. Later that day, her daughter-in-law Marie sent her a telegram to say that the funeral had been 'most impressive' and that the dowager Empress Maria had 'bore up with remarkable fortitude'.[7] It was Alix who preyed on Victoria's mind though and that evening she thought constantly about her and wondered how she was feeling after what must have been an exhausting and stressful day, especially for someone as reserved and shy as Alix. As soon as the funeral was over, preparations for the royal wedding gathered pace and, by the 20th, work on Alix's silver-brocade wedding-dress had advanced enough for her sister Ella to draw two sketches of it, which she added to a letter to their grandmother, who was beside herself with worry as the wedding day approached and wished that she could have been there to support her granddaughter. 'Tomorrow, poor Alicky's fate will be sealed,' she wrote to her eldest daughter Vicky on the eve of the wedding. 'The dangers and responsibilities fill me with anxiety and I shall be constantly thinking of them with anxiety.'[8] She also felt protective of Nicholas and on 22 November wrote to him to thank him for the letters and telegrams that he had sent to her since his father's death and to express her great sympathy for the ordeal he must have suffered at his father's funeral. 'You must have gone through such terrible trying and harrowing scenes,' she wrote. 'The various processions, the whole journey – and the last fearful ordeal! How your poor dear Mama could go through it all is a marvel! All speak and write of your devotion to her and of your kindness and goodness to all! I need say nothing about your being a good husband to my darling Alix. I know how safe she is with you and how you will watch over her!... I fear it will be a sad wedding and yet a happy one for yourselves! God bless you, dearest Nicky.'[9] Perhaps the memory of Alix's parents' melancholy wedding ceremony was also on Victoria's mind at this time as she worried about the tragedy-tinged nuptials that were about to take place in Russia.

'My thoughts constantly with dear Alicky, whose wedding takes place today,' Victoria wrote in her journal on 26 November. 'I prayed most earnestly for her and felt so sad that I could not be with her.'[10] There is no doubt that her presence would have been most welcome as Alix tearfully prepared for her big day on that icy cold morning in St Petersburg. She spent her last night as an unmarried woman in her usual bedchamber in Ella and Sergei's Beloselsky-Belozersky Palace before making her way to the Winter Palace, where she was dressed for her wedding in the Malachite Drawing Room, with her future mother-in-law adding the final touch of the diamond nuptial crown worn by all Romanov brides, which was placed carefully on the beautiful lace wedding veil that had first been worn by her mother Princess Alice and then by all of her sisters. Although the court was still officially in mourning for Alexander III, the decision to hold the wedding on Empress Maria's birthday meant that etiquette could be relaxed and the court ladies could appear in pale silk gowns and their most dazzling jewels so that the wedding procession made an impressively splendid sight as it slowly made its way past the 8,000 courtiers who lined the route as Nicholas and Alexandra walked through the state apartments of the Winter Palace to the chapel where they were to be married at last. Although she would ordinarily have some stiff competition from some of the beauties at the Russian court, Alix was generally agreed to be by far the most lovely woman there. '"How beautiful she is!" That exclamation followed her all along her path and it is true that her appearance was positively magnificent as she stood there in her bridal array of silver cloth and old lace,' one guest recalled later on. 'Her unusual height helped her to bear the weight of her dress and set off its splendour in its best light. Her mouth quivered a little, and this relieved her habitual hard expression that was the one defect of an otherwise perfectly beautiful face, the straight classical features of which reminded one of an antique Greek statue. The glow upon her cheeks only added to the loveliness of her countenance and her eyes, modestly lowered, gave to her whole figure a maidenly shyness that made it wonderfully attractive.'[11] When the ceremony was over, the couple changed out of their heavy wedding apparel and climbed into a carriage, which took them to the Anichkov Palace, which was still the chief residence of Nicholas' mother, the Dowager Empress, who awaited them in their rooms with the traditional Russian welcome gift of bread and salt. It was to be a quiet wedding night. 'We sat the whole evening answering telegrams,' Nicholas wrote in his journal. 'We dined at 8 o' clock and went to bed early as she had a bad headache!'[12]

Far away at Windsor Castle, Queen Victoria was being kept updated throughout the day by a regular stream of telegrams from various family members at the wedding, beginning with one from Alix herself, who sent one in the morning before setting off for the ceremony. 'Heard from Bertie that the wedding was just over and had gone off extremely well,' she wrote in her journal that evening. 'Alicky looked lovely. Soon after got a telegram… and others from Marie and Alix, saying what a trying ceremony it had been and that darling Alicky had looked "too wonderfully lovely." Oh, how I wish I had been there.'[13] While Alix and Nicholas enjoyed the first private supper of their married life together, Victoria was holding a grand dinner party in honour of their wedding in the state dining room at Windsor Castle. 'I proposed the healths of Nicky and Alicky in the following words: "I wish to propose the healths of their

Majesties the Emperor and Empress of Russia, my dear grandchildren"
and I stood, whilst the Russian anthem was played. How I thought of
Darling Alicky and how impossible it seemed that that gentle simple
little Alicky should be the great Empress of Russia!'[14] The evening
ended with a final telegram, this time from Nicholas, who was beside
himself with astonishment and delight at Victoria's wedding present –
she had made him Colonel in Chief of the Scots Greys after noting his
particular admiration of this regiment during their visit to Aldershot
earlier that year. 'Words fail me to express to you how deeply thankful
I am to you for appointing me… The wedding went off well. Dearest
Alicky not tired, tender love from us both.'[15] A few days later, Victoria
would receive Alix's heartfelt thanks for her own wedding presents,
which had been rather less exciting but nonetheless welcome. 'How can
I ever thank you enough for your sweet letter with good wishes and
blessings, for the lovely presents. The pendant with your dear portrait
is *too* beautiful and I shall prize it very much – the lovely ring I wore for
the wedding and ever since, and when I look at it I have to think of the
beloved giver. The stuffs, shawls and cape are charming and will be most
useful – alas I shall long not be able to have the dresses made up.'[16] The
rest of the letter, Alix's first to her grandmother since her wedding, is
indicative of the delirious happiness that she felt now that she was finally
married to Nicholas at long last. 'It is a comfort being married. I can be
more with him and try and comfort and help him in all. He is so awfully
good and dear to me, and my great love for him increases daily. We
both are so intensely happy you gave him that splendid regiment and so
deeply touched your having thought of giving him that great pleasure…
I shall send you some of the myrtle and orange blossom I wore at the
wedding, and a bit of the dress as soon as I can… Thanking you again for
all the kindness you expressed in your dear letter and for the presents, I
remain, beloved Grandmama dear, your ever deeply devoted and dutiful,
loving child… We were immensely touched that you gave a dinner the
day of our wedding.'[17] Thwarted in her desire to see her beloved Alicky
married at last, Victoria had decided to commission the Danish artist
Laurits Tuxen to travel to St Petersburg in order to paint the wedding
(he sat with the choir during the service, which provided him with an
excellent vantage point as he made his preparatory sketches) and hung

the finished work, which depicts Alix and Nicholas standing together, candles in their hands, as the Metropolitan Archbishop of St Petersburg makes the sign of the cross over them, in Osborne House.

Sadly, despite the fact that they both hoped to be reunited as soon as possible, Alix and her grandmother would not see each other again for almost two years, during which time she would become a mother herself. Their affectionate correspondence continued, however, with Alix assuring Victoria of her happiness and contentment, while her grandmother kept her up to date with all the family news, which involved the usual endless round of engagements, births and deaths. 'I am lying on the sopha (sic) after having been for a delightful walk with Nicky in the park,' one of Alix's early letters to Victoria began. 'He is sitting near me and reading through his papers... I never can thank God enough for having given me such a husband – and his love to you touches me also so deeply, for have you not been as a mother to me, since beloved Mama died... I always wear your pretty ring. But now I must say goodbye, beloved Grandmama. Kissing your hand most tenderly... Nicky sends his best love.'[18] Both Alix and Nicholas felt cast adrift and apprehensive as they adjusted to their new life and although Nicholas' mother was still alive and close enough to offer help if they needed it, they naturally turned to Victoria, who was not just their beloved 'granny' but also the most experienced ruler in Europe, for advice and support – both of which she willingly gave. In exchange, Victoria felt able to gently remonstrate when articles critical of England appeared in the Russian press, prompting Nicholas to protest that: 'I must say that I cannot prevent people from putting their opinions openly in the newspapers. How often have I not been worried to read in English gazettes rather unjust statements in connection with my country! Even books are being constantly sent to me from London, misinterpreting our actions in Asia, our interior politics etc. I am sure there is as little hostility intended in these writings, as there is in the above mentioned ones.'[19] The always uneasy relations between Britain and Russia may have been slightly improved by Nicholas and Alix's marriage but ultimately, the two great nations still regarded each other with suspicious distrust – which was exacerbated in January 1895 when Nicholas gave a speech denouncing those who sought a more democratic, liberal regime as 'carried away by senseless dreams of taking part in the business of government' before affirming that he would 'retain the principles of autocracy as firmly and unbendingly as my unforgettable late father,'[20] quashing the hopes of all those who had hoped that the new young Tsar would be less conservative than his father and prompting the disappointed Victoria, who was naturally concerned that this repressive approach would provoke another wave of assassination attempts, to write to his sister-in-law Princess Victoria that 'I regret Nicky's speech the other day which is contrary to the way he began.'[21] Her fears for Alix were not assuaged by Ella, who wrote to reassure their grandmother that if only she could see for herself just how popular Alix and Nicholas were with their people and how loved they were in Russia, 'it would be a true comfort to you as I see you are worrying about them'.

By spring 1895, Alix was pregnant with her first child – an anxious and exciting time for any newly-married couple. Victoria was convinced of the superiority of British doctors when it came to childbirth and would recommend them whenever any of her female relatives were pregnant, becoming quite irate if they decided to use German doctors instead. The traumatic first labour of her eldest daughter Vicky, which had been presided over by a German doctor and resulted in the injury of her son Wilhelm, had only increased Victoria's prejudice. The fact that Alix was planning to use the Imperial midwife Madame Günst and Dr Dmitri Ott, who was favoured by the Romanov family rather than her own favoured British practitioners, appalled Victoria who confided to Alix's eldest sister in October that as the time for Alix's confinement grew closer she was feeling 'very anxious all should go off well' before adding 'I dread that Russian doctor!'[22] However, she was very satisfied to learn that most of Alix's care during her pregnancy, which involved severe and protracted morning sickness, was carried out by the faithful Miss Orchard, who had been with her since childhood and accompanied her to Russia. As she grew increasingly unwieldly and uncomfortable, Alix was forced to spend much of her time resting on sofas, where she occupied herself reading books or planning the redecoration of her new home. She and Nicholas had decided to take over the apartments in the west wing of the stately Alexander Palace at Tsarskoe Selo, where they could be assured of complete privacy. Alix disliked St Petersburg society and, mainly due to her own loneliness and sense of isolation, was becoming increasingly inclined to resent anyone or anything, including his state duties and those dreaded meetings with ministers, which prevented Nicholas from spending the majority of his time with her. She desperately missed the cosy, cheerful intimacy of the Neues Palais with its simple lemonwood furniture, pale-coloured walls, English style and lack of ostentation and determined to recreate it as much as possible for herself, Nicholas and their family. To the mingled consternation and amusement of their Romanov relatives as well as the court, who had already dismissed their new Empress as a boring and unsophisticated little nobody, Alix ignored the vast and opulent furniture reserves owned by the Imperial family and instead ordered the furnishings for their new home from Maples on Tottenham Court Road in London, just as her own mother had done, while the busily-floral wallpapers and chintz soft furnishings in the rooms were very definitely of the florid English style favoured by her grandmother Victoria in her private rooms in Windsor Castle and Osborne House. Just as her mother Princess Alice had once written about her own home in Darmstadt that 'the decoration and domestic arrangements are so English that it is hard to believe that one is in Germany,' so too was it a struggle to stand in Nicholas and Alix's apartments in the Alexander Palace and believe that you were actually in Russia rather than visiting an average middle-class residence in London filled with plants, family photographs, trinkets and clutter.

Alix's determination to recreate her own childhood did not end there, for she also planned to procure an English nurse for her baby, although the process turned out to be trickier than she had anticipated. 'If I can only find a good one,' she complained to her sister-in-law Xenia, who had also recently given birth to her first child, Irina. 'They mostly dread going so far away, and have extraordinary ideas about the wild Russians and I don't know what other nonsense – the nursery maid will of course be a Russian.'[23] Until a proper nurse could be found, the nursery would be presided over by Alix's own former nanny, her beloved 'Orchie'. Although the baby had been expected to arrive in the middle of October, Alix's pregnancy dragged on until the beginning of November, much to her despair. 'Baby won't come,' she wrote miserably to her brother Ernie. 'It is at the door but has not yet wished to appear and I do so terribly long for it.'[24] To everyone's relief, she finally went into labour in the early hours of 15 November and after a protracted and stressful twenty-hour labour that had ended with a forceps delivery, gave birth to a 10lb daughter at 9 pm. 'A day I will remember forever, during which I suffered a great deal,'[25] a dazed and delighted Nicholas wrote in his journal that evening after sending off a telegram to Victoria, who was anxiously awaiting news as she travelled down from Balmoral to Windsor Castle. 'Darling Alix has just given birth to a lovely enormous little daughter, Olga; My joy is beyond words. Mother and child doing well.'[26] Nicholas was entranced by his baby daughter and for the next few months could write about very little else in his journal, while his family letters became exceedingly dull as he regaled his mother and siblings with details of Olga's progress. To Victoria's dismay, Alix decided to breastfeed her daughter herself, although a Russian wet nurse was also hired for times when she was not available. To everyone's amusement, although she initially struggled to get Olga to latch on, she easily managed to breastfeed the wet nurse's son, which Nicholas deemed to be 'very funny!'[27] Fully aware of Victoria's disapproval, when Nicholas wrote to her after Olga's birth, he made a point of informing her that Alix 'finds such a pleasure in nursing our sweet baby herself. For my part I consider it the most natural thing a mother can do and I think the example an excellent one!'[28] Both he and Alix had been very touched as always by Victoria's interest in them and so it was only natural that they invited her to be one of their daughter's godmothers when she was christened on their wedding anniversary, 26 November. 'We are both so pleased that you accepted to be godmother of our first child, because I am sure it will provide a happiness to her after your constant signs of kindness and of motherly affection towards us,'[29] Nicholas wrote to Victoria, before assuring her that he was in a 'state of utter happiness' and promising to send a lock of the baby's hair to her as soon as possible.

As Alix didn't have much luck finding an English nanny for her baby, her grandmother Victoria took over and after reviewing several candidates, settled upon the highly-experienced Mrs Inman, who was duly despatched from England and arrived at Tsarskoe Selo in December. Both Alix and Nicholas took an immediate dislike to her, but felt unable to dismiss her without causing offence to Victoria. 'Yesterday a nanny arrived from England, whom we do not particularly like the look of,' Nicholas complained to his younger brother Georgy. 'She has something hard and unpleasant in her face and looks like a stubborn woman. In general she's going to be a lot of trouble and I am ready to bet that things are not going to go smoothly. For instance, she has already decided that our daughter does not have enough rooms, and that, in her opinion, Alix pops into the nursery too often. How do you like that?'[30] Meanwhile, Alix was venting her annoyance about Mrs Inman to her own favourite confidante, her brother Ernie. 'I am not at all enchanted with the nurse,' she told him. 'She is good and kind with Baby, but as a woman most antipathetic, and that disturbs me sorely. Her manners are neither very nice, and she will mimic people in speaking about them, an odious habit, which would be awful for a child to learn… I foresee no end of troubles.'[31] Unfortunately, although they both heartily detested Mrs Inman and longed to dismiss her, they were unable to do so until the following May, at which point she would be replaced by the far more congenial Mrs Coster.

Although Alix and Nicholas longed to remain cocooned in their new home forever, at the end of the year they were forced to return to St Petersburg and the very different ambience of the Winter Palace in order to preside over the court's winter season, which involved an endless calendar of balls, formal receptions, concerts and parties. Alix absolutely loathed being on show, especially now that she was sure that the Russian aristocracy disliked her, and although Nicholas was far more outgoing, under her influence he too was becoming remote and disinclined to socialise, which dismayed his family and advisors. For now though their happy family life could continue as before, with Alix giving Olga her daily breastfeed while drinking her morning coffee and Nicholas bathing the baby in the evening, but as their coronation, which was scheduled to take place in Moscow on 26 May, approached, changes had to be made and Alix was reluctantly forced to give up breastfeeding, while Nicholas, who regarded the coronation as a 'great trial sent to us by God',[32] could not spend as much time as he would have liked with his family. Both he and Alix were immensely relieved when the coronation had taken place, but still had to endure over a week of official celebrations, which left them both exhausted. To make matters worse, four days after the ceremony, a public banquet at the Khodynka Meadow, on the outskirts of Moscow, ended in tragedy when a rumour spread through the enormous crowd of attendees that there wasn't enough food to go around, which resulted in a stampede which left over 1,300 people dead and around the same amount seriously injured. Nicholas was horrified and wanted to cancel his attendance at a ball to be held at the French Embassy that evening but his uncles Vladimir and Sergei, who bullied him relentlessly, persuaded him that it would be a fatal error to offend the French and so he very unwillingly went, which meant offending his own people, who saw his behaviour as frivolous and uncaring – not knowing that he had wanted to leave after half an hour and had had to be bullied by his uncles into staying for longer. When Victoria learned of the incident, she was horrified, not just by the scale of the 'most horrible and ghastly catastrophe',[33] which the British newspapers blamed upon poor management on the part of the organisers, in particular Ella's husband Sergei, who was Governor General of Moscow and had appeared to behave with an almost callous indifference that deeply distressed many members of his own family, but also Nicholas' decision to go to a ball that evening, which she believed looked 'unfeeling'.[34] As always, she was also extremely worried about Alix's reputation and safety in the aftermath of the tragedy, writing in her journal that: 'The papers say that the people of Moscow are showing signs of anger and exasperation at the frightful mismanagement of the authorities. It makes me anxious.'[35]

To Queen Victoria's great delight, in the summer of 1896, Alix informed her that it might be possible for them to make the long-wished-for visit to Britain as part of a general tour of Europe that autumn. As they were already scheduled to visit Denmark and France then it made sense for them to come to Victoria in between, if only for just over a week. Not only that, but to Victoria's happiness, they would also be bringing their baby Olga with them for the trip – although Nicholas was rather less pleased by the prospect. 'First of all we are going to Austria, then Kiev, Germany, Denmark, England, France and finally Darmstadt... An attractive prospect, don't you think?' he wrote to his brother Georgy. 'On top of it, we shall have to drag our poor little daughter with us, as all the relatives want to see her.'[36] In many ways though, Olga's presence turned out to be a blessing, not just because it meant that her parents could see her every day (at almost the same age, the current queen, while Princess Elizabeth of York, was left behind with her grandparents while her parents were away on a Royal Tour for several months) but because the presence of the baby Grand Duchess, who was an exceedingly adorable infant, did much to compensate for the social awkwardness of her parents, who caused offence more than once over the course of the tour by not engaging with well-wishers or appearing frosty and uninterested when actually they were just shy and exhausted. Lady Lytton, Queen Victoria's Lady of the Bedchamber, was able to observe the young couple during their stay in Scotland and recorded that: 'The Emperor very shyly whispered a few words of thanks but he ought to learn to do this sort of thing better. She smiles but neither of them takes trouble enough to bow to all assembled as our Queen did SO well.'[37] About little Olga, however, she had nothing but praise. 'Oh you never saw such a darling as she is... a very broad face, very fat, in a lovely high St Joshua baby bonnet – but with bright intelligent eyes, a wee mouth and so happy and contented the whole day... bursting with life and happiness and a perfect knowledge how to behave.'[38]

On the morning of Tuesday, 22 September, word arrived at Balmoral that the imperial yacht *Standart* was within sight of Leith, a port to the north of Edinburgh, where it docked just before 10 am. Although Victoria had wanted the Tsar's arrival to be as low-key as possible to reflect the private nature of the visit, her son Bertie, who headed the welcoming committee at Leith, disagreed and so Alix and Nicky were welcomed to Scotland by a flotilla of small boats, several battleships and a twenty-one gun salute. Compared to Alix's previous trips to Scotland, it must have been a most surreal and strange moment to be welcomed back with so much fuss and fanfare – neither of which she welcomed. However, her embarrassment was quickly dispelled by the sight of her uncles Bertie and Arthur, Duke of Connaught, coming towards them on the ship's tender. In honour of the occasion, Bertie had squeezed himself into a Russian dragoon uniform, while Nicholas wore his Scots Greys uniform, which he loved but made him feel awkward on this occasion as he considered it 'unpleasant'[39] to leave his own crew while wearing the uniform of a foreign regiment. Although Alix was keen to be reunited with her beloved Grandmama, they did not leave immediately but instead had luncheon onboard the *Standart* before going to shore on the tender. The weather was shockingly bad even by Scottish standards, which cast a damper on proceedings although everyone nonetheless bravely soldiered through the official welcome from the Lord Provost on the dock, after which they were taken to Leith railway station where they could thankfully clamber into their train for the journey up to Balmoral. Although every effort had been made to ensure their comfort, the long train journey up to Aberdeenshire, which took them across the Forth Bridge and through Dundee, Arbroath and Aberdeen, was still fairly miserable with Nicholas describing it in his journal as 'cold, drizzling, shivering on the train'.[40] His mood did not improve when they finally arrived at Ballater station, where their cousin George was valiantly waiting for them, to be greeted by torrential rain and the prospect of an 8-mile journey to the castle by open carriage.

As they neared Balmoral Castle, the church bells began to ring and beacons were lit on the hills overlooking the estate, alerting Victoria, who was anxiously awaiting them, that they were near. 'Punctually, at 8, the procession reached the door,' Victoria recalled in her journal. 'The escort of Scots Greys came first, then the pipers and torch bearers, and finally the carriage containing Nicky, Alicky, Bertie and Arthur. I was standing at the door and Nicky got out first, whom I embraced, and then darling Alicky, all in white, looking so well, whom I likewise embraced most tenderly.'[41] It was the first time that they had seen each other since their visit in the summer of 1894 and Nicholas was able to report to his mother later that as always 'Granny' was 'marvellously kind and amiable to us'[42] and that he didn't 'think her much changed except that she seemed a little smaller'.[43] He had wanted to visit Balmoral Castle for quite some time, having heard so much about it thanks to Alix that, according to the British Ambassador to Russia, 'he felt as if he were quite familiar with its beautiful surroundings'.[44] Sadly, the rain and lateness of the hour meant that he did not see the castle at its best that evening but Victoria hoped that once the weather had brightened, he would love it just as much as she did, no doubt recalling how much Alix's father had enjoyed his visits there over the years. Nicholas would have had an opportunity to survey his surroundings as the family gathered in the drawing room, where they were joined by Olga, who was much admired by her great grandmother. 'The dear baby was then brought in, a most beautiful child and so big,'[45] Victoria wrote in her journal. Olga was not yet eleven months old and already weighed over 30lbs, much to the pride of her parents. 'The baby is magnificent,'[46] Victoria wrote approvingly to her eldest daughter Vicky after the visit, adding that she was bigger than Alix and Ella ever were and was a 'lovely lively' great-grandchild. After Olga had been admired by everyone, she was whisked away to the nursery while the adults prepared for dinner, which was a family affair taken in the castle's dining room. 'It seems quite like a dream having dear Alicky and Nicky here,'[47] Victoria wrote in her journal that evening, obviously very pleased and contented to have them restored to her again, albeit for just ten days.

The following morning, Victoria was delighted when Alix joined her for breakfast, just as she had always done in the past and even more pleased when the 'dear sweet Baby was brought in'[48] to see them. Although the royal children were not considered mature enough to join the adults for dinner in the evening until they had been confirmed, Victoria always loved to have their company at breakfast, which was the most informal meal of the day, and even babies were welcome to join her – so long as they behaved themselves. It had once amused Nicholas very much that Victoria's daily routine never seemed to change no matter whether she happened to be in residence at Windsor Castle or Osborne House and he was no doubt pleased to note that this was also true when she was at Balmoral where it was business as usual with daily carriage rides and luncheon lasting no more than half an hour. While he reluctantly braved the 'awful'[49] weather in order to go out shooting with Uncle Bertie and the other gentlemen, Alix accompanied her grandmother on her daily carriage ride, making the most of a brief pause in the heavy rainfall, which had kept the queen indoors all morning. The following day, however, he joined his wife and her grandmother on their carriage ride, during which Victoria spoke to him about the conflict between Turkey and Armenia and the possibility that Russia and Britain could work together to bring about peace between the two. Nicholas felt somewhat ambushed by Victoria but meekly agreed that 'he would see what he could do, although it was most difficult'.[50] As soon as he and Alix had become engaged, Victoria and some of her ministers had tended to regard the union, however unwelcome it might have been on a personal level, as akin to one of the great dynastic marriages that had always been a crucial feature of European politics, not quite grasping that as the nineteenth century drew to an end such matches held far less weight and significance than they had done a century earlier and that the union of Alix and Nicholas did not in fact translate to a stronger bond between Britain and Russia but rather highlighted and exacerbated the differences between the two. For Victoria, who had become the longest reigning English sovereign the previous day, it had seemed completely natural to corner Nicholas during a convivial carriage ride and ask him to intervene in a dispute between Turkey and Armenia, but the Russians did things very differently and he did not appreciate being put on the spot. Sadly for him, his attempts to avoid any future political discussions with Victoria for the rest of the visit were doomed to failure and he even found himself forced into two lengthy discussions with the Prime Minister, Lord Salisbury, much to his discomfiture although he still managed to assure Salisbury that he was deeply desirous that Russia should be on the best of terms with Britain and furthermore had no 'unfriendly intentions'[51] towards India. Meanwhile, his shooting excursions with Bertie were similarly uncomfortable because his uncle also kept drawing him into political discussions in an overbearing way that reminded the young Tsar of his Romanov uncles back in Russia, who were the bane of his life.

While her husband was doing his best to avoid political discussions, enduring hideous shooting expeditions with his uncle Bertie and complaining in his journal about the weather, which on 27 September was so bad that Victoria gloomily described it in her own diary as 'the most terrible pouring wet morning, with great darkness,'[52] Alix was very much enjoying the nostalgic pleasures of visiting Balmoral and being with her grandmother once again. While another woman of her age (Alix was just twenty-four years old) might have found the lifestyle at Balmoral intolerably slow and dull, Alix had very little complaints and as always was happy to act as Victoria's companion. It was also a pleasure to be able to show her own daughter around the Balmoral estate, although the poor weather meant that Olga spent most of her time indoors in the nursery, where she was introduced to her cousins David (the future Edward VIII), who was her father's godson, and Bertie (the future George VI), the sons of George and May, Duke and Duchess of York, who were staying at the nearby Glenmuick estate and frequently came over for lunch or dinner. Their eldest son David, who was third in line to the throne, was another great favourite with Victoria, who noted in her journal that he was 'a most attractive little boy and so forward and clever'.[53] Much later on, there would be talk about David marrying one of his Russian cousins but if the thought occurred to Victoria on this occasion, she did not commit it to paper, although it was said that on one occasion when little David was patiently helping Olga toddle across the drawing room carpet, Victoria turned to Nicholas and stage-whispered that it was *La Belle Alliance*.[54] Alix's difficulties finding a suitable nanny for her daughter had not entirely abated after the welcome departure of Mrs Inman earlier that year as although she was happy with her replacement, Mrs Coster, she informed Lady Lytton that 'she cannot keep her'.[55] When she wasn't involved in domestic matters, Alix was also sitting for the artist Heinrich von Angeli, who had painted her twice before as a child, for a portrait commissioned by her grandmother. The original plan had been for Angeli to paint Nicholas as well but unfortunately they ran out of time and so Alix sits alone, serene but melancholy, in delicate white lace, a shimmering sautoir of pearls and with yellow roses pinned to the front of her gown.

On 29 September, Alix, Nicholas, Olga, Bertie and Victoria posed for a photograph that for many people epitomises the relationship between the British and Russian royal families at this time. In the centre of the photograph sits Victoria, her face turned towards the splendidly plump baby Olga, who sits on the lap of her mother. Even by the standards of Victorian photography, where almost everyone looks exceptionally grave, Alix looks sombre, even melancholy as she stares into the distance, while her husband, wearing his beautifully tailored Scots Greys uniform, gazes directly and earnestly into the camera. Uncle Bertie, looking faintly bemused as always, completes the composition, his confident manner and stocky build highlighting the nervous fragility of the young Tsar. If Nicholas looked decidedly sickly in the photograph then he had good reason for he was beginning to suffer from one of the terrible toothaches with which he was often afflicted due to his loathing of dentists. As if that wasn't bad enough, soon after the photograph had been taken, he was once again cornered by Lord Salisbury for yet another intense political discussion, which went rather less well than the last one as this time Nicholas had been primed by the Russian Ambassador, Baron Egorovich

Staal, to be less compliant and more than once changed the subject so that Salisbury went away feeling frustrated and rather annoyed. Like many of Nicholas' own relatives and ministers, he came to the conclusion that the young Tsar was dangerously weak and pliable, with a worrying tendency to parrot the opinions of whoever was fortunate or cunning enough to be the last person he had spoken to – which obviously had the potential to lead to disaster. The concerned Salisbury went off and related the whole conversation to Victoria who then made matters worse by bringing the subject up during that afternoon's excursion, while Alix and Nicholas were trapped in a carriage with her and could not escape. She had assured Salisbury that in her view, Nicholas' personal devotion to herself would ensure peace between their two nations but even so, she couldn't help but be alarmed by how impressionable Nicholas was.

Nicholas' toothache was much worse the following day and when he reluctantly allowed Victoria's physician, Dr James Reid to examine him, it was discovered that he had an infection around a decayed tooth, which required treatment with iodine. On the plus side, his toothache gave Nicholas an excuse to avoid going out shooting with the other gentlemen and instead he accompanied his wife and Victoria on a gentle carriage ride to visit his cousin Louise, Duchess of Fife at Mar Lodge, where they had lunch. When they returned to Balmoral Castle, Alix showed her jewellery collection to her grandmother, who noted in her journal later that 'she has quantities – all her own private property'.[56] This distinction between private and state jewels was important to Victoria, who was already beginning to think about the dispersal of her own significant jewellery collection after her death, with some less important pieces being earmarked for personal family bequests while other, more significant ones, were to be passed down to each successive queen after her as the property of the Crown. As Empress of Russia, Alix had access to some of the most extraordinary jewels in the world and although Victoria had admonished her after her engagement, when Nicholas was already beginning to shower her with dazzling gifts, not to 'get too proud', she revelled in her new wealth and could not help but enjoy this reversal in her fortunes – whereas once she had felt unable to afford to come to London for her cousin's wedding, now she had untold riches at her command and could afford to go wherever she chose. However, if Victoria had feared that Alix would be made unbearably proud and haughty by her new status, the visit to Balmoral at least reassured her that her granddaughter was much the same as always. Nonetheless, whereas Alix's stiff and distant manner had been acceptable when she was a mere Princess of Hesse, it was a little unbecoming for an Empress and Victoria, who had long since mastered the knack of engaging with great and small alike, took her granddaughter aside and gently advised her to smile more and make more of an effort to look friendly when meeting people. Her advice fell on deaf ears.

Nicholas missed dinner that evening because of his tooth but was feeling much better next morning, which meant that he was able to have breakfast with his wife and Victoria, after which they made the most of the beautiful weather by going for a drive up to Craig Gowan, where Victoria and Albert had celebrated the completion of their new castle at Balmoral by building a cairn of rough stones. After luncheon, 'the dear fat beautiful Baby was brought in as usual… and sat playing on the floor'.[57] Now that his tooth was feeling better and both Lord Salisbury and his uncle Bertie had departed, Nicholas' spirits noticeably rose and he enjoyed the last few days of their stay considerably more than the rest of their visit. The following day, he went stalking with Alix's uncle Prince Arthur, Duke of Connaught, while his wife accompanied her grandmother on her daily carriage drive, making it home just before it began to rain again. That evening, Victoria, who was completely captivated by her new great granddaughter, accompanied Olga's proud parents to the nursery in order to 'see the dear Baby in its bath'[58] adding in her journal that she was a 'splendid child and so full of life'.[59] After this, however, she took Nicholas off to her rooms for what would prove to be their final political discussion – this time she considered the results to be 'satisfactory'[60] and they parted on good terms as Nicholas now appeared to be in agreement with her about the issues in Turkey and also consented to act as an intermediary for Britain and France, whose relationship had become strained, during his state visit to Paris in a few days' time. The following day, 3 October, was Alix and Nicholas' last day at Balmoral and after breakfast, they commemorated the occasion by participating in the creation of a short film. 'At twelve went down to below the Terrace, near the Ball Room and were all photographed by Downey by the new cinematograph process, which makes moving pictures by winding off a reel of films,'

Victoria wrote in her journal. 'We were walking up and down and the children jumping about.'[61] The result is jerky and rather awkward but nonetheless curiously moving as Nicholas and Alix, looking not a little embarrassed, trot alongside Victoria's buggy. After this, Nicholas and Alix rather ineptly planted trees, which obviously occasioned a great deal of laughter, as the photographs of the occasion testify. Luckily there was time for another drive, this time to Invercauld and back via the Balloch Bhui, tea and then a family dinner before Alix and Nicholas finally took their leave of Victoria at the rather late hour of 10 pm – 'to my regret,' as Victoria noted later in her journal, 'as I am so fond of them both.'[62] She accompanied them to the door and remained there, a tiny, black-clad figure as they drove away past a long line of Highlanders bearing aloft flaming torches.

Although they hoped to be reunited again the following year, it was to be the last time that Alix and Victoria saw each other. 'It has been such a very short stay and I leave dear kind Grandmama with a heavy heart,' Alix wrote later to her former governess Miss Jackson. 'Who knows when we may meet again and where?'[63]

Chapter Eleven

'A dearer kinder being never was.'

1896–1901

'It seems so strange that all is over now, all our guests gone and the party in the house become quite small,' Victoria wrote in her journal a few days later. 'Everything passes so quickly, all is bustle, excitement and expectation, and then after a few days all is over and quiet again.'[1] The following day, Alix and Nicholas were welcomed to Paris by enormous cheering crowds, keen to celebrate the rapport between France and Russia – but if Victoria had truly expected Nicholas to speak on Britain's behalf during his stay in the French capital, she was to be disappointed, for he did no such thing. 'Kindly use your influence and let the French understand that you do not intend to support them in their constant inimicality towards England, which is the cause of much annoyance and difficulty to us,'[2] Victoria reminded him by letter. However, Nicholas was clearly not inclined to involve himself and completely failed to act, which disappointed her very much. 'Politics… are not the same as private or domestic affairs and they are not guided by personal or relationship feelings,'[3] Nicholas wrote to her from Darmstadt, after explaining his position on the matter. 'History is one's real positive teacher in these matters and for me personally, except that, I have always got the sacred example of my beloved father and also the result and proof of all his deeds!' As Victoria had been no great admirer of the autocratic, conservative and 'tyrannical' Alexander III, she was in no way comforted by Nicholas' determination to emulate his statesmanship as much as possible and must have wondered just how long the currently good relations between their own two nations would continue even if, for now at least, Nicholas still considered himself to be her 'most loving and devoted grandson'.

By the time she arrived back in Russia, Alix knew for certain that she was once again pregnant. She had loved her stay in Paris, which had involved sleeping in Marie Antoinette's own bedchamber at Versailles, and the quiet nineteen-day-long visit to her brother and sister-in-law in Darmstadt afterwards had been a most welcome respite before returning home to her duties as Empress. She kept in constant contact with Victoria during her travels, sending daily telegrams when she was too busy to write a proper letter, although she kept the news of her pregnancy to herself for longer than usual this time as she felt so desperately ill and was in severe pain from a sciatica flare up that forced her to spend several weeks in bed and miss the all-important winter season – which she did not regret in the least, but it did nothing for her aloof and unfriendly reputation with her husband's family and courtiers. At the same time, she was forced to deal with rumours that she and her sister Ella had had a falling out. When Ella learned that a fabricated story about her being so filled with envy for her youngest sister that she had refused to kiss her hand at the coronation had reached Victoria's ears, she had felt compelled to write and set the record straight, assuring her grandmother that she and Alix were as friendly as ever and that 'it was a real joy'[4] to see Alix crowned Empress for 'she being so much younger than I has always been more like a child than a sister' while in her view it was good that they lived in different cities for it would make Alix more independent. Not only that but the talk about Sergei's unpopularity in Moscow after the Khodynka tragedy was, according to Ella, completely untrue for 'although it sounds vain, people here like us and again proved their affection by receiving us most warmly when we arrived the other day here.' As for Alix, Ella was keen to assure Victoria that 'she is already dearly loved in her new home and it is for me the greatest joy'.[5] Although Victoria would have loved to have Alix and Nicholas in England for her Diamond Jubilee celebrations in June 1897, Alix's pregnancy made it impossible for them to attend, although they were there in spirit, having clubbed together with Ella, Sergei, Ernie, Ducky, Victoria and Louis to order the queen a beautiful diamond and sapphire Fabergé brooch, which took the form of a silver heart enclosing the number sixty in Slavonic characters with two large cabochon sapphires suspended underneath. Victoria loved it and wore it during the official celebrations, which touched Alix very much.

On 10 June 1897, Alix gave birth to a second daughter, Tatiana. Although Nicholas loyally referred to the event in his journal as 'the second bright happy day in our family life',[6] the reactions within their wider family were distinctly mixed, with many privately expressing disappointment that the new baby was not the much-longed-for son and heir to the Romanov throne. In England, Victoria was no less muted in her reaction, recording in her journal that she had 'received the good news that dear Alicky had given birth to another daughter, which is rather a disappointment, but both are doing well',[7] while to her daughter Beatrice, she wrote rather fatalistically that she had 'fully expected'[8] Alix to have another little girl. Once again, Victoria was horrified by Alix's decision to breastfeed her baby herself and expressed her disapproval to her eldest sister, Princess Victoria. 'I hear Alicky is grown very large. Does she still go on nursing? I think it a great mistake in her position.'[9] The reference to Alix's size might be due to the fact that there were rumours at the time that she was once again pregnant, although if this was indeed the case then the pregnancy would sadly come to an end before it was officially announced. Alix's cousin and friend, Princess Helena Victoria of Schleswig Holstein (known within the family as Thora) was visiting her in St Petersburg at the time and made no mention of Alix's pregnancy in her letters to Victoria, who was naturally keen to know about such matters as soon as possible and was especially anxious that Alix should produce a son. Victoria was still concerned that Alix and, to a lesser extent, Nicholas were not doing enough to endear themselves to their people and as a second winter season passed without the Empress making an appearance in St Petersburg, she put Thora on the spot by asking if it was true that they were rarely seen outside Tsarskoe Selo. Thora had been a good and loyal friend to Alix since childhood but like almost everyone else was far too much in awe of Victoria to lie and so did her best to ameliorate the truth. 'As to what you say about Alix and Nicky seeing so few people,' she responded. 'I think she quite knows how important it is she should get to know more of the society but the truth is she and Nicky are so absolutely happy together that they do not like to give up their evenings to receiving people.'[10] Meanwhile, when their aunt Marie, Duchess of Saxe-Coburg Gotha visited St Petersburg the following summer, she reported to one of her daughters that 'it seems that Nicky and Alix shut themselves up more than ever and never see a soul.'[11]

This was absolutely not good enough for Victoria – she too had been wildly happy with Albert but had nonetheless made a point of being seen by her courtiers and the wider populace as often as possible, while the births of nine children had not prevented her from presiding over court balls and making regular official appearances. She also understood now that her long reclusive period after Albert's death had seriously affected her popularity and also, more importantly, the stability of the crown and it deeply troubled her that Alix had seemingly already withdrawn from public life at a time when she should be highly visible. Her remonstrations fell on deaf ears though as Alix was highly reluctant to stray beyond the cosy, private family life that she had created for Nicholas and certainly had no desire to do so in order to mix with the Russian aristocrats who attended the dazzling balls and parties during the St Petersburg season. Her mother-in-law Minnie was very much at home with so much frivolity, gossip and extravagance, but Alix was repelled by it and resented any suggestions that she should leave her babies for the night in order to rub shoulders with people that she despised. Their dislike of her did not trouble her as much as it should have done either for she had convinced herself that the aristocracy were not 'true Russians' and their opinions did not matter at all so long as the Russian people themselves still loved their Emperor and Empress – which indeed they did, for now at least.

In the autumn of 1898, Nicholas was able to report to his mother that 'with God's help – we expect a new happy event next May'[12] but that as always Alix was very unwell and in need of complete peace and quiet, which meant that once again she would not be making any appearances in St Petersburg that winter. Like everyone else, Victoria was delighted by the news and most anxious that the new baby should be a boy as she feared for her granddaughter's already shaky popularity in Russia should it prove to be another girl. The correspondence between herself and Nicholas had tapered off considerably since his failure to act on Britain's behalf in France and although she remained confident that he would ultimately never work against British interests, still she feared that other influences might ruin the fragile relationship between their two nations. In particular, she was concerned that her grandson, Wilhelm II, was working behind the scenes to cause problems between them. In the middle of March 1899, Victoria felt compelled to pick up a pen and write to Nicholas about the subject in a letter which began by acknowledging how infrequently they now wrote to each other. 'It is ages since you wrote to me and I to you, but I am sure that you have not forgotten your old Grandmama who wishes much we could see each other again. I long to see darling Alicky so much,'[13] she began, before moving quickly on to the point. 'But I feel now there is *something* that I *must* tell you, which you *ought* to know and which perhaps you do *not*. It is, I am very sorry to say, that William takes *every* opportunity of impressing… that Russia is doing all in her power to work *against* us saying she offers Alliances to other powers and has made one with the Amir of Afghanistan against us!… I need not say that I do not believe a word of this… With many loves to dear Alicky and kisses to the little girls believe me always your devoted Grandmama.'[14] Nicholas' quick response was affectionate and reassuring. 'I thank you with all my heart for your kind letter which touched me deeply… I feel quite ashamed at not having written to you for such a long time and beg you to excuse me,' he began before moving on to the always thorny topic of Wilhelm. 'I am so happy you told me in that open way about William. Now I fully understand what he is up to – it is a dangerous double game he is playing at… I am very glad you did not believe the story of the alleged alliance between us and the Amir of Afghanistan, for there is not a syllable of truth in it. As you know dearest Grandmama, all I am striving at now is for the longest possible prolongation of peace in this world… All that Russia wants is to be left quiet and to develop her position in the sphere of interest which concerns her being so close to Siberia.'[15] Once the political matters were dealt with, he returned to more personal matters by informing Victoria that 'if all is well we should so much like to pay you a private visit at Balmoral with our babies this autumn; we hope this plan will suit you.'[16] Sadly this much-longed-for visit never happened.

Alix and Nicholas' third daughter, Maria, another bouncing ten pounder, was born after a very quick labour on 26 June 1899 and once again everyone's relief that mother and baby were well was tempered by disappointment that the new Imperial infant was not the much longed for son and heir. In England, Victoria's response to the announcement of the birth of a third Romanov great-granddaughter was phlegmatic: 'I am so thankful that dear Alicky has recovered so well, but I regret the third girl for the country.'[17] She did not note Maria's birth in her journal that day, although that is hardly surprising considering the fact that Victoria had long since begun to lose interest in her ever increasing brood of great-grandchildren, remarking that as they came at 'the rate of three a year, it becomes a cause of mere anxiety… and of no great interest'.[18] In Maria's case, she was mentioned in Victoria's journal for the first time at the end of June when Sir Charles Scott, the British Ambassador to St Petersburg, came to dinner at Windsor Castle and discussed this latest disappointment with her. 'He fears the Russians will be much disappointed at Alicky's having a third daughter,' Victoria wrote. 'He deplores very much they see so few people.'[19] This concern was echoed by Crown Princess Marie of Romania, who was a cousin of both Alix and Nicholas. 'Now I suppose she will have to begin over again and then once more she will shut herself up and it discontents everyone,'[20] she wrote to her formidable mother, Marie. Alix's long absences from St Petersburg and frosty demeanour whenever she was forced to appear in public were making her increasingly unpopular and no amount of remonstration from her grandmother or anyone else made any difference, so long as Nicholas was happy.

In the autumn of 1899, the British once again became embroiled in a conflict with the Boer states in South Africa, which developed into the second Boer War. Although Victoria expected Nicholas to be firmly on her side, he actually sympathised with the Boers, whom he regarded as 'a small people… desperately defending their country, a part of their land is devastated, their families flocked together in camps, their farms burnt… it looks more like a war of extermination.'[21] He later confided to his uncle Bertie that he had 'often wanted to write to dear Grandmama to ask her quite privately whether there was any possibility of stopping the war in South Africa. Yet I never wrote to her, fearing to hurt her and always hoping it would soon cease.'[22] When he wrote to her in May 1900, his only reference to the war was a fervent hope that she had 'less worries now'[23] about it along with the information that his own regiment, the Scots Greys had sent him a telegram from Kronstadt on his birthday, which 'astonished me and at the same time gave me great pleasure'.[24] Equally delightful was the birthday letter that he had received from Victoria, who never allowed a birthday, even those of her granddaughters' husbands, to pass without some sort of recognition. 'I cannot tell you how touched I was to receive your dear kind letter on the eve of my birthday,' Nicholas wrote. 'I thank you from the depth of my heart for all the love and great kindness you show me.'[25] Although the trip to Scotland the previous autumn had failed to happen, Alix and Nicholas were obviously still very keen to come and see Victoria as soon as possible for he added: 'You mentioned in your letter about the possibility of our meeting this year. That is our constant wish to come over to England and see you. This summer and autumn I am afraid will be taken up by the tiresome Shah of Persia and manoeuvres in different parts of Russia, But if there was a possibility of coming and seeing you we would be happy of doing so.'[26] Alix was sorely disappointed that they would not be able to go to England and even considered going by herself, which was quite unprecedented as she had hitherto been keen to remain as close to possible to Nicholas' side no matter what and suggests that she, who had been kept fully updated about Victoria's failing health, thought that time might well be running out for a reunion. 'My grandmother invites us to come to England, but now is certainly not the moment to be out of the country,' she wrote to Princess Bariatinsky in July 1900. 'How intensely I long to see her dear old face, you can imagine; never have we been separated so long, four whole years, and I have the feeling as tho' I should never see her any more. Were it not so far away, I should have gone off all alone for a few days to see her and left my children and my husband, as she has been as a mother to me, ever since Mama's death twenty two years ago.'[27] Sadly, if she was thinking about going that autumn, she would also be disappointed for in October she discovered that she was once again pregnant and then not long afterwards, while the family were staying at Livadia Palace, Nicholas fell seriously ill with typhoid – an illness that she understandably, thanks to her family's history, found especially alarming. If a visit was to be made to England then it would have to be the following year, once her baby was born and could safely be left behind in Russia.

Queen Victoria was always a thoughtful and generous present giver, who loved to spoil those that she loved with gifts. The Christmas and birthday present tables for her family were always covered with wonderful presents and her household and servants also received many tokens of Victoria's appreciation during their time in service and beyond. Her grandchildren and then great grandchildren also benefitted from this largesse and even Alix and her siblings in Darmstadt were treated to a regular supply of treats from Granny, including books, simple jewellery (including pearls on their birthdays, which were collected and then put together to create a necklace), clothes, toys and, usually for their tenth birthday, a gold watch. Victoria had sent a Shetland pony to Princess Elisabeth, the daughter of Ernie and Victoria Melita and in November of 1900 decided to do the same for Alix's children, possibly as a Christmas present. She chose the pony herself on 24 November[28] and it was duly despatched to Russia from Windsor Castle. Victoria's presents were not usually quite so extravagant but in this instance perhaps it was fitting as it was destined to be the last present that she would send to them.

'Another year begun,' Queen Victoria wrote in her journal on 1 January 1901 at Osborne House. 'I am feeling so weak and unwell that I enter upon it sadly.'[29] The year 1900 had not been a good one for her thanks to the conflict in South Africa, the death of her son Prince Alfred in July, the terminal illness of her eldest daughter Vicky and the usual round of personal and political anxieties and disappointments. Although she felt confident about the future of her own dynasty, which she believed would be in good hands for generations to come, she was desperately worried about the wider reaches of the family, about Alix and Nicholas who seemed to be heading towards disaster in Russia and about Wilhelm in Prussia, who was so determined to create trouble and divisions. The world that Victoria was about to leave was very different to the one that she had been born into, where Europe was still healing from the scars left by Napoleon's ambitions, and the one that she had so delightedly learned about as an inexperienced new queen in 1837, and she felt exhausted by the effort of trying to understand it. As the days went by, Victoria visibly weakened and gradually began to lose her appetite as well as her sight, while her mental faculties became impaired and she found it increasingly difficult to sleep, waking often during the night. The daily carriage rides which had once so amused Nicholas and been the bane of her grandchildren's lives as they were forced to accompany her even when it was raining, became increasingly rare and when she did manage to go out, it exhausted her so much that she was forced to nap for two hours afterwards in order to recover. By the time Victoria wrote her final journal entry on 13 January, her daughters Helena and Beatrice, who were with her, were forced to accept that she was dying and the letters and telegrams began to fly around Europe letting everyone know that the time had come to prepare themselves for the end. 'I don't want to die yet. There are several things I want to arrange,'[30] Victoria said to her physician Sir James Reid, who was forced to assure her that the end was not yet nigh even as she became progressively more confused and drowsy with every passing day. However, within a few days, Victoria suffered the first of a series of strokes and her family were hastily summoned to her bedside.

In Russia, Alix was devastated when the telegram announcing Victoria's imminent demise arrived and she would have set out immediately for the Isle of Wight if it hadn't been for the fact that as usual pregnancy had left her feeling incredibly unwell. Her presence would almost certainly have been more welcome than that of her cousin Wilhelm, who left Berlin as soon as the news arrived, as determined to be at his grandmother's side as she drew her last breath as the rest of the family were keen to prevent him. In the end, Wilhelm got his way as always and he was there beside her when Victoria drew her last breath at 6.30 pm on Tuesday, 22 January at the age of eighty-one. 'What a sorrow for the whole of England and the poor family,' Nicholas' sister Xenia wrote in her journal when the news arrived in Russia. 'The Queen was everything that was best about England, she was so much-loved, and exuded such enormous charm!… I feel terribly sorry for poor Alix. She did so love her grandmother.'[31] Victoria's death was indeed a terrible blow to Alix, who had basked in her grandmother's affection and attention for as long as she could remember and even if she had not, in latter years, paid much heed to Victoria's advice, she still regarded her as one of the most important and influential people in her life. She and Nicholas were at Sebastopol when the news arrived, waiting to board the imperial train back to the capital after the end of their Crimean holiday. Alix wanted to leave for England in order to attend Victoria's funeral, which took place at Windsor on 2 February, but was persuaded not to because of her pregnancy – hopes were high that this time she would give birth to a boy (unfortunately, once again their hopes were destined to be dashed as instead of a boy, Grand Duchess Anastasia would be born that June and the long-awaited Tsesarevich would not make an appearance until 1904) and so the imperial doctors were unwilling to allow her to take any risks by leaving the country. When they returned to St Petersburg, the court was immediately ordered to go into mourning and on the day of the funeral, Alix and Ella were the chief mourners at a special memorial service in the English Church in St Petersburg where, to everyone's astonishment, the usually cold and apparently unemotional Empress broke down in tears. Nicholas was also deeply distressed by Victoria's death. 'It is difficult for me to realise that beloved Grandmama has been taken away from this world,' he wrote to his uncle Bertie. 'She was so remarkably kind and touching towards me since the first time I ever saw her, when I came to England for George's and May's wedding. I felt quite like at home when I lived at Windsor and later in Scotland near her and I need not say that I shall forever cherish her memory. I am quite sure that with your help, dear Bertie, the friendly relations between our two countries shall become still closer than in the past... May the new century bring England and Russia together for their mutual interests and for the general peace of the world.'[32]

For Alix, Victoria's death was more than the end of an era, it was the severance of one of the last remaining links between herself and her mother Alice as well as the removal of one of the most constant, stable and reliable influences upon her life. Ever since her mother's death, Victoria had been there – nagging, advising, guiding and loving not just Alix but her four surviving siblings, all of whom had been left shocked and distressed by Alice's sudden death. Although she knew that Victoria had not approved of some of the choices that she had made since her marriage, she had nonetheless known that she could always count upon her grandmother for support if it was needed. 'I cannot really believe she has gone, that we shall never see her any more,' she wrote to her sister Victoria. 'Since one can remember, she was in our life and a dearer kinder being never was... England without the Queen seems impossible.'[33]

Acknowledgements

In 1917, while she and her family were under house arrest in the Alexander Palace in Tsarskoe Selo, Empress Alexandra Feodorovna of Russia took the precaution of burning fire to most of her private papers, which included much of her correspondence with her grandmother, Queen Victoria – thus destroying evidence of one of the most fascinating relationships in royal history. Ever since Alexandra's mother, Princess Alice, the second daughter of Queen Victoria, died in 1878, her formidable grandmother had taken over the reins, encouraging her bewildered, distressed Hesse grandchildren to regard her as a substitute mother and taking a close interest in their lives, which extended as much to attempting to organise their marriages as it did to ensuring they were properly educated. This relationship between two female rulers, who were so different in ability and personality but bound together by blood and genuine affection, has always fascinated me and the result of this interest is this book.

I've spent the last year immersed in Queen Victoria's journals and letters and those of her children and grandchildren, hunting for glimpses of Alexandra as well as piecing together what I hope will be a vivid picture of Victoria's private family life with all of its ups and downs. Any historian researching Queen Victoria is truly privileged because she left behind such a wealth of written material – not least her fascinating journals, which she updated almost every day, roping her daughters and granddaughters in to help when her eyesight began to fail in her later years. It is a most wonderful source, packed full of information, not just about her domestic life but also her views on current affairs. I could not have written this book without it. However, Victoria's spelling and punctuation could be erratic (and after all, who is going to tell Queen Victoria that she should be using more commas?) so I have made some minor corrections where appropriate so that the pieces quoted make more sense.

Although this book was intended to simply be a study of the relationship of Queen Victoria and her granddaughter Empress Alexandra, I decided to begin with the marriage of Alexandra's parents, Alice and Louis and then after some reflection, chose to start even further back with Alice's birth as I felt like her relationship with her mother shaped that between Victoria and Alexandra and was highly relevant to the events that occurred later on. Therefore, although the title refers only to Alexandra and Victoria, I feel like this book is also, in part at least, about Alice too. In the name of clarity and simplicity, I also made the decision to use only New Style (NS) dating throughout the book, converting OS dates on Russian letters and journals if necessary.

I couldn't have written this book without the support and encouragement of my friends and lovely followers online, who have been a real Godsend on those occasions when I have started to doubt myself and wonder about my life choices. Helen Rappaport and Estelle Paranque deserve special mention for being really lovely and helpful, also Holly Snaith, Amy Licence and Sara Sheridan for amazing pep talks when things weren't going so well. Thanks too to PopComms in Bristol for letting me hang out and use your pool table in your lovely office every day while I was writing – I really REALLY couldn't have done it without you. Many thanks also to Her Majesty Queen Elizabeth II for permission to use images from the Royal Collection to illustrate this book.

This book is dedicated to Simon Hayden and my awful boys in thanks for putting up with me being insanely grumpy while I wrote it.

Notes

Chapter 1

1. RA VIC/MAIN/QVJ/1842: 10 August.
2. RA VIC/MAIN/QVJ/1842: 22 October.
3. RA VIC/MAIN/QVJ/1842: 31 October.
4. RA VIC/MAIN/QVJ/1842: 1 September.
5. RA VIC/MAIN/QVJ/1842: 15 September.
6. RA VIC/MAIN/QVJ/1843: 11 March.
7. RA VIC/MAIN/QVJ/1843: 13 April.
8. RA VIC/MAIN/QVJ/1843: 25 April.
9. RA VIC/MAIN/QVJ/1843: 25 April.
10. Stratfield Saye MS, quoted in *Victoria R.I.*, Longford, Elizabeth (1966).
11. RA VIC/MAIN/QVJ/1843: 14 May.
12. RA VIC/MAIN/QVJ/1843: 12 May.
13. RA VIC/MAIN/QVJ/1843: 2 June.
14. RA VIC/MAIN/QVJ/1843: 24 May.
15. RA VIC/MAIN/QVJ/1843: 24 May.
16. RA VIC/MAIN/QVJ/1844: 25 April.
17. RA VIC/MAIN/QVJ/1851: 25 April.
18. RA VIC/MAIN/QVJ/1853: 25 April.
19. RA VIC/MAIN/QVJ/1852: 25 April.
20. RA VIC/MAIN/QVJ/1856: 25 April.
21. RA VIC/MAIN/QVJ/1844: 18 March.
22. Letter to Louis, Grand Duke of Hesse, 22 November 1866 taken from Helena Victoria, Princess (ed.), *Alice, Grand Duchess of Hesse: Biographical Sketch and Letters* (John Murray, 1884).

Chapter 2

1. RA VIC/MAIN/QVJ/1858: 25 January.
2. RA VIC/MAIN/QVJ/1858: 2 February.
3. Fulford, Roger (ed.), *Dearest Child: Letters between Queen Victoria and the Princess Royal, 1858–1861* (Evans Brothers, 1964).
4. Benson, Arthur Christopher and Esher, Viscount (edited by), *The Letters of Queen Victoria, Vol. III* (John Murray, 1907).
5. RA VIC/MAIN/QVJ/1839: 27 May.
6. RA VIC/MAIN/QVJ/1860: 1 June.

7. RA VIC/MAIN/QVJ/1860: 6 June.
8. Martin, Theodore, *The Life of His Royal Highness the Prince Consort, Vol. 5* (Smith, Elder & Co., London, 1880).
9. Martin, Theodore, *The Life of His Royal Highness the Prince Consort, Vol. 5* (Smith, Elder & Co., London, 1880).
10. RA VIC/MAIN/QVJ/1860: 25 September.
11. Fulford, Roger (ed.), *Dearest Child: Letters between Queen Victoria and the Princess Royal, 1858–1861* (Evans Brothers, 1964).
12. RA VIC/MAIN/QVJ/1860: 11 October.
13. RA VIC/MAIN/QVJ/1860: 11 October.
14. RA VIC/MAIN/QVJ/1860: 24 November.
15. RA VIC/MAIN/QVJ/1860: 28 November.
16. RA VIC/MAIN/QVJ/1860: 30 November.
17. RA VIC/MAIN/QVJ/1860: 30 November.
18. RA VIC/MAIN/QVJ/1860: 4 December.
19. RA VIC/MAIN/QVJ/1860: 4 December.
20. Martin, Theodore, *The Life of the Prince Consort, Vol. 5* (Smith, Elder & Co., London, 1880).
21. Helena Victoria, Princess (ed.), *Alice, Grand Duchess of Hesse: Biographical Sketch and Letters* (John Murray, 1884).
22. RA VIC/MAIN/QVJ/1861: 26 June.
23. RA VIC/MAIN/QVJ/1861: 6 October.
24. RA VIC/MAIN/QVJ/1861: 4 December.
25. Strafford, Henry Greville, vol.3, p.420 quoted in Rappaport, Helen, *Magnificent Obsession* (Windmill, 2012).
26. Morris, Charles and Halstead, Murat, *Life and Reign of Queen Victoria: including the Lives of King Edward VII and Queen Alexandra* (1901).
27. Morris, Charles and Halstead, Murat, *Life and Reign of Queen Victoria: including the Lives of King Edward VII and Queen Alexandra* (1901).
28. RA VIC/ADDU/396, undated letter, c. 17 December, from the Hon. Victoria Stuart Worsley quoted in Rappaport, Helen, *Magnificent Obsession* (Windmill, 2012).
29. Fulford, Roger (ed.), *Dearest Child: Letters between Queen Victoria and the Princess Royal, 1858–1861* (Evans Brothers, 1964).
30. Knightley, Lady Louisa, *The Journals of Lady Knightley of Fawsley 1856–1884* (John Murray, 1924).
31. RA VIC/MAIN/QVJ/1862: 14 June.
32. RA VIC/MAIN/QVJ/1862: 23 June.
33. RA VIC/MAIN/QVJ/1862: 30 June.
34. RA VIC/MAIN/QVJ/1862: 30 June.
35. RA VIC/MAIN/QVJ/1862: 30 June.
36. RA VIC/MAIN/QVJ/1862: 1 July.
37. RA VIC/MAIN/QVJ/1862: 1 July.

38. RA VIC/MAIN/QVJ/1862: 1 July.
39. Fulford, Roger (ed.), *Dearest Child: Letters between Queen Victoria and the Princess Royal, 1858–1861* (Evans Brothers, 1964).

Chapter 3

1. RA VIC/MAIN/QVJ/1862: 8 July.
2. Noel, Gerard, *Princess Alice: Queen Victoria's Forgotten Daughter* (Constable, 1974).
3. Helena Victoria, Princess (ed.), *Alice Grand Duchess of Hesse: Biographical Sketch and Letters* (John Murray, 1884).
4. Helena Victoria, Princess (ed.), *Alice Grand Duchess of Hesse: Biographical Sketch and Letters* (John Murray, 1884).
5. RA VIC/MAIN/QVJ/1863: 10 March.
6. RA VIC/MAIN/QVJ/1863: 5 April.
7. RA VIC/MAIN/QVJ/1863: 16 April.
8. RA VIC/MAIN/QVJ/1864: 1 November.
9. Letter from Victoria to Alice 12/10/64 quoted in Pakula, Hannah, *An Uncommon Woman: The Empress Frederick* (W&N, 2006).
10. RA VIC/MAIN/QVJ/1866: 26 June.
11. Helena Victoria, Princess (ed.), *Alice Grand Duchess of Hesse: Biographical Sketch and Letters* (John Murray, 1884).
12. Helena Victoria, Princess (ed.), *Alice Grand Duchess of Hesse: Biographical Sketch and Letters* (John Murray, 1884).
13. Fulford, Roger (ed.), *Your Dear Letter: Private Correspondence of Queen Victoria and the Crown Princess of Prussia 1865–1871*.
14. Fulford, Roger (ed.), *Your Dear Letter: Private Correspondence of Queen Victoria and the Crown Princess of Prussia 1865–1871*.
15. Fulford, Roger (ed.), *Your Dear Letter: Private Correspondence of Queen Victoria and the Crown Princess of Prussia 1865–1871*.
16. Fulford, Roger (ed.), *Your Dear Letter: Private Correspondence of Queen Victoria and the Crown Princess of Prussia 1865–1871*.
17. Noel, Gerard, *Princess Alice: Queen Victoria's Forgotten Daughter* (Constable, 1974).
18. Fulford, Roger (ed.), *Your Dear Letter: Private Correspondence of Queen Victoria and the Crown Princess of Prussia 1865–1871*.
19. Ponsonby, Frederick (ed.), *The Letters of the Empress Frederick* (Macmillan and Co., 1928).
20. RA VIC/MAIN/QVJ/1871: 14 September.
21. RA VIC/MAIN/QVJ/1871: 14 September.
22. RA VIC/MAIN/QVJ/1871: 18 September.
23. RA VIC/MAIN/QVJ/1871: 29 November.
24. Helena Victoria, Princess (ed.), *Alice Grand Duchess of Hesse: Biographical Sketch and Letters* (John Murray, 1884).

25. Helena Victoria, Princess (ed.), *Alice Grand Duchess of Hesse: Biographical Sketch and Letters* (John Murray, 1884).

Chapter 4
 1. Helena Victoria, Princess (ed.), *Alice Grand Duchess of Hesse: Biographical Sketch and Letters* (John Murray, 1884).
 2. Buxhoeveden, Sophie, *The Life and Tragedy of Alexandra Feodorovna: Empress of Russia* (Longmans, Green & Co., 1928).
 3. Helena Victoria, Princess (ed.), *Alice Grand Duchess of Hesse: Biographical Sketch and Letters* (John Murray, 1884).
 4. Buxhoeveden, Sophie, *The Life and Tragedy of Alexandra Feodorovna: Empress of Russia* (Longmans, Green & Co., 1928).
 5. Private letter to Sir Theodore Martin in 1870, quoted in Croft, Christina, *Alice, The Enigma* (Hilliard & Croft, 2013).
 6. Private letter to Sir Theodore Martin in 1870, quoted in Croft, Christina, *Alice, The Enigma* (Hilliard & Croft, 2013).
 7. Helena Victoria, Princess (ed.), *Alice Grand Duchess of Hesse: Biographical Sketch and Letters* (John Murray, 1884).
 8. Helena Victoria, Princess (ed.), *Alice Grand Duchess of Hesse: Biographical Sketch and Letters* (John Murray, 1884).
 9. Helena Victoria, Princess (ed.), *Alice Grand Duchess of Hesse: Biographical Sketch and Letters* (John Murray, 1884).
10. Helena Victoria, Princess (ed.), *Alice Grand Duchess of Hesse: Biographical Sketch and Letters* (John Murray, 1884).
11. RA VIC/MAIN/QVJ/1873: 2 June.
12. RA VIC/MAIN/QVJ/1873: 2 June.
13. Helena Victoria, Princess (ed.), *Alice Grand Duchess of Hesse: Biographical Sketch and Letters* (John Murray, 1884).
14. RA VIC/MAIN/QVJ/1873: 29 November.
15. RA VIC/MAIN/QVJ/1873: 30 November.
16. RA VIC/MAIN/QVJ/ 1873: 19 December.
17. RA VIC/MAIN/QVJ/1875: 13 April.
18. RA VIC/MAIN/QVJ/1875: 13 April.
19. RA VIC/MAIN/QVJ/ 1875: 22 April.
20. RA VIC/MAIN/QVJ/ 1875: 2 May.
21. RA VIC/MAIN/QVJ/ 1875: 9 May.
22. RA VIC/MAIN/QVJ/ 1875: 25 April.
23. RA VIC/MAIN/QVJ/ 1875: 11 May.
24. RA VIC/MAIN/QVJ/ 1875: 11 May.
25. RA VIC/MAIN/QVJ/ 1876: 5 April.
26. RA VIC/MAIN/QVJ/ 1876: 5 April.
27. RA VIC/MAIN/QVJ/ 1876: 20 September.
28. Noel, Gerard, *Princess Alice: Queen Victoria's Forgotten Daughter* (Constable, 1974).

29. Noel, Gerard, *Princess Alice: Queen Victoria's Forgotten Daughter* (Constable, 1974).
30. Helena Victoria, Princess (ed.), *Alice Grand Duchess of Hesse: Biographical Sketch and Letters* (John Murray, 1884).
31. RA VIC/MAIN/QVJ/ 1878: 12 July.
32. RA VIC/MAIN/QVJ/ 1878: 12 July.
33. RA VIC/MAIN/QVJ/ 1878: 16 July.
34. RA VIC/MAIN/QVJ/ 1878: 16 July.
35. Marie, Queen of Roumania, *The Story of My Life* (Cassell, 1934).
36. RA VIC/MAIN/QVJ/ 1878: 16 August.
37. RA VIC/MAIN/QVJ/ 1878: 16 August.
38. RA VIC/MAIN/QVJ/ 1878: 20 August.
39. RA VIC/MAIN/QVJ/ 1878: 13 November.
40. RA VIC/MAIN/QVJ/ 1878: 15 November.
41. RA VIC/MAIN/QVJ/ 1878: 16 November.
42. RA VIC/MAIN/QVJ/ 1878: 16 November.
43. RA VIC/MAIN/QVJ/ 1878: 17 November.
44. Helena Victoria, Princess (ed.), *Alice Grand Duchess of Hesse: Biographical Sketch and Letters* (John Murray, 1884).
45. Helena Victoria, Princess (ed.), *Alice Grand Duchess of Hesse: Biographical Sketch and Letters* (John Murray, 1884).
46. Helena Victoria, Princess (ed.), *Alice Grand Duchess of Hesse: Biographical Sketch and Letters* (John Murray, 1884).
47. RA VIC/MAIN/QVJ/ 1878: 8 December.
48. RA VIC/MAIN/QVJ/ 1878: 12 December.
49. RA VIC/MAIN/QVJ/ 1878: 13 December.
50. RA VIC/MAIN/QVJ/ 1878: 14 December.
51. RA VIC/MAIN/QVJ/ 1878: 14 December.
52. RA VIC/MAIN/QVJ/ 1878: 14 December.
53. RA VIC/MAIN/QVJ/ 1878: 14 December.

Chapter 5
1. Hough, Richard, (ed.), *Advice to My Grand-daughter: Letters from Queen Victoria to Princess Victoria of Hesse* (Simon & Schuster, 1976).
2. Hough, Richard, (ed.), *Advice to My Grand-daughter: Letters from Queen Victoria to Princess Victoria of Hesse* (Simon & Schuster, 1976).
3. RA VIC/MAIN/QVJ/ 1878: 15 December.
4. RA VIC/MAIN/QVJ/ 1878: 21 December.
5. RA VIC/MAIN/QVJ/ 1878: 28 December.
6. Hough, Richard, (ed.), *Advice to My Grand-daughter: Letters from Queen Victoria to Princess Victoria of Hesse* (Simon & Schuster, 1976).
7. RA VIC/MAIN/QVJ/ 1879: 21 January.
8. Hough, Richard, (ed.), *Advice to My Grand-daughter: Letters from Queen Victoria to Princess Victoria of Hesse* (Simon & Schuster, 1976).

9. RA VIC/MAIN/QVJ/ 1879: 2 February.
10. RA VIC/MAIN/QVJ/ 1879: 8 February.
11. RA VIC/MAIN/QVJ/ 1879: 7 May.
12. RA VIC/MAIN/QVJ/ 1879: 28 February.
13. RA VIC/MAIN/QVJ/ 1879: 28 February.
14. Hough, Richard, (ed.), *Advice to My Grand-daughter: Letters from Queen Victoria to Princess Victoria of Hesse* (Simon & Schuster, 1976).
15. RA VIC/MAIN/QVJ/ 1879: 20 October.
16. Hough, Richard, (ed.), *Advice to My Grand-daughter: Letters from Queen Victoria to Princess Victoria of Hesse* (Simon & Schuster, 1976).
17. RA VIC/MAIN/QVJ/ 1880: 31 March.
18. RA VIC/MAIN/QVJ/ 1880: 17 September.
19. RA VIC/MAIN/QVJ/ 1880: 18 October.
20. Hough, Richard, (ed.), *Advice to My Grand-daughter: Letters from Queen Victoria to Princess Victoria of Hesse* (Simon & Schuster, 1976).
21. Hough, Richard, (ed.), *Advice to My Grand-daughter: Letters from Queen Victoria to Princess Victoria of Hesse* (Simon & Schuster, 1976).
22. Hough, Richard, (ed.), *Advice to My Grand-daughter: Letters from Queen Victoria to Princess Victoria of Hesse* (Simon & Schuster, 1976).
23. Hough, Richard, (ed.), *Advice to My Grand-daughter: Letters from Queen Victoria to Princess Victoria of Hesse* (Simon & Schuster, 1976).
24. Hough, Richard, (ed.), *Advice to My Grand-daughter: Letters from Queen Victoria to Princess Victoria of Hesse* (Simon & Schuster, 1976).
25. Hough, Richard, (ed.), *Advice to My Grand-daughter: Letters from Queen Victoria to Princess Victoria of Hesse* (Simon & Schuster, 1976).
26. Hough, Richard, (ed.), *Advice to My Grand-daughter: Letters from Queen Victoria to Princess Victoria of Hesse* (Simon & Schuster, 1976).
27. Hough, Richard, (ed.), *Advice to My Grand-daughter: Letters from Queen Victoria to Princess Victoria of Hesse* (Simon & Schuster, 1976).
28. Hough, Richard, (ed.), *Advice to My Grand-daughter: Letters from Queen Victoria to Princess Victoria of Hesse* (Simon & Schuster, 1976).
29. Hough, Richard, (ed.), *Advice to My Grand-daughter: Letters from Queen Victoria to Princess Victoria of Hesse* (Simon & Schuster, 1976).
30. Hough, Richard, (ed.), *Advice to My Grand-daughter: Letters from Queen Victoria to Princess Victoria of Hesse* (Simon & Schuster, 1976).
31. RA VIC/MAIN/QVJ/ 1884: 17 April.
32. Hough, Richard, (ed.), *Advice to My Grand-daughter: Letters from Queen Victoria to Princess Victoria of Hesse* (Simon & Schuster, 1976).
33. Cadbury, Deborah, *Queen Victoria's Matchmaking* (Bloomsbury, 2017).

Chapter 6

1. Mironenko, Sergei and Maylunas, Andrei, *A Lifelong Passion: Nicholas and Alexandra* (Doubleday, 1997).

2. Mironenko, Sergei and Maylunas, Andrei, *A Lifelong Passion: Nicholas and Alexandra* (Doubleday, 1997).
3. Mironenko, Sergei and Maylunas, Andrei, *A Lifelong Passion: Nicholas and Alexandra* (Doubleday, 1997).
4. Mironenko, Sergei and Maylunas, Andrei, *A Lifelong Passion: Nicholas and Alexandra* (Doubleday, 1997).
5. Cadbury, Deborah, *Queen Victoria's Matchmaking* (Bloomsbury, 2017).
6. Mironenko, Sergei and Maylunas, Andrei, *A Lifelong Passion: Nicholas and Alexandra* (Doubleday, 1997).
7. Hough, Richard, (ed.), *Advice to My Grand-daughter: Letters from Queen Victoria to Princess Victoria of Hesse* (Simon & Schuster, 1976).
8. RA VIC/MAIN/QVJ/ 1885: 23 April.
9. RA VIC/MAIN/QVJ/ 1885: 23 April.
10. Hough, Richard, (ed.), *Advice to My Grand-daughter: Letters from Queen Victoria to Princess Victoria of Hesse* (Simon & Schuster, 1976).
11. RA VIC/MAIN/QVJ/ 1885: 30 April.
12. RA VIC/MAIN/QVJ/ 1885: 20 July.
13. RA VIC/MAIN/QVJ/ 1885: 20 July.
14. RA VIC/MAIN/QVJ/ 1885: 23 July.
15. RA VIC/MAIN/QVJ/ 1885: 21 August.
16. RA VIC/MAIN/QVJ/ 1887: 21 June.
17. RA VIC/MAIN/QVJ/ 1887: 6 September.
18. Hough, Richard, (ed.), *Advice to My Grand-daughter: Letters from Queen Victoria to Princess Victoria of Hesse* (Simon & Schuster, 1976).
19. Hough, Richard, (ed.), *Advice to My Grand-daughter: Letters from Queen Victoria to Princess Victoria of Hesse* (Simon & Schuster, 1976).
20. Hough, Richard, (ed.), *Advice to My Grand-daughter: Letters from Queen Victoria to Princess Victoria of Hesse* (Simon & Schuster, 1976).
21. RA VIC/MAIN/QVJ/ 1888: 31 July.
22. Hough, Richard, (ed.), *Advice to My Grand-daughter: Letters from Queen Victoria to Princess Victoria of Hesse* (Simon & Schuster, 1976).
23. Cadbury, Deborah, *Queen Victoria's Matchmaking* (Bloomsbury, 2017).
24. Cadbury, Deborah, *Queen Victoria's Matchmaking* (Bloomsbury, 2017).

Chapter 7

1. Cadbury, Deborah, *Queen Victoria's Matchmaking* (Bloomsbury, 2017).
2. Mironenko, Sergei and Maylunas, Andrei, *A Lifelong Passion: Nicholas and Alexandra* (Doubleday, 1997).
3. Cadbury, Deborah, *Queen Victoria's Matchmaking* (Bloomsbury, 2017).
4. Hough, Richard, (ed.), *Advice to My Grand-daughter: Letters from Queen Victoria to Princess Victoria of Hesse* (Simon & Schuster, 1976).
5. Hough, Richard, (ed.), *Advice to My Grand-daughter: Letters from Queen Victoria to Princess Victoria of Hesse* (Simon & Schuster, 1976).

6. Cadbury, Deborah, *Queen Victoria's Matchmaking* (Bloomsbury, 2017).
7. Cadbury, Deborah, *Queen Victoria's Matchmaking* (Bloomsbury, 2017).
8. Cadbury, Deborah, *Queen Victoria's Matchmaking* (Bloomsbury, 2017).
9. Cadbury, Deborah, *Queen Victoria's Matchmaking* (Bloomsbury, 2017).
10. Hough, Richard, (ed.), *Advice to My Grand-daughter: Letters from Queen Victoria to Princess Victoria of Hesse* (Simon & Schuster, 1976).
11. Hough, Richard, (ed.), *Advice to My Grand-daughter: Letters from Queen Victoria to Princess Victoria of Hesse* (Simon & Schuster, 1976).
12. Kurth, Peter, *Tsar: The Lost World of Nicholas and Alexandra* (Doubleday, 1995).
13. Mironenko, Sergei and Maylunas, Andrei, *A Lifelong Passion: Nicholas and Alexandra* (Doubleday, 1997).
14. Hough, Richard, (ed.), *Advice to My Grand-daughter: Letters from Queen Victoria to Princess Victoria of Hesse* (Simon & Schuster, 1976).
15. Hough, Richard, (ed.), *Advice to My Grand-daughter: Letters from Queen Victoria to Princess Victoria of Hesse* (Simon & Schuster, 1976).
16. Hough, Richard, (ed.), *Advice to My Grand-daughter: Letters from Queen Victoria to Princess Victoria of Hesse* (Simon & Schuster, 1976).
17. Hough, Richard, (ed.), *Advice to My Grand-daughter: Letters from Queen Victoria to Princess Victoria of Hesse* (Simon & Schuster, 1976).
18. Hough, Richard, (ed.), *Advice to My Grand-daughter: Letters from Queen Victoria to Princess Victoria of Hesse* (Simon & Schuster, 1976).
19. Hough, Richard, (ed.), *Advice to My Grand-daughter: Letters from Queen Victoria to Princess Victoria of Hesse* (Simon & Schuster, 1976).
20. Hough, Richard, (ed.), *Advice to My Grand-daughter: Letters from Queen Victoria to Princess Victoria of Hesse* (Simon & Schuster, 1976).
21. Hough, Richard, (ed.), *Advice to My Grand-daughter: Letters from Queen Victoria to Princess Victoria of Hesse* (Simon & Schuster, 1976).
22. Cadbury, Deborah, *Queen Victoria's Matchmaking* (Bloomsbury, 2017).
23. RA VIC/MAIN/QVJ/ 1891: 19 June.
24. RA VIC/MAIN/QVJ/ 1892: 13 March.
25. RA VIC/MAIN/QVJ/ 1892: 13 March.

Chapter 8

1. RA VIC/MAIN/QVJ/ 1892: 17 March.
2. RA VIC/MAIN/QVJ/ 1892: 17 March.
3. Hough, Richard, (ed.), *Advice to My Grand-daughter: Letters from Queen Victoria to Princess Victoria of Hesse* (Simon & Schuster, 1976).
4. RA VIC/MAIN/QVJ/ 1892: 22 March.
5. RA VIC/MAIN/QVJ/ 1892: 22 March.
6. RA VIC/MAIN/QVJ/ 1892: 26 April.
7. RA VIC/MAIN/QVJ/ 1892: 27 April.
8. Hough, Richard, (ed.), *Advice to My Grand-daughter: Letters from Queen Victoria to Princess Victoria of Hesse* (Simon & Schuster, 1976).

9. Hough, Richard, (ed.), *Advice to My Grand-daughter: Letters from Queen Victoria to Princess Victoria of Hesse* (Simon & Schuster, 1976).
10. RAVIC/MAIN/QVJ/ 1892: 21 September.
11. RAVIC/MAIN/QVJ/ 1892: 25 September.
12. RAVIC/MAIN/QVJ/ 1892: 10 October.
13. Cadbury, Deborah, *Queen Victoria's Matchmaking* (Bloomsbury, 2017).
14. Mironenko, Sergei and Maylunas, Andrei, *A Lifelong Passion: Nicholas and Alexandra* (Doubleday, 1997).
15. Mironenko, Sergei and Maylunas, Andrei, *A Lifelong Passion: Nicholas and Alexandra* (Doubleday, 1997).
16. Mironenko, Sergei and Maylunas, Andrei, *A Lifelong Passion: Nicholas and Alexandra* (Doubleday, 1997).
17. Mironenko, Sergei and Maylunas, Andrei, *A Lifelong Passion: Nicholas and Alexandra* (Doubleday, 1997).
18. Mironenko, Sergei and Maylunas, Andrei, *A Lifelong Passion: Nicholas and Alexandra* (Doubleday, 1997).
19. RAVIC/MAIN/QVJ/ 1893: 1 July.
20. RAVIC/MAIN/QVJ/ 1893: 1 July.
21. Mironenko, Sergei and Maylunas, Andrei, *A Lifelong Passion: Nicholas and Alexandra* (Doubleday, 1997).
22. Mironenko, Sergei and Maylunas, Andrei, *A Lifelong Passion: Nicholas and Alexandra* (Doubleday, 1997).
23. Mironenko, Sergei and Maylunas, Andrei, *A Lifelong Passion: Nicholas and Alexandra* (Doubleday, 1997).
24. RAVIC/MAIN/QVJ/ 1893: 5 July.
25. Mironenko, Sergei and Maylunas, Andrei, *A Lifelong Passion: Nicholas and Alexandra* (Doubleday, 1997).
26. Mironenko, Sergei and Maylunas, Andrei, *A Lifelong Passion: Nicholas and Alexandra* (Doubleday, 1997).
27. Hough, Richard, (ed.), *Advice to My Grand-daughter: Letters from Queen Victoria to Princess Victoria of Hesse* (Simon & Schuster, 1976).
28. Mironenko, Sergei and Maylunas, Andrei, *A Lifelong Passion: Nicholas and Alexandra* (Doubleday, 1997).
29. Mironenko, Sergei and Maylunas, Andrei, *A Lifelong Passion: Nicholas and Alexandra* (Doubleday, 1997).
30. Mironenko, Sergei and Maylunas, Andrei, *A Lifelong Passion: Nicholas and Alexandra* (Doubleday, 1997).
31. Mironenko, Sergei and Maylunas, Andrei, *A Lifelong Passion: Nicholas and Alexandra* (Doubleday, 1997).
32. Mironenko, Sergei and Maylunas, Andrei, *A Lifelong Passion: Nicholas and Alexandra* (Doubleday, 1997).
33. Mironenko, Sergei and Maylunas, Andrei, *A Lifelong Passion: Nicholas and Alexandra* (Doubleday, 1997).

34. Mironenko, Sergei and Maylunas, Andrei, *A Lifelong Passion: Nicholas and Alexandra* (Doubleday, 1997).
35. Hough, Richard, (ed.), *Advice to My Grand-daughter: Letters from Queen Victoria to Princess Victoria of Hesse* (Simon & Schuster, 1976).
36. Cadbury, Deborah, *Queen Victoria's Matchmaking* (Bloomsbury, 2017).
37. Cadbury, Deborah, *Queen Victoria's Matchmaking* (Bloomsbury, 2017).
38. Cadbury, Deborah, *Queen Victoria's Matchmaking* (Bloomsbury, 2017).
39. Cadbury, Deborah, *Queen Victoria's Matchmaking* (Bloomsbury, 2017).
40. Mironenko, Sergei and Maylunas, Andrei, *A Lifelong Passion: Nicholas and Alexandra* (Doubleday, 1997).
41. Mironenko, Sergei and Maylunas, Andrei, *A Lifelong Passion: Nicholas and Alexandra* (Doubleday, 1997).
42. Mironenko, Sergei and Maylunas, Andrei, *A Lifelong Passion: Nicholas and Alexandra* (Doubleday, 1997).
43. Mironenko, Sergei and Maylunas, Andrei, *A Lifelong Passion: Nicholas and Alexandra* (Doubleday, 1997).
44. Mironenko, Sergei and Maylunas, Andrei, *A Lifelong Passion: Nicholas and Alexandra* (Doubleday, 1997).

Chapter 9
1. RA VIC/MAIN/QVJ/ 1894: 20 April.
2. RA VIC/MAIN/QVJ/ 1894: 20 April.
3. RA VIC/MAIN/QVJ/ 1894: 20 April.
4. RA VIC/MAIN/QVJ/ 1894: 20 April.
5. RA VIC/MAIN/QVJ/ 1894: 20 April.
6. Mironenko, Sergei and Maylunas, Andrei, *A Lifelong Passion: Nicholas and Alexandra* (Doubleday, 1997).
7. RA VIC/MAIN/QVJ/ 1894: 21 April.
8. Mironenko, Sergei and Maylunas, Andrei, *A Lifelong Passion: Nicholas and Alexandra* (Doubleday, 1997).
9. Mironenko, Sergei and Maylunas, Andrei, *A Lifelong Passion: Nicholas and Alexandra* (Doubleday, 1997).
10. RA VIC/MAIN/QVJ/ 1894: 26 April.
11. Mironenko, Sergei and Maylunas, Andrei, *A Lifelong Passion: Nicholas and Alexandra* (Doubleday, 1997).
12. Mironenko, Sergei and Maylunas, Andrei, *A Lifelong Passion: Nicholas and Alexandra* (Doubleday, 1997).
13. Mironenko, Sergei and Maylunas, Andrei, *A Lifelong Passion: Nicholas and Alexandra* (Doubleday, 1997).
14. Mironenko, Sergei and Maylunas, Andrei, *A Lifelong Passion: Nicholas and Alexandra* (Doubleday, 1997).
15. Mironenko, Sergei and Maylunas, Andrei, *A Lifelong Passion: Nicholas and Alexandra* (Doubleday, 1997).

16. Mironenko, Sergei and Maylunas, Andrei, *A Lifelong Passion: Nicholas and Alexandra* (Doubleday, 1997).

17. Mironenko, Sergei and Maylunas, Andrei, *A Lifelong Passion: Nicholas and Alexandra* (Doubleday, 1997).

18. Mironenko, Sergei and Maylunas, Andrei, *A Lifelong Passion: Nicholas and Alexandra* (Doubleday, 1997).

19. Mironenko, Sergei and Maylunas, Andrei, *A Lifelong Passion: Nicholas and Alexandra* (Doubleday, 1997).

20. Mironenko, Sergei and Maylunas, Andrei, *A Lifelong Passion: Nicholas and Alexandra* (Doubleday, 1997).

21. Hough, Richard, (ed.), *Advice to My Grand-daughter: Letters from Queen Victoria to Princess Victoria of Hesse* (Simon & Schuster, 1976).

22. Mironenko, Sergei and Maylunas, Andrei, *A Lifelong Passion: Nicholas and Alexandra* (Doubleday, 1997).

23. Mironenko, Sergei and Maylunas, Andrei, *A Lifelong Passion: Nicholas and Alexandra* (Doubleday, 1997).

24. Mironenko, Sergei and Maylunas, Andrei, *A Lifelong Passion: Nicholas and Alexandra* (Doubleday, 1997).

25. Hough, Richard, (ed.), *Advice to My Grand-daughter: Letters from Queen Victoria to Princess Victoria of Hesse* (Simon & Schuster, 1976).

26. Mironenko, Sergei and Maylunas, Andrei, *A Lifelong Passion: Nicholas and Alexandra* (Doubleday, 1997) (Alice would go on to become mother to Prince Philip, Duke of Edinburgh).

27. Mironenko, Sergei and Maylunas, Andrei, *A Lifelong Passion: Nicholas and Alexandra* (Doubleday, 1997).

28. Mironenko, Sergei and Maylunas, Andrei, *A Lifelong Passion: Nicholas and Alexandra* (Doubleday, 1997).

29. Mironenko, Sergei and Maylunas, Andrei, *A Lifelong Passion: Nicholas and Alexandra* (Doubleday, 1997).

30. RA VIC/MAIN/QVJ/ 1894: 26 June.

31. Mironenko, Sergei and Maylunas, Andrei, *A Lifelong Passion: Nicholas and Alexandra* (Doubleday, 1997).

32. Mironenko, Sergei and Maylunas, Andrei, *A Lifelong Passion: Nicholas and Alexandra* (Doubleday, 1997).

33. RA VIC/MAIN/QVJ/ 1894: 29 June.

34. Mironenko, Sergei and Maylunas, Andrei, *A Lifelong Passion: Nicholas and Alexandra* (Doubleday, 1997).

35. Mironenko, Sergei and Maylunas, Andrei, *A Lifelong Passion: Nicholas and Alexandra* (Doubleday, 1997).

36. Mironenko, Sergei and Maylunas, Andrei, *A Lifelong Passion: Nicholas and Alexandra* (Doubleday, 1997).

37. Mironenko, Sergei and Maylunas, Andrei, *A Lifelong Passion: Nicholas and Alexandra* (Doubleday, 1997).

38. RA VIC/MAIN/QVJ/ 1894: 22 July.
39. RA VIC/MAIN/QVJ/ 1894: 23 July.
40. Mironenko, Sergei and Maylunas, Andrei, *A Lifelong Passion: Nicholas and Alexandra* (Doubleday, 1997).
41. Mironenko, Sergei and Maylunas, Andrei, *A Lifelong Passion: Nicholas and Alexandra* (Doubleday, 1997).
42. Mironenko, Sergei and Maylunas, Andrei, *A Lifelong Passion: Nicholas and Alexandra* (Doubleday, 1997).
43. Mironenko, Sergei and Maylunas, Andrei, *A Lifelong Passion: Nicholas and Alexandra* (Doubleday, 1997).
44. RA VIC/MAIN/QVJ/ 1894: 31 July.
45. Mironenko, Sergei and Maylunas, Andrei, *A Lifelong Passion: Nicholas and Alexandra* (Doubleday, 1997).
46. Mironenko, Sergei and Maylunas, Andrei, *A Lifelong Passion: Nicholas and Alexandra* (Doubleday, 1997).
47. Mironenko, Sergei and Maylunas, Andrei, *A Lifelong Passion: Nicholas and Alexandra* (Doubleday, 1997).
48. Mironenko, Sergei and Maylunas, Andrei, *A Lifelong Passion: Nicholas and Alexandra* (Doubleday, 1997).
49. RA VIC/MAIN/QVJ/ 1894: 30 September.
50. Hough, Richard, (ed.), *Advice to My Grand-daughter: Letters from Queen Victoria to Princess Victoria of Hesse* (Simon & Schuster, 1976).
51. RA VIC/MAIN/QVJ/ 1894: 30 October.
52. Mironenko, Sergei and Maylunas, Andrei, *A Lifelong Passion: Nicholas and Alexandra* (Doubleday, 1997).
53. Mironenko, Sergei and Maylunas, Andrei, *A Lifelong Passion: Nicholas and Alexandra* (Doubleday, 1997).
54. Mironenko, Sergei and Maylunas, Andrei, *A Lifelong Passion: Nicholas and Alexandra* (Doubleday, 1997).
55. RA VIC/MAIN/QVJ/ 1894: 1 November.

Chapter 10
1. Mironenko, Sergei and Maylunas, Andrei, *A Lifelong Passion: Nicholas and Alexandra* (Doubleday, 1997).
2. Mironenko, Sergei and Maylunas, Andrei, *A Lifelong Passion: Nicholas and Alexandra* (Doubleday, 1997).
3. Mironenko, Sergei and Maylunas, Andrei, *A Lifelong Passion: Nicholas and Alexandra* (Doubleday, 1997).
4. Hough, Richard, (ed.), *Advice to My Grand-daughter: Letters from Queen Victoria to Princess Victoria of Hesse* (Simon & Schuster, 1976).
5. Mironenko, Sergei and Maylunas, Andrei, *A Lifelong Passion: Nicholas and Alexandra* (Doubleday, 1997).
6. RA VIC/MAIN/QVJ/ 1894: 19 November.

7. RA VIC/MAIN/QVJ/ 1894: 19 November.
8. Cadbury, Deborah, *Queen Victoria's Matchmaking* (Bloomsbury, 2017).
9. Mironenko, Sergei and Maylunas, Andrei, *A Lifelong Passion: Nicholas and Alexandra* (Doubleday, 1997).
10. RA VIC/MAIN/QVJ/ 1894: 26 November.
11. King, Greg, *The Last Empress: The Life and Times of Alexandra Feodorovna, Tsarina of Russia* (Aurum Press, 1996).
12. Mironenko, Sergei and Maylunas, Andrei, *A Lifelong Passion: Nicholas and Alexandra* (Doubleday, 1997).
13. RA VIC/MAIN/QVJ/ 1894: 26 November.
14. RA VIC/MAIN/QVJ/ 1894: 26 November.
15. RA VIC/MAIN/QVJ/ 1894: 26 November.
16. Mironenko, Sergei and Maylunas, Andrei, *A Lifelong Passion: Nicholas and Alexandra* (Doubleday, 1997).
17. Mironenko, Sergei and Maylunas, Andrei, *A Lifelong Passion: Nicholas and Alexandra* (Doubleday, 1997).
18. Mironenko, Sergei and Maylunas, Andrei, *A Lifelong Passion: Nicholas and Alexandra* (Doubleday, 1997).
19. Mironenko, Sergei and Maylunas, Andrei, *A Lifelong Passion: Nicholas and Alexandra* (Doubleday, 1997).
20. Mironenko, Sergei and Maylunas, Andrei, *A Lifelong Passion: Nicholas and Alexandra* (Doubleday, 1997).
21. Hough, Richard, (ed.), *Advice to My Grand-daughter: Letters from Queen Victoria to Princess Victoria of Hesse* (Simon & Schuster, 1976).
22. Hough, Richard, (ed.), *Advice to My Grand-daughter: Letters from Queen Victoria to Princess Victoria of Hesse* (Simon & Schuster, 1976).
23. Rappaport, Helen, *Four Sisters: The Lost Lives of the Romanov Grand Duchesses* (Picador, 2014).
24. Rappaport, Helen, *Four Sisters: The Lost Lives of the Romanov Grand Duchesses* (Picador, 2014).
25. Mironenko, Sergei and Maylunas, Andrei, *A Lifelong Passion: Nicholas and Alexandra* (Doubleday, 1997).
26. RA VIC/MAIN/QVJ/ 1895: 15 November.
27. Mironenko, Sergei and Maylunas, Andrei, *A Lifelong Passion: Nicholas and Alexandra* (Doubleday, 1997).
28. Mironenko, Sergei and Maylunas, Andrei, *A Lifelong Passion: Nicholas and Alexandra* (Doubleday, 1997).
29. Mironenko, Sergei and Maylunas, Andrei, *A Lifelong Passion: Nicholas and Alexandra* (Doubleday, 1997).
30. Mironenko, Sergei and Maylunas, Andrei, *A Lifelong Passion: Nicholas and Alexandra* (Doubleday, 1997).
31. Rappaport, Helen, *Four Sisters: The Lost Lives of the Romanov Grand Duchesses* (Picador, 2014).

32. Mironenko, Sergei and Maylunas, Andrei, *A Lifelong Passion: Nicholas and Alexandra* (Doubleday, 1997).
33. RA VIC/MAIN/QVJ/ 1896: 2 June.
34. Hough, Richard, (ed.), *Advice to My Grand-daughter: Letters from Queen Victoria to Princess Victoria of Hesse* (Simon & Schuster, 1976).
35. RA VIC/MAIN/QVJ/ 1896: 3 June.
36. Mironenko, Sergei and Maylunas, Andrei, *A Lifelong Passion: Nicholas and Alexandra* (Doubleday, 1997).
37. Welch, Frances, *The Imperial Tea Party: Family, Politics and Betrayal* (Short Books, 2018).
38. Welch, Frances, *The Imperial Tea Party: Family, Politics and Betrayal* (Short Books, 2018).
39. Welch, Frances, *The Imperial Tea Party: Family, Politics and Betrayal* (Short Books, 2018).
40. Welch, Frances, *The Imperial Tea Party: Family, Politics and Betrayal* (Short Books, 2018).
41. RA VIC/MAIN/QVJ/ 1896: 22 September.
42. Welch, Frances, *The Imperial Tea Party: Family, Politics and Betrayal* (Short Books, 2018).
43. Welch, Frances, *The Imperial Tea Party: Family, Politics and Betrayal* (Short Books, 2018).
44. Welch, Frances, *The Imperial Tea Party: Family, Politics and Betrayal* (Short Books, 2018).
45. RA VIC/MAIN/QVJ/ 1896: 22 September.
46. Welch, Frances, *The Imperial Tea Party: Family, Politics and Betrayal* (Short Books, 2018).
47. RA VIC/MAIN/QVJ/ 1896: 22 September.
48. RA VIC/MAIN/QVJ/ 1896: 23 September.
49. Welch, Frances, *The Imperial Tea Party: Family, Politics and Betrayal* (Short Books, 2018).
50. RA VIC/MAIN/QVJ/ 1896: 24 September.
51. RA VIC/MAIN/QVJ/ 1896: 28 September.
52. RA VIC/MAIN/QVJ/ 1896: 27 September.
53. RA VIC/MAIN/QVJ/ 1896: 28 September.
54. Rappaport, Helen, *Four Sisters: The Lost Lives of the Romanov Grand Duchesses* (Picador, 2014).
55. Welch, Frances, *The Imperial Tea Party: Family, Politics and Betrayal* (Short Books, 2018).
56. RA VIC/MAIN/QVJ/ 1896: 30 September.
57. RA VIC/MAIN/QVJ/ 1896: 1 October.
58. RA VIC/MAIN/QVJ/ 1896: 2 October.
59. RA VIC/MAIN/QVJ/ 1896: 2 October.
60. RA VIC/MAIN/QVJ/ 1896: 2 October.

61. RA VIC/MAIN/QVJ/ 1896: 3 October.

62. RA VIC/MAIN/QVJ/ 1896: 3 October.

63. Welch, Frances, *The Imperial Tea Party: Family, Politics and Betrayal* (Short Books, 2018).

Chapter 11

1. RA VIC/MAIN/QVJ/ 1896: 5 October.

2. Mironenko, Sergei and Maylunas, Andrei, *A Lifelong Passion: Nicholas and Alexandra* (Doubleday, 1997).

3. Mironenko, Sergei and Maylunas, Andrei, *A Lifelong Passion: Nicholas and Alexandra* (Doubleday, 1997).

4. Mironenko, Sergei and Maylunas, Andrei, *A Lifelong Passion: Nicholas and Alexandra* (Doubleday, 1997).

5. Mironenko, Sergei and Maylunas, Andrei, *A Lifelong Passion: Nicholas and Alexandra* (Doubleday, 1997).

6. Mironenko, Sergei and Maylunas, Andrei, *A Lifelong Passion: Nicholas and Alexandra* (Doubleday, 1997).

7. RA VIC/MAIN/QVJ/1897: 10 June.

8. Rappaport, Helen, *Four Sisters: The Lost Lives of the Romanov Grand Duchesses* (Picador, 2014).

9. Hough, Richard, (ed.), *Advice to My Grand-daughter: Letters from Queen Victoria to Princess Victoria of Hesse* (Simon & Schuster, 1976).

10. Rappaport, Helen, *Four Sisters: The Lost Lives of the Romanov Grand Duchesses* (Picador, 2014).

11. Rappaport, Helen, *Four Sisters: The Lost Lives of the Romanov Grand Duchesses* (Picador, 2014).

12. Mironenko, Sergei and Maylunas, Andrei, *A Lifelong Passion: Nicholas and Alexandra* (Doubleday, 1997).

13. Mironenko, Sergei and Maylunas, Andrei, *A Lifelong Passion: Nicholas and Alexandra* (Doubleday, 1997).

14. Mironenko, Sergei and Maylunas, Andrei, *A Lifelong Passion: Nicholas and Alexandra* (Doubleday, 1997).

15. Mironenko, Sergei and Maylunas, Andrei, *A Lifelong Passion: Nicholas and Alexandra* (Doubleday, 1997).

16. Mironenko, Sergei and Maylunas, Andrei, *A Lifelong Passion: Nicholas and Alexandra* (Doubleday, 1997).

17. Mironenko, Sergei and Maylunas, Andrei, *A Lifelong Passion: Nicholas and Alexandra* (Doubleday, 1997).

18. Worsley, Lucy, *Queen Victoria: Daughter, Wife, Mother, Widow* (Hodder & Stoughton, 2018).

19. RA VIC/MAIN/QVJ/1899: 30 June.

20. Rappaport, Helen, *Four Sisters: The Lost Lives of the Romanov Grand Duchesses* (Picador, 2014).

21. Mironenko, Sergei and Maylunas, Andrei, *A Lifelong Passion: Nicholas and Alexandra* (Doubleday, 1997).
22. Mironenko, Sergei and Maylunas, Andrei, *A Lifelong Passion: Nicholas and Alexandra* (Doubleday, 1997).
23. Mironenko, Sergei and Maylunas, Andrei, *A Lifelong Passion: Nicholas and Alexandra* (Doubleday, 1997).
24. Mironenko, Sergei and Maylunas, Andrei, *A Lifelong Passion: Nicholas and Alexandra* (Doubleday, 1997).
25. Mironenko, Sergei and Maylunas, Andrei, *A Lifelong Passion: Nicholas and Alexandra* (Doubleday, 1997).
26. Mironenko, Sergei and Maylunas, Andrei, *A Lifelong Passion: Nicholas and Alexandra* (Doubleday, 1997).
27. Buxhoeveden, Sophie, *The Life and Tragedy of Alexandra Feodorovna: Empress of Russia* (Longmans, Green & Co., 1928).
28. RA VIC/MAIN/QVJ/1900: 24 November.
29. RA VIC/MAIN/QVJ/1901: 1 January.
30. Worsley, Lucy, *Queen Victoria: Daughter, Wife, Mother, Widow* (Hodder & Stoughton, 2018).
31. Mironenko, Sergei and Maylunas, Andrei, *A Lifelong Passion: Nicholas and Alexandra* (Doubleday, 1997).
32. Mironenko, Sergei and Maylunas, Andrei, *A Lifelong Passion: Nicholas and Alexandra* (Doubleday, 1997).
33. Massie, Robert K., *Nicholas and Alexandra* (W&N, 2000).

Bibliography

Baird, Julia, *Victoria the Queen: An Intimate Biography of the Woman Who Ruled an Empire* (Blackfriars, 2016).

Benson, Arthur Christopher and Esher, Viscount (edited by), *The Letters of Queen Victoria, Vol. III* (John Murray, 1907).

Buxhoeveden, Sophie, *The Life & Tragedy of Alexandra Feodorovna: Empress of Russia* (Longmans, Green & Co., 1928).

Cadbury, Deborah, *Queen Victoria's Matchmaking: The Royal Marriages That Shaped Europe* (Bloomsbury, 2017).

Croft, Christina, *Alice, The Enigma: A Biography of Queen Victoria's Daughter* (Hilliard & Croft, 2013).

Dennison, Matthew, *The Last Princess: The Devoted Life of Queen Victoria's Youngest Daughter* (Apollo, 2019).

Duff, David, *Hessian Tapestry* (TBS, 1967).

Edwards, Anne, *Matriarch: Queen Mary and the House of Windsor* (Rowman & Littlefield, 2014).

Fulford, Roger (ed.), *Dearest Child: Letters Between Queen Victoria and the Princess Royal, 1858–1861* (Evans Brothers, 1964).

Fulford, Roger (ed.), *Your Dear Letter: Private Correspondence of Queen Victoria and the Crown Princess of Prussia* 1865–1871 (Evans Brothers, 1971).

Gelardi, Julia, *Born to Rule: Granddaughters of Victoria, Queens of Europe* (Headline, 2006).

Gray, Annie, *The Greedy Queen: Eating with Victoria* (Profile Books, 2017).

de Guitaut, Caroline, *Russia: Art, Royalty and the Romanovs* (Royal Collection Trust, 2018).

Hawksley, Lucinda, *The Mystery of Princess Louise: Queen Victoria's Rebellious Daughter* (Vintage, 2014).

Helena Victoria, Princess (ed.), *Alice, Grand Duchess of Hesse: Princess of Great Britain and Ireland, Biographical Sketch and Letters* (John Murray, 1884).

Hibbert, Christopher, *Queen Victoria: A Personal History* (HarperCollins, 2010).

Hough, Richard (ed.), *Advice to My Grand-daughter: Letters from Queen Victoria to Princess Victoria of Hesse* (Simon & Schuster, 1976).

King, Greg, *Last Empress: The Life and Times of Alexandra Feodorovna Tsarina of Russia* (Aurum Press, 1996).

Kurth, Peter, *Tsar: The Lost World of Nicholas and Alexandra* (Doubleday, 1995).

Van der Kiste, John, *Queen Victoria's Children* (The History Press, 2011).

Longford, Elizabeth, *Victoria R.I.* (Heron Books, 1964).

Marie, Queen of Romania, *The Story of My Life* Vol. 1. (1934).

Martin, Theodore, *The Life of His Royal Highness the Prince Consort, Vol. 5* (Smith, Elder & Co., London, 1880).

Massie, Robert K., *Nicholas and Alexandra* (W&N, 2000).

Mironenko, Sergei and Maylunas, Andrei, *A Lifelong Passion: Nicholas and Alexandra* (Doubleday, 1997).

Noel, Gerard, *Princess Alice: Queen Victoria's Forgotten Daughter* (Constable, 1974).

Pakula, Hannah, *An Uncommon Woman: The Empress Frederick* (Weidenfeld & Nicolson, 2006).

Ponsonby, Frederick (ed.) *The Letters of the Empress Frederick* (Macmillan and Co., 1928).

Radzinsky, Edvard, *The Last Tsar: The Life and Death of Nicholas II* (Hodder & Stoughton, 1992).

Rappaport, Helen, *Four Sisters: The Lost Lives of the Romanov Grand Duchesses* (Picador, 2014).

Rappaport, Helen, *Magnificent Obsession* (Windmill Books, 2012).

Rappaport, Helen, *The Race to Save the Romanovs* (Windmill Books, 2019).

Ridley, Jane, *Bertie: A Life of Edward VII* (Vintage, 2013).

Sebag Montefiore, Simon, *The Romanovs* (W&N, 2017).

Strafford, Alice, Countess of (ed.), *Leaves from the Diary of Henry Greville, vol.3* (Smith Elder & Co., 1904).

Tinniswood, Adrian, *Behind the Throne: A Domestic History of the Royal Household* (Jonathan Cape, 2018).

Welch, Frances, *The Imperial Tea Party: Family, Politics and Betrayal* (Short Books, 2018).

Wilson, A. N., *Victoria: A Life* (Atlantic Books, 2014).

Worsley, Lucy, *Queen Victoria: Daughter, Wife, Mother, Widow* (Hodder & Stoughton, 2018).

York, H.R.H. the Duchess of, and Storey, Benita, *Victoria and Albert: Life at Osborne House* (W&N, 1991).

Index